D0148323

The Psychology
of the
Psychic

The Psychology of the Psychic

By David Marks
and
Richard Kammann
Foreword by Martin Gardner

ℙ *Prometheus Books*
Buffalo, New York 14215

Published 1980 by Prometheus Books
1203 Kensington Avenue, Buffalo, N.Y. 14215

Library of Congress Catalog Number: 80-7458
Cloth: ISBN 0-87975-121-5
Paper: ISBN 0-87975-122-3

Printed in the United States of America

CONTENTS

FOREWORD

MARTIN GARDNER

Extraordinary claims in science are usually established by extraordinarily careful experiments designed to eliminate the unconscious biasing of data by strong hopes and beliefs—experiments that can be repeated over and over again by open-minded researchers who have no intense interest in the outcome. This "repeatability" of an experiment, like almost all concepts in the methodology of science, is a matter of degree, and not easy to define sharply. Two examples will make this clear.

About forty years after the famous Michelson-Morly experiment, so pivotal in the development of relativity theory, a respected U.S. physicist, Dayton C. Miller, tried to replicate the historic test. He found variations in the speed of light that, if valid, would refute relativity. Miller repeated his experiment many times, always with similar results, and until his death, believed he had disproved Einstein's theory. Why does no physicist today accept these results? It is because Miller's work has to be evaluated in the light of tens of thousands of experiments by others that confirm light's unvarying relative velocity. It is not enough that an experiment be repeatable by the *same* scientist.

Nor is it enough that an experiment be repeatable by a small group of scientists who share the same emotional allegiance to an unorthodox view. The history of phrenology provides a splendid illustration. In the nineteenth century, an enormous number of intelligent, well-educated people, including many prominent scientists, considered phrenology an established truth. Alfred Russel Wallace and Karl Marx were true believers. Famous writers (Coleridge, Poe, Whitman, Doyle, and others) were equally persuaded. The pages of an international flood of learned books and journals on phrenology swarmed with impressive test replications. Wallace's essay on "The Neglect of Phrenology" can be summed up by that hoary one-liner: "Anyone who doubts phrenology ought to have his head examined." Let us not waste time on the trivial fact that different parts of the brain do indeed have different functions. Phrenology claimed something far more remarkable. It claimed that the sizes of bumps in specific locations on the skull are correlated with specific personality traits. There are no such correlations. Yet throughout the nineteenth century, endless replications of apparently well-controlled tests confirmed the theory.

When parapsychologists talk about the repeatability of their experiments, it is good to remember the lesson of phrenology. It is not enough that experiments supporting extraordinary claims be repeatable only by true believers. They must be repeatable by nonbelievers. The saddest and most striking fact about parapsychology is that, after a hundred years of intensive investigation, not one experiment has been produced that can be regularly replicated by skeptics. Of course, parapsychologists have all sorts of rationalizations. The one most often invoked by parapsychologists is that doubt on the part of an experimenter (or even an observer!) somehow inhibits psi abilities. Frequently, a psychic who demonstrates fantastic powers in poorly controlled tests will mysteriously lose his or her ability when subjected to tighter controls by the same parapsychologist who initially got strong results. This failure to replicate, which cannot be blamed on skepticism, is seldom taken as evidence against the early informal results. Parapsychologists prefer to believe that, for unknown reasons, psychics tend to mysteriously lose their powers.

Skeptics of psi, and this includes the great majority of professional psychologists around the world, have simpler explanations for psi replication failures. I know of no work that gives in clearer or more persuasive detail why the doubters prefer their simpler explanations than this explosive, timely book. The authors, two knowledgeable research psychologists, tried their best to duplicate the much-publicized remote viewing experiments made at the Stanford Research Institute by Harold Puthoff and Russell Targ. Results were negative. A painstaking investigation of the SRI tests revealed huge flaws in their design. The authors did their best to find evidence that Uri Geller, the most famous self-styled psychic of the past decade, possesses genuine psi powers. They conclude that he has none.

But this book is much more than just an expose of the conjuring methods of modern "mentalists" such as Kreskin and Geller, or of the gaping holes in the remote viewing investigations at SRI. The authors also discuss, supporting their opinions with little-known but eye-opening research, the reasons why so many people today are prone to believe not only in the reality of psi phenomena, but also in astrology, extraterrestrial UFOs, palmistry, biorhythms, poltergeists, dowsing, and all the other popular delusions that make up the current "occult explosion." A final chapter on "The Art of Doubt" explores the positive role of skepticism in the progress of genuine science. It is essential for avoiding what the authors call those "self-perpetuating beliefs" in pseudoscience that can at times severely damage a society—one has only to think of the crazy anthropology of Nazi Germany—and that always sap a nation's intellectual energies and rip off its gullible citizens.

The Psychology of the Psychic is a book that should have been printed and promoted with trumpets by a major publishing house. Alas, such is the temper of our times that the manuscript was side-stepped by a great number of publishers before the authors found Prometheus Books. The obvious reason — skeptical books, even (or especially) high-quality books, rarely sell. For every person who reads this valuable book, there are hundreds of näive souls who would prefer to have their spines tingled by a sensational but worthless potboiler by some hack journalist of the paranormal. You who now read these sentences thoughtfully join a small but wiser minority.

Martin Gardner

PREFACE

ESP is just around the next corner. When you get there, it is just around the next corner. Having now turned over one hundred of these corners, we decided to call it quits and report our findings for public review.

We report our investigation of three of the boldest claims of psychic power in the 1970s. The first is a laboratory study of "remote viewing" as conducted at Stanford Research Institute in California. In this case, poor methodology is responsible for the false alarm. The next two cases are concerned with psychic superstars, Kreskin and Uri Geller who, we conclude, use magicians' tricks to create psychic illusions. We are not the first to charge Geller with deception, but we hope we have laid out the most comprehensive review of all the evidence. Our results confirm the pattern of experimental errors and probable deceptions that Professor C.E.M. Hansel has documented for the best available ESP experiments reported in the four preceding decades in his book, *ESP: A Scientific Evaluation* (Scribner's, 1966).

In chapter eleven we take up two more traditional kinds of ESP demonstrations: one, an unconvincing psychic experiment conducted by Professor Alister Hardy in England; and the other, the case history approach provided by the writings of Arthur Koestler, the well-known author and scientific gadfly.

In the last three chapters, we try to answer the question, "Why do so many people believe so deeply in phenomena that, as far as we can tell, do not exist?" Our brief study of natural biases and errors in human perception and judgment suggests that the entire spectrum of psychism, occultism, and pseudoscience are products of these illusions. We have tried to provide the reader with some tools for recognizing these fallacies,

4

whether they occur in normal or in paranormal beliefs.

We did not set out to shoot ESP down. On the contrary, we vaguely hoped that all the public acclaim, news stories, and even scientific reports signaled a new era of supernormal communication and understanding between people. In short, we fell for the where-there's-smoke-there-must-be-fire fallacy, although not for long. Our only skepticism was the healthy kind that any scientiest is required to show toward any phenomenon he does not understand.

Some people will conclude that we don't believe in *anything*. That this is entirely false is demonstrated by our other research activities. One of us (DM) is the cofounder of a research organization known as the Isis Research Centre, committed to the application of psychology to problems of living such as smoking, obesity, and stress. And one of us (RK) is committed to the study of human happiness, ecology, and the environment. There are many exciting developments occurring in psychology and other social sciences, and it is unfortunate that these are not often enough described in language that the public can understand and identify with. We believe that the truly impressive powers of mind and consciousness lie elsewhere than in mind reading and spoon bending.

We have tried to write this book for the intelligent nonpsychologist and the beginning psychology student. We also hope that the last three chapters will encourage fellow psychologists to give more attention to several promising, but somewhat underdeveloped lines of research.

To reach the widest possible audience, we were tempted from time to time to draw literary swords and enter into a battle of personalities and events, giving our conclusions in passionate "pows" and "zaps." We knew that explaining how an experiment is done, or giving our results in numerical averages and percentages would only make our argument seem *weaker* in the minds of some.

We rejected this approach in its extreme form. It seemed better to reach that more select audience of people who like to think for themselves. At the same time, we have gone out of our way to keep scientific methodology to the barest essentials, and to avoid all academic jargon, except for a few terms that would help the reader get a handle on a new concept or new way of thinking. Here and there, in an effort to make ourselves clear, or perhaps in a moment of exasperation, we state our own opinions in fairly blunt words.

In the early days of this research—on Kreskin and Uri Geller—we worked side by side at every step, making the same observations, running the same experiments, and coordinating our follow-up inquiries. But, this all had to be worked around our university teaching and our existing research programs in other areas, and our progress was correspondingly slow. At that point we decided to take on separate assignments: David Marks undertook to examine the SRI remote viewing experiments, while Dick Kammann undertook a review of psychological experiments that might help explain the origins of psychic beliefs. In these cases, the other coauthor acted as a consultant and devil's advocate on the research and as critic and editor of the written chapters, until we reached a complete agreement.

An apology is due to all female readers for our frequent use of "he" and "his" when we talk about a hypothetical person. We tried writing everything in the two-gender mode, saying "he or she," and so forth, but that distracted from the topic. We tried using sentences that avoided such pronouns altogether, but this created cumbersome constructions. In the end we regretfully fell back into old language habits. Whenever we say man, mankind, he, his, or him, we mean equally *woman, womankind, she, hers, or her.*

It is not possible for us to give due recognition to the countless individuals who offered a helping hand in so many different ways during our research and writing. To all of them we say, "Thank you sincerely."

But, we would be remiss not to list some of the people who gave especially large doses of time, assistance, wisdom, or encouragement. We are glad to acknowledge the special contributions of Linda Addis, Peter Bradshaw, Isabel Campbell, Mary Davison, Gillian Denny, Barry Dingwall, Martin Fisher, Martin Gardner, Uri Geller, Margaret Gilkison, Arthur Hastings, Ian Hodgson, Carol Hunter, Ray Hyman, Robyn Irwin, Max Lowry, Margaret McGoldrick, Peter McKellar, Ray Mitchell, Gillian Pow, James Randi, Roxane Smith, Pavel Tichy, Chris Trotter, Marcello Truzzi, Sally Watson, and Manson Wright.

1

THE GROWING WORLD
OF THE OCCULT

ESP either does or does not occur.
Nothing I can do will change the reality.
Therefore, I had better find out the truth and accommodate my
thinking to it.

R.A. McConnell

Nothing in our histories as experimental psychologists has ever suggested that one day we would end up studying the feats of psychic superstars. The tide turned in 1973 when many of our students challenged us to explain the psychic miracles that were displayed with frightening regularity each week on television by the internationally known mentalist, Kreskin. At first, we asked, "Who's Kreskin?" and our students went away disappointed. But our students were persistent in their claims that there was definitely something there that psychology couldn't explain, and so we took a look for ourselves one night in March 1974, when, somewhat impulsively, we went to see a Kreskin stage show.

Kreskin seemed to be traveling on the crest of a wave of growing interest in the world of the occult. Back in mid-1973 we came across a news story in a local newspaper, reprinted from the *Christian Science Monitor.* Some excerpts from the article went as follows:

OCCULTISM ON U.S. CAMPUS
by David Mutch

A lot of bright American college students think the future is in the palm of their hand, says Professor David C. Lindberg. That doesn't mean they think they have the world on a string, he explains.

What it does mean—"and it boggled my mind at first," he adds—is that 20 percent of 231 university juniors and seniors he questioned at the University of Wisconsin expressed trust in palmistry.

Some 23 percent said they believe in witches, and 18 percent in astrology. No less than 74 percent said they believe in extrasensory perception.

A specialist in the history of science, he teaches a course in the history of the occult and pseudoscience at the Madison campus. Teaching the course with him is a colleague in the same field, Professor Robert Siegfried.

It is only their second year at it, but a hundred students had to be turned away when this year's course began in August. The students surveyed are the ones who enrolled and may be more prone to such beliefs, the professors agree.

TURMOIL SPOTLIGHTED

Both of these teachers warn that the next generation could be "absolute believers" in the power of occult.

Why? One fundamental reason given by Professor Lindberg is that today's rapid social and intellectual change produces the turmoil and anxieties that breed belief in the occult.

"Popularity of the occult rises and falls in the course of history," Professor Lindberg says, "but it flourishes most during times like these." A specialist in the history of the Renaissance, a turbulent period of social and intellectual change, he notes it was a time when the occult flourished.

Today, Professor Lindberg continues, "the press and these sixth-sense television shows are doing an amazing job of indoctrinating young people." He goes on: "I understand that it is fun to listen to stories about ESP. Eastern religion is involved in this interest in the occult, but I'm not sure which is cause and effect. But, I'd be gratified if the press would include some articles on the other side, showing scientific reasons why there are so many misconceptions in this area."

POSSIBLE ABUSE SEEN

Professor Lindberg says that some kind of extranormal mental perceptions are "plausible," but he adds, "the case is not made yet—and it could, of course, be much abused if it were so."

While the figures Professors Lindberg and Siegfried cite for belief in occult powers on the Madison campus are striking, the evidence suggests an equally high prevalence of occult beliefs throughout the world. In 1975, we ran a survey in one of our own psychology classes at the University of Otago in New Zealand. A total of 304 psychology students answered our survey that covered a variety of occult skills and phenomena. The evidence suggests that beliefs in the occult among our own students in New Zealand are even stronger than was the case at Wisconsin, United States, two years earlier. More than four in five of our psychology class believed in the ability to read minds (mental telepathy) and over half believed in the ability of the mind to leave the body (astral traveling). Thirty-eight percent believed in witchcraft and 31 percent reported having personal psychic powers. It's a small wonder that so many of them felt restless in our classes that tended to neglect the parapsychological in favor of naturalistic approaches to the study of man. While we were doing our best to account for man's mental life in terms of the conventional senses and cognitive processes, Kreskin and Geller were busily demonstrating their powers of extrasensory perception on national television. Perhaps the most striking statistic of all is the fact that approximately *one in three of our students believed that they too had psychic powers.*

This latter point was brought home even more vividly in another survey conducted on our university campus by three colleagues, Louis Leland, John Patterson, and John Clark. Using the *Clark Information Sheet,* they asked 619 students from four separate faculties (physics, English, commerce, and psychology) if they personally possessed any of ten so-called "supernatural" abilities. *Approximately 50 percent of the students claimed one or more psychic abilities.* Even if the two "religious" abilities are removed from the list (ability to communicate with God—18 percent—and the ability to invoke God's assistance through prayer—17 percent), 40 percent of the sample claimed at least one of the other nonreligious abilities. Most frequently claimed was the ability to perceive future events by premonition, dreams, or other methods (26 percent) and the two religiously inclined powers were second and third in popularity. Casting horoscopes (1 percent) and telling fortunes (4 percent) were least claimed. These trends were true for four different types of students, although there was a difference between majors in the overall rate of claimed powers as follows: English, 68 percent; psychology, 50 percent; physics, 44 percent; and commerce, 39 percent.

University students don't seem very different from the general American population in which three out of four people believe in ESP or clairvoyance, according to a national random sample sponsored by *Playboy* in 1976. Perhaps college students are not typical of all young people of their age. For example, a random Gallup poll in 1975 found that 23 percent of American adults believe in astrology, but in the 18-24 group, this jumped to an impressive 38 percent (Gallup, 1978). If we suppose that the beliefs of young people are more vulnerable to social change and manipulation by the media, the result for astrology belief supports the idea that the nation is undergoing a large swing toward occult and psychic beliefs. It is perfectly plausible that Viet Nam, Watergate, and the economic doldrums of the 1970s have seriously eroded American pride and optimism, and young people are turning to quasi-religious beliefs to find a new sense of meaning and purpose.

Professor Gustav Jahoda of the University of Strathclyde, Scotland, has presented figures for occult beliefs in England, Germany, Scotland, and the United States covering a forty-year period since 1925. He cites a study done by Garwood who noted the behavior of people when confronted by a ladder in position over a pavement. Of fifty-one persons passing the spot during fifteen minutes, only fourteen walked under the ladder and the rest stepped into the road to avoid it, exposing themselves to danger from the traffic. As there was nobody up the ladder at the time, any realistic risk was excluded. "Superstition is still very much with us," Jahoda concludes, "and it is even possible that some forms of it may be on the increase."

We agree with Jahoda; not walking under safe ladders may well be a superstition, but what of telepathy, clairvoyance, and premonition? Can all those students, intelligent people to be sure, claiming supernatural powers *all* be wrong? It is the main goal of this book to answer this question.

Traditionally, scientists and psychologists have, with a few exceptions, been chary of exploring the area of the supernatural or *paranormal,* the currently more fashionable term. A fair definition of this term given in a recent handbook edited by White (1974) goes as follows: "PARANORMAL: As related to psychic research, faculties and phenomena that are beyond 'normality' in terms of cause and effect as currently understood." It seems that nowadays many more scientists believe that research on the psychic or paranormal sphere is urgently warranted. This apparent change of heart in the scientific community was revealed most clearly in a survey conducted by Dr.Christopher Evans through the columns of a popular English science magazine, *New Scientist*. Evans received 1500 replies from the 71,000-72,000 copies of the magazine sold. Sixty-three percent of the sample possessed degrees, and 29 percent higher degrees. To quote Evans: "A solid 350 respondents (25 percent of the total) held ESP to be 'an established fact,' with a further 590 (42 percent) declaring it to be 'a likely possibility.' Only 3 percent of the total believed ESP to be an impossibility." Obviously, the sample of readers replying to the questionnaire could easily have been biased, but the figures Evans obtained are impressively high. A massive 88 percent considered ESP to be "a legitimate scientific undertaking," but only 30 percent considered that psychic researchers were tackling the problem in the right way. There were numerous suggestions as to the optimum approach to psychic research and the most popular of these was that "research should concentrate on people known, or claiming to have ESP."

Part of this book is devoted to the study of two such people, Kreskin and Uri Geller. Both are internationally known celebrities with well-established careers as professional psychics. We believe that people such as Kreskin and Geller have an important and influential role in molding and shaping our minds. Through their amazing skill and endless energy, our imagination for a world beyond mundane reality develops and grows. This hidden, secret world of the occult may itself become part of, or even replace, what we hitherto took for granted. Such men as Kreskin and Uri Geller have much to teach us, in an unexpected way, about the workings of the human mind.

Before the chapters on these famous psychic performers, we describe and evaluate some important recent experiments on psychic functioning conducted at the Stanford Research Institute in California. These experiments conducted by two physicists, Harold Puthoff and Russell Targ, have been widely acclaimed; yet, they too lead us to a surprising conclusion about the science of psychic powers.

2

REMOTE VIEWING

I didn't even change from my civilian clothes. I sat there on the couch and Russell Targ said, "We don't care what you do outside this room, but while you're here, you have permission to be psychic."

Richard Bach

PLACE: STANFORD RESEARCH INSTITUTE, MENLO PARK, CALIFORNIA.
TIME: 18:03:28 P.S.T., April 27, 1973.
MISSION: EXPLORATION OF PLANET JUPITER.
TRAVELER: INGO SWANN.
GROUND CONTROL: HAROLD PUTHOFF, RUSSELL TARG.

...three...two...one...lift-off. Swann is on his way to Jupiter. Unlimited by normal laws of time and space, in seconds Swann is flying through Jupiter's thick atmosphere of hydrogen, one hundred thousand miles from the planet's surface. He sees the glittering yellow crystals from which emanate rainbows of color. Traveling through the planet's thick cloud, Swann arrives on the surface to discover huge, reddish-brown, volcanic peaks that are sparking red-hot, with tremendous winds, ice, water, and powerful magnetic forces. Within thirty minutes Swann has returned to earth, mission completed.

Imaginative science fiction? Not so. At least not according to two scientists in Menlo Park, California. "Remote viewing," the ability to perceive information from remote sources not available to any known sense, has been recorded and measured in the laboratories of one of the

12

world's foremost scientific institutions, the Stanford Research Institute (SRI). Mr. Russell Targ and Dr. Harold Puthoff, two senior physicists at SRI's Radio Physics Laboratory, have published their astonishing research in the world's oldest and most prestigious scientific journal *Nature*, and in their book *Mind-Reach.*

In earlier times this ability would have been called "extrasensory perception," or ESP, but Targ and Puthoff prefer the terms "remote viewing" or "remote sensing." The new term conveys a break with traditional psychic research that has stagnated through lack of progress in the form of positive, repeatable results. In their headline-making research, Targ and Puthoff claim to have discovered a powerful and reliable phenomenon that defies reason or known laws. To "see" the invisible extends and broadens our concept of knowledge, our world view, and what we fondly term "reality."

How often have we dreamed that we have miraculously traveled to other time-space regions and grappled with strange events and phenomena beyond the limits of our mundane reality? According to Targ and Puthoff, remote viewing is an ability available to everybody whose mind is open to the possibility. They claim that nobody they have tested failed to accurately describe selected locations that could not possibly be viewed or known directly via normal sensory means. Targ and Puthoff claim to have carried out "more than one hundred experiments" on remote viewing, "most of them successful" *(Mind-Reach,* pp. 9-10). The methods used are claimed to be foolproof and fraud-proof and, therefore, are demanding of serious attention. Nine different subjects participated in the original series of experiments. Of these, none produced more dramatic results than the first, Mr. Patrick Price. Price, an ex-police commissioner and vice-mayor of Burbank, California, claimed he used his psychic powers to detect the whereabouts of wanted criminals and other undesirables. Puthoff and Targ ran a series of nine experiments with Price, and, as these were the prototypes for a six-year research program at SRI, we shall describe and evaluate this series in some detail.

In each experiment, one of the experimenters (usually Targ) remained with the subject at SRI while the other experimenter and one to three observers traveled to an undisclosed location selected from a list of twelve. All of the twelve natural target locations were different and within thirty minutes driving time from the laboratory. They had been chosen from 100 available locations by Mr. Bonnar Cox, Director of the Division of Information Science and Engineering at SRI. Both the experimenters and the subject were kept ignorant, or "blind," as to the contents of the target list and, once selected, a place was not chosen again.

The third experiment with Pat Price illustrates the procedures used. Targ and an assistant, Hugh Crane, are with Price in a shielded room at SRI. The shielded room is a Faraday cage which eliminates much of the electromagnetic spectrum. At 10:26 A.M., having synchronized watches with Targ, Puthoff drives to a location selected by Bart Cox. Mrs. Ann Price and Cox accompany Puthoff to this location, which is the Radio Telescope in Portola Valley. Thirty minutes are allowed for traveling. At 10:56 A.M. Price begins his description, which is recorded on audiotape. Puthoff, Mrs. Price, and Cox who are the target "demarcation team" remain at the Radio Telescope for thirty minutes where they roam around the area, making as complete an inspection as possible and acting as "psychic beacons" of on-site information. The team walk from the parking lot up to a catwalk, horizontally bisecting the antenna dish, and observe the surrounding area. Meanwhile, back at SRI Targ and Crane, who are themselves ignorant of the target, question Price to help him clarify his description. At the end of the thirty-minute period allowed for remote viewing, Targ and Crane wait with Price for the demarcation team to return to SRI. Puthoff then takes Price to the Radio Telescope so that comparisons can be made between the description and the place itself. This basic procedure was repeated nine times, with minor changes occurring from time to time.

Unedited transcripts of Price's descriptions were presented to an independent judge, Dr. Arthur Hastings, together with a listing of the targets. Dr. Hastings visited the locations and arranged the nine descriptions in rank order against each of the targets. The transcript that gave the best or most accurate description of a given place was ranked first, and the one that provided the worst description was ranked ninth. Intermediate descriptions were ranked between those two extremes.

The results obtained from Hastings are staggering. *Seven of the nine transcripts were ranked perfectly, in first position.* The remaining two descriptions received ranks of six and three, giving a sum of ranks of sixteen. A purely random or chance association between targets and transcripts (as would be obtained if the descriptions contained no information about their positioning in the series of targets) would produce a sum of ranks of forty-five. In a statistical procedure developed by Morris (1972), this result has a probability of 2.9×10^{-5} or odds of less than *1 in 30,000.* As a back-up procedure, five other judges were asked to match the nine transcripts against the nine targets. A total of twenty-four correct matches occurred instead of the expected total of five, giving odds of less than one in one billion!

Considering the generality and ambiguity of many of Price's descriptions, this result is all the more remarkable. Most of Price's descriptions contained references to trees, buildings, hills, and water in some form or another, and lots of irrelevant information, such as what the experimenters were wearing or saying. And occasionally, Price would home-in on some distant part of the globe—such as Hong Kong Harbor or Santiago—which didn't help the judge much in his task of matching the description against the targets in the list. Yet despite the many irrelevancies, inconsistencies, and plain inaccuracies, Price's descriptions were sufficiently informative to permit the judge to match the transcripts against targets with a dramatic and compelling degree of accuracy.

Following their highly successful experiments with Pat Price, Targ and Puthoff obtained the assistance of an inexperienced subject, Mrs. Hella Hammid. In a series of six mock experiments in which a walkie-talkie was used, Mrs. Hammid was found to show considerable promise at remote viewing; so, Targ and Puthoff conducted a nine-experiment series with Hammid, in which the remote viewing period was reduced from thirty to fifteen minutes. As with the Price series, unedited transcripts were submitted to Dr. Hastings, who ranked them in order of accuracy at each of the nine locations. Again the results were staggering. Hastings obtained five direct hits and four second ranks, which gives odds of better than 500,000 to 1!

Hammid performed so successfully in these experiments that Targ and Puthoff asked her back to the laboratory for more. The second series of experiments were even more remarkable than the first: the subject was actually required to describe the remote location *before* the target had been selected! This ability to predict future events that cannot be known through rational inference is known as "precognition." Many people will have, on occasion, noted a strange feeling that they "have been here before," in a location where logically they know they have not been (the "déjà vu" experience), or they have dreamed about something strange and unusual that happened the next day. Targ and Puthoff adapted their remote viewing protocol to permit a measurement of precognition under laboratory conditions. Hammid was required to describe the remote location during a fifteen-minute period, beginning twenty minutes before the target was selected and thirty-five minutes before the outbound experimenter was to arrive at the target location. Four such experiments were carried out, and Targ and Puthoff claim that each was a "striking success." Three judges were able to match the four unedited transcripts against the targets without error. The Targ-Puthoff effect, therefore, defies not only accepted physical laws of space and matter, but the laws of time as well.

In addition to the research with Price and Hammid (two series), the Targ-Puthoff effect was successfully obtained in four other series of experiments made up by combining results from seven other subjects. One series was made up of twelve remote viewings from five different subjects of seven pieces of equipment in the laboratory. This series, contrasting with the others which utilized natural outdoor targets, was judged by combining multiple responses to the same target, giving seven batches of material for seven targets. In only one series (number 4) did the results fail to reach statistical significance. (See Table 1.)

These mind-boggling results defy any of the usual, simple explanations that might be raised to account for them. The experimenter who stayed with the subject couldn't have cued him or led him to a correct description because he, like the subject, was blind to the target. Another possibility is that the experimenters selected only the positive results for publication and conveniently ignored any negative findings, but Targ and Puthoff state that every experiment they ran was included in the statistical evaluations. A third possibility is that data for the reported experiments could have been edited before the judge saw them to bias them in the direction of accuracy by discarding the nonmatching elements. But Targ and Puthoff state that the transcripts of all subjects' descriptions remained *unedited* and that all data were included in the information given to the judge *(Mind-Reach,* p. 101). If all these statements are true, the Targ-Puthoff effect is the single most significant and convincing discovery in over one hundred years of psychic research. Like Ingo Swann, all of us could become space travelers.

The Targ-Puthoff effect gains its significance from two main features: (1) It does not depend on the selection of specially gifted psychics to serve as subjects. Although two of the best results were obtained from individuals whose paranormal abilities were previously studied or known (Swann and Price), the other results belong to seven subjects, including visiting government scientists, who had not considered themselves to be specially gifted or psychic. Targ and Puthoff repeatedly emphasize that *we can all be successful remote viewers if we want to be.* (2) The remote

TABLE 1

Targ and Puthoff's
Remote Viewing Experiments

Series	Targets	Subjects	Number of Experiments	Total Number of Experiments in the Series	Probability Value
1	Natural	Price	9	9	.000029
2	Natural	Hammid	9	9	.0000018
3	Natural	Swann Elgin	4 } 4	8	.00038
4	Natural	Pease Cole	4 } 4	8 [a]	.08
5	Natural	V1 (unnamed) V2 (unnamed)	3 } 2	5	.017
6	Equipment	Elgin Swann Hammid V2 (unnamed) V2 (unnamed)	1 4 5 1 1	12 [b]	.036
7	Natural (Precognitive)	Hammid	4	4	.05

a. Series 4 was judged as a series of 7, as one target was selected twice, once for Pease and once for Cole.
b. Series 6 was judged as a series of 7, as 4 targets were used by 2 or more of the subjects.

viewing effect, unlike most other findings in parapsychology, can be *replicated* or repeated. In other words, the finding is *reliable,* and not a will-of-the-wisp affair, occurring once or twice under freak conditions. Targ and Puthoff claim over one hundred successful experiments. The experiments, therefore, deserve a serious, in-depth scrutiny.

Inspired by these unique features, we decided to replicate the Targ-Puthoff experiments in our own laboratory at the University of Otago, situated in the beautiful South Island of New Zealand. We were assisted in this research by Ray Mitchell. Against a background of scorning skepticism from most of our colleagues, who must have believed the two of us had finally gone completely kookie, we began our preparations by asking our research assistants, Roxane Smith and Gillian Denny, to spend a few days driving around the area finding suitable target sites. This was done in such a way that we wouldn't know which sites had been chosen. Altogether one hundred targets were selected within twenty minutes drive from our laboratory, and the target locations were named, numbered, and placed in envelopes in a locked storage room controlled by our Technical Officer, Barry Dingwall.

In the period of 1976-1978, we ran a total of thirty-five experiments, all similar to Targ and Puthoff's as far as we could tell. Each series utilized a different subject as follows: a graduate psychology student (Ian Hodgson), a hypnotist (Bert Loser), a housewife (Lila MacGregor), a medical student (Pat Tuchy), and an arts major (Chris Trotter). All believed they might be psychic to some degree.

A summary of the experiments is given in Table 2. For each experiment, the experimenter monitoring the subject synchronized watches with the demarcation team and then waited with the subject in a pleasant lounge room or office for twenty minutes. The demarcation team obtained a randomly chosen location envelope (without replacement through all thirty-five experiments) from the Staff Technical Officer and proceeded directly to the target site where they started observing the location. Twenty minutes later the subject reported whatever images or thoughts came to mind and added any pencil drawings he wished to include. This "remote viewing" phase usually lasted fifteen minutes (ten minutes in series 5).

When the traveling experimenters returned, they took the subject back to the site to provide feedback and reinforcement. Subjects were generally pleased by the results and, occasionally, deeply moved or excited. Our first subject, Ian Hodgson, stated at the end of his series of nine experiments that "if the judges can't match my descriptions correctly, there will be something wrong with them." Another subject, Chris Trotter, stated that his second experiment, for which the target was a grave, was an experience he would always remember. Our subjects were mostly convinced that something psychic had happened, and at first, so were we. Until we had the transcripts judged, that is!

For series 1-4, the transcripts and drawings were judged by a different set of five judges for each subject, except that one judge was used for both series 1 and 3. The judges for series 1-4 consisted of graduate students,

TABLE 2

Summary of the Otago
Remove Viewing Experiments

| Series | Subject | Experimenters | | Number of | Number |
		With Subject	On-Site	Experiments in the Series	of Judges
1	Hodgson	Marks	Denny & Smith	9	5
2	Loser	Mitchell	Denny & Smith	5	5
3	MacGregor	Mitchel	Denny & Smith	9	5
4	Tuchy	Mitchell	Denny & Smith	5	5
5	Trotter	Marks (plus observers)	Watson (plus various others)	7	1

research psychologists, and nine volunteers from the community. For series 5, which we shall describe separately in some detail, a single judge was utilized, Professor Pavel Tichy of the Philosophy Department in the University of Otago.

All the transcripts were undated, marked with a random code letter, and had been carefully checked for any cues that could aid the judge, such as references to previous targets. No such cues were available in any of the transcripts. Having studied the transcripts in the series, each judge went independently to each of the target locations and rank-ordered all transcripts for appropriate fitness to the location. *None, repeat none, of the results was statistically significant.* In not a single case did a judge do better than chance at ranking the transcripts—a total of twenty sets of judgments and not a single, significant result. How could this be when our subjects had been so sure they had described the targets accurately? It certainly was no easy task trying to explain to our now insulted and hurt subjects that our statistical tests indicated that nothing psychic had taken place. The reaction of one subject, Chris Trotter, was typical of them all: "Your statistics are obviously wrong—I never believed in them anyway." Here was an arts-science clash *par excellence:* a sensitive young psychic, having done his level best to travel the ether, being statistically disproven, unvalidated. Far out.

Strangely enough, the judges were often as surprised as the subjects that the rankings weren't correct; so we had their displeasure to contend with as well! What a mess—the subjects blamed the judges, the judges blamed the subjects, and inevitably all psychic believers will somehow blame *us!*

An insight into how this conflict of evidence came about was obtained when we broke the normal protocols and decided to accompany the subject during the feedback stage of the experiment. We did this in series 5 with Chris Trotter. Another unique feature of the Trotter series was that with the help of a television company (TV-1), we filmed the first three experiments using two crews, one filming the subject and the other, the on-site observations of the sender, Sally Watson. For the first time we would have an objective record of the movements, perceptions, and reactions of the sender at the target site. In addition, one film crew followed the judge around and recorded some of his reactions. Then, suddenly, everything began to fit together.

The first target, the A-Frame House and Steps, was situated at the foot of a hillside, and the steps beside the house wound their way up the hillside to the foot of a road at the top of the hill (see Figure 1). Trotter described his impressions as follows, "A very open sort of feeling. Something like hills...sensation of being quite high up." He felt a sense of movement, as though Sally was walking about. He felt that the predominant color was green and that there was a tree somewhere around, a single tree. His drawing for this target is shown in Figure 1B.

When we went with Chris Trotter to the target site, Sally said she had walked up the steps to a position above the roof of the house. There we discovered the view shown in Figure 1D. Chris was stunned by the surprising panoramic view from above the A-Frame, which he believed could have been the same one he had imaged and drawn. From Chris's point of view, this first experiment was a partial success and he felt encouraged to go on with the experiments.

The second target was a triangular grave in a local cemetery. The grave was surrounded by a triangular iron fence with a tree at each corner (see Figure 2). The complete transcript for the experiment went as follows:

CT: Definitely getting an oblong shape...just a flash of the Town Hall, but I don't know whether that's right or not. Mm...seems to be fairly enclosed space. Yes. I'll do a drawing. (Starts first drawing.)

DM: O.K.

CT: I definitely get the impression of something sort of high, something going up...

DM: You said it was an enclosed space...do you still feel that?

CT: Yes, I do. Yes, I think there are buildings present. I see. Yes, I see some kind of monument and some kind of large tall structure. It's pretty indeterminant at the moment. Sally's quite close to it. (Starts second drawing.)

DM: Do you pick up any colors?

CT: Dark...that's all. I feel quite strongly that this area here's quite close, quite imposing.

DM: Use another page if you want to. Is it possible you can try and draw what it might look like from above? (Starts third drawing.) Are there any people there...or is there any activity associated with that place?

CT: No, I feel that Sally's eyes are drawn to this shape, this object...(draws X).

DM: Not much color, you say.

CT: No, I don't get much color. Except for the brightness of the sky.

DM: One more minute to go now. Jot down anything else you feel, any mood, or feeling.

CT: A somber feeling.

DM: A somber feeling?

CT: Mm...I initially picked up a feeling of close proximity of quite large objects, quite tall, but apart from that there's just this thing here.

DM: Indoors or outdoors?

CT: I think outdoors. Once again, I get the feeling she's looking up. Yes, that's my initial impression.

DM: There's a few seconds to go. Five seconds.

CT: Something large.

Clearly, this experiment had a profound effect on Chris, who was naturally a bit shaken by what had happened—apparently he was just about 100 percent accurate, right down to the "somber feeling" he experienced as Sally wandered around the graveyard. At that stage everybody concerned seemed to believe that Chris and Sally had communicated at an extrasensory level, or else it was an extraordinarily powerful coincidence.

With one partial success and one complete success behind him, Chris was now much more relaxed and confident about his ability to perform the rather strange task we had set for him. The third target was Dunedin Railway Station, a rather large, grand old building about one mile from the laboratory (see Figure 3). Chris's description and drawings indicated a series of geometric patterns and forms, mainly triangles and pyramids, but he was uncertain about what they represented (see Figure 3C). When we arrived at the station, Chris was again stunned by what he saw. Looking up to the roof over the platform, there were dozens of triangular forms. Sally said she had gone out onto the track and looked up at the railway line and so we all did the same. The correspondence to Chris's final drawing seemed quite remarkable. The apparent accuracy of Chris's drawings, particularly for the second and third targets, was not only affecting the subject, it was having considerable impact on the experimenter as well!

Our decision to break normal protocol and accompany the subject to the target at the end of each experiment was an attempt to gain a better understanding of *why our subjects consistently reported successful remote viewing while judges consistently failed to make correct matches.* This procedure was working only too well—on the basis of the first three experiments in this series (i.e., prior to the objective judging), the experimenter's own belief in remote viewing had increased considerably. Four whole series before this one, with completely negative results, had taken their toll, and by the start of this fifth and final series we had become quite skeptical of ever getting a significant result. Now at last we seemed to be on to something, or at least we thought so at the time.

As the series progressed, Chris's performance seemed to become less convincing, although each time we visited a site together we seemed to be able to make something Chris had said or drawn match some aspect of the target. But it seemed to be getting more and more tenuous as we went along—we seemed to be really straining our imaginations to make things match. This seemed to be especially true when Sally didn't see Chris's description and then came to the site with us to tell us things she'd noticed or attended to. Chris and I both felt that maybe she was cuing us after the fact, perhaps forcing matches that weren't really there. On the seventh and final experiment, Chris and Sally, who had started out so willing and positive, had become disheartened.

The judge for this series was carefully chosen. Professor Pavel Tichy of the Philosophy Department, University of Otago, is a man known locally for his brilliant ability as a logician. Open-minded himself about ESP and psychic powers, we were delighted that he was prepared to assist us in the judging task. If anybody was motivated and capable of making accurate matches, Dr. Tichy was.

For those of us still hoping for a positive result, Tichy's matchings were a disaster. As a demonstration of one of the important principles in the psychology of the psychic, however, his rankings were truly enlightening. A summary of the results is shown in Table 3.

TABLE 3
Results Obtained for Each Target Location
in the Trotter/Watson
Remote Viewing Experiments.

Target Location	Rank of Associated Transcript	Transcript Ranked First
A-Frame House and Steps	7	Railway Station
Triangular Grave	3	A-Frame House
Railway Station	7	Ross Home
Robert Burns Statue	6	Triangular Grave
Provincial Hotel	3	Robert Burns Statue
Ross Home	2	Railway Station
Chimney, Woolen Mill	6	Triangular Grave
Total sum of ranks	34	

Not one of the transcripts was ranked in the correct position. The transcript and drawings ranked against the A-Frame House and Steps were the ones Chris produced for the Railway Station (see Figure 1). The strong predominance of triangles in the latter drawings convinced Pavel Tichy he had made the correct choice. In fact, he felt more sure of this one than any of the others. The correct transcript, which Tichy described as "the only one which didn't contain triangles," was ranked *seventh* (i.e., last). The A-Frame transcript Tichy placed in first position for the second target, the Triangular Grave (see Figure 2). Tichy felt that Chris's drawings and description for the grave matched far better against the Robert Burns Statue and the chimney, and he ranked them in *third place* for the grave itself.

At the Railway Station, Tichy again placed the correct transcript in *seventh* place. He complained that in the "correct" transcript there was no movement, no trains, no people, nothing to do with the station whatsoever. A fair comment, but quite different from the subject's perspective (see Figure 3). *Just as definitely and easily as the subject and experimenter had seen correspondences between the subject's descriptions and their associated targets, the judge had seen still greater correspondences with completely different targets, and no correspondence whatsoever to the correct targets.*

This phenomenon is an example of a basic process we have termed *subjective validation.* This occurs when two unrelated events are perceived to be related because a belief, expectancy, or hypothesis demands or requires a relationship. In the context of remote viewing experiments, the subject obviously hopes to do well and produce an accurate description of the target. When he goes to see the target site after finishing his description, *he tends to notice the matching elements and ignore the nonmatching elements.* Equally, when the judge compares transcripts to the target and makes a relative judgment, he can easily make up his mind that a particular transcript is the correct one and fall into the same trap: he will validate his hypothesis by attending strongly to the matching elements. The fact is that *any* target can be matched by *any* description to some degree. Confidence in the correctness of the match has more to do with the degree of commitment to the idea that there is or should be a match, than it does to the degree of correspondence *per se.*

In *Mind-Reach,* Targ and Puthoff suggest a "recipe" for remote viewing in which the reader is invited to ask a friend to go to a secret location for fifteen minutes, and then have a shot at describing that location. Targ and Puthoff claim they "have not found a single person who could not do remote viewing to satisfaction" (*Mind-Reach,* p. 104). With subjective validation on their side, we are not surprised if a näive person, unfamiliar with the power of subjective validation, visits a location with a description fresh in his mind—*any description*—he will easily and effortlessly find that the description will match.

Subjectively, the experience of accurate remote viewing is not doubted. Only if the process is repeated several times under experimental conditions can any conclusions be reached. Our own extensive experiments have failed to find any evidence of remote viewing ability. This leads to the obvious question: On what basis did Targ and Puthoff obtain their positive results? We turn to this issue in the next chapter.

3

THE TARG-PUTHOFF
EFFECT EXPLAINED

As is your sort of mind,
So is your sort of search; you'll find
What you desire.

Robert Browning

The Price Series

The complete failure of our experiments, in contrast to the complete success of Targ's and Puthoff's, left us groping in the dark for explanations. Had we done the experiments right? Was there something wrong with our subjects—perhaps they weren't sufficiently psychic? Was there something wrong with our judges—were they really motivated to do the task successfully? Worse, was there something wrong with us? Were we missing the point somewhere along the line? We racked our brains for answers but reached a complete mental block. But not long after, Dr. Ed Karnes, a psychologist at Metropolitan State College in Denver, Colorado, reported an extensive remote viewing experiment in which he also could not get any evidence whatsoever for the ESP effect.

Then one day we suddenly had a crazy idea. Maybe it wasn't *our* experiments that were wrong, but Targ and Puthoff's. This led us to search for the differences between our experiments and theirs. No two experiments done in different laboratories are ever identical, even if one is tagged with the label, "replication study." We kept returning to one seemingly relevant detail: when we produced transcripts of each subject's descriptions, we occasionally found it necessary *to edit out certain phrases and remarks referring to previously visited locations in the series.* This was necessary as such references could cue the judges about which target did not go with the given transcript. For example, if transcript X mentioned a church visited the day before, and a church did appear in the target list, the judge could obviously assume safely that the transcript X did not go with the church. This reduced his range of uncertainty by one unit. So if there were nine targets in the series, the judge's chance of matching transcript X correctly became one in eight instead of one in nine.

We checked the two transcripts Targ and Puthoff had published in *Mind-Reach* to discover that in the transcript of experiment 7 with Pat Price there a specific reference by Price to "the marina," and a marina is listed as the fourth target in the series. Price states, "They don't feel as far away. I'd say that it is about—not half the distance they were to the marina..." (p.65).

We also noted that the other transcripts published in *Mind-Reach,* the first of Phyllis Cole's, is actually dated "October Seventh" (p.104). *This would have been a useful cue if the judge knew the order in which the targets were visited. If transcripts are dated, placing them in correct order obviously becomes a highly trivial exercise.*

A third transcript available in publication occurs in Wilhelm's *The Search for Superman* (pp.213-218). This transcript is purported to be a complete transcript of Price's description of the fourth target, Redwood City Marina. Incredulous, we noted that on page 217 Targ actually states the following: "I've been trying to picture it in my mind and where you went yesterday on the nature walk." Obviously, this could cue the judge in several ways:

1. it tells him that this transcript does not go with the nature walk (Baylands Nature Preserve, experiment 2);

2. it tells him that this transcript goes with a target visited the day after the visit to the Nature Preserve;

3. (the wild one)—if the judge knew, or could determine the correct sequence of targets, then this cue tells him that this transcript goes with a target occuring soon after the Nature Preserve in the sequence, i.e., a target one or two places down the list.

With this latter possibility at the front of our minds, it became highly desirable to find out what the judge knew and what his instructions were, before he ranked the transcripts. It was also necessary to obtain a copy of the complete set of transcripts for the Price series of experiments to see how many of them contained cues such as those already found in the published transcripts. If several of the transcripts contained cues referring to previous targets, *and* if the judge could determine the original sequence of targets, then, obviously, we have an explanation of the whole Targ-Puthoff effect. Our own negative results would also be explained, as in our experiments we had taken great care to *(a)* remove all cues and *(b)* randomize the listing of targets given to the judge, assuming at the time that Targ and Puthoff had done the same.

Over a sixteen-month period we wrote to Targ and Puthoff on four different occasions asking for a copy of the information given to the judge (letters dated 7 January 1976; 13 April 1977; 17 May 1977; and 26 May 1977). We received no reply to three of these requests and to the fourth we were told: "Although not available for general dissemination, our data has been made available to serious investigators attempting to replicate our work." As no transcripts accompanied this curt reply, we took cold comfort from the implication that we were not serious! Two telephone calls to Targ at SRI in May 1977 were no more successful than our letters, and finally in a personal visit to SRI on 18 June 1977, Targ informed me (DM) that he was *not* prepared to hand over the series of Price transcripts. Richard Kammann and John Wilhelm had also previously failed to obtain copies of these crucial transcripts despite repeated requests.

Fortunately, the consultant to the SRI remote viewing project, Dr. Arthur Hastings, was much more cooperative. He agreed to let me see the Price transcripts and agreed on the desirability that others be allowed to judge them. Moreover, in a letter dated 26 May 1977, Hastings told us that, for the Price series of experiments, *he had been given a typed list of targets in the same order as the table in* Mind-Reach, *i.e., in the correct order.* Hastings gave me a copy of the target list that he received from Targ and Puthoff and, indeed, the targets were listed in correct experimental order.

We now had the information necessary to test our initially improbable hypothesis that the judges in the SRI remote viewing experiments were able to successfully match transcripts against the target list because of cues available in the unedited transcripts.

One preliminary method of testing the cuing hypothesis was to rejudge the Price series of transcripts, utilizing only the cues and the target list. If all the descriptive material is ignored, and the cues are powerful enough, it should be possible to correctly match transcripts against targets *without even visiting the target locations themselves.* We call this technique, "remote judging." Although he didn't know our hypothesis at that stage,

Hastings agreed to let me rejudge five of the Price transcripts that had not been published (either fully or in part). These were transcripts for the Baylands Nature Preserve, Stanford University Radio Telescope, Dumbarton Bridge Toll Plaza, Palo Alto Drive-in Theatre, and the Church of Our Lady on Portola Road.

Careful examination of the transcripts indicated that a large number of cues were available indicating the position of a transcript in the series; e.g., (1) Price expresses apprehension and an inability to do this kind of experiment (target 1); (2) a reference is made to the fact that this experiment is the "second place of the day" (target 2); (3) a reference is made to "yesterday's two targets" (target 3); (4) Targ says encouragingly, "Nothing like having three successes behind you" and mentions the Nature Reserve visited the day before (target 4); (5) Price refers to the marina that was the fourth target (target 7).

In addition to these highly specific cues, the transcripts were laden with possible cues of a much more general, subtle, or contextual nature. These cues included the following: (1) time of day (useful for ordering transcripts fixed on the same day); (2) names of experimenters visiting the target site and those staying with the subject at SRI (personnel tend to remain the same for a block of two-four experiments and then change); (3) the location of the subject at SRI (starts outdoors, then moves indoors); (4) the inclusion of drawings along with the verbal material in two cases (towards the end of the series only); (5) specification of how the target was selected (becomes more sophisticated); and (6) variations in the length of the verbal transcripts in pages (they tend to be relatively long early in the series and shorter near the end). How useful these types of cues are depends upon knowing, or making intelligent guesses at, the information contained in parentheses in each case. Most of the parenthetical information is logical enough and would be available to the discerning professional judge familiar with the Targ-Puthoff experiments. How much of this information Hastings knew is open for debate but it seems reasonable that, as a consultant to the SRI research team, he would have been at least as familiar with the project as the present authors.

Utilizing the cues listed above, I correctly matched all five transcripts, making five direct hits ($p < .0005$). In this procedure it should be noted that *this task was completed solely on the basis of the cues contained in the transcripts, and no visits to target locations were made prior to the successful matchings.*

This "remote judging" procedure has since been replicated with subjects who blind-matched the whole series of transcripts approximately twelve thousand kilometers from the target locations. All judges were given a copy of the sequence of targets in their correct order, as provided to the judge in the original SRI experiment. Judges were also given randomly numbered abstracts of the original transcripts containing contextual and sequential cues present in the originals. The results obtained from eight independent judges A-H along with the original data are shown in Table 4.

Cues listed above enable the judge to place transcripts in groups by making a series of intuitive but accurate guesses about how the experiment was probably run. For example, Mrs. Ann Price (the subject's wife) visited the targets along with Dr. Puthoff on four trials but not on the remaining five. Judges tend to group these four transcripts together—assuming they are more likely to occur in a block than randomly during the sequence. Typically the judge then guesses (correctly) that this block is more probable at the beginning than at the end. These contextual cues, along with the specific sequential cues, converge toward a single correct solution for matching the first four transcripts against their associated targets. All judges matched the first four transcripts perfectly and judges A-H did this remotely, utilizing the cues available. If the remaining five transcripts are ranked randomly against the remaining five targets giving a sum of ranks of fifteen for this block of five, the total sum of ranks for the whole series of nine would be nineteen ($p < .0005$). The results for judges B, F, G, and H, however, show that it is possible to do even better than this.

In a further experiment, we determined whether identification of target sites could be made from the transcripts without utilization of the extraneous cues. To ensure that judges were blind to the correct matchings, it was again necessary to exclude the four transcripts already published. Two judges, both research psychologists, visited these targets in a random sequence and independently ranked the five transcripts at each location, extraneous cues having been removed.

Each judge made a careful and detailed content analysis of the descriptive information provided in the transcripts and ranked on the basis of the descriptive accuracy of the information available. The two judges produced sums of ranks of sixteen and thirteen, neither of which departs significantly from the chance expectation of fifteen. We reported these

Table 4 Distribution of rankings assigned to transcripts associated with each target location in the Price series for judges A–H. Column SRI gives the results for the original judge.

Target Location	Rank of Associated Transcript								
	A	B	C	D	E	F	G	H	SRI
Hoover Tower	1	1	1	1	1	1	1	1	1
Baylands Nature Preserve	1	1	1	1	1	1	1	1	1
Radio Telescope	1	1	1	1	1	1	1	1	1
Redwood City Marina	1	1	1	1	1	1	1	1	1
Bridge Toll Plaza	3	6	4	3	4	6	4	1	6
Drive-in Theatre	5	2	5	4	3	1	1	1	1
Arts and Crafts Plaza	3	2	2	3	3	1	1	3	1
Church	4	2	5	2	5	3	3	2	3
Rinconada Park	2	2	2	4	4	1	1	1	1
Total sum of ranks	21	18	22	20	23	16	14	12	16
P values	10^{-3}	10^{-4}	2.1×10^{-3}	5.1×10^{-4}	2.1×10^{-3}	2.9×10^{-5}	10^{-5}	10^{-6}	2.9×10^{-5}

findings in *Nature* (17 August 1978).

These results provide a striking contrast to the correct matchings obtained when the cues from the unedited transcripts were utilized in making the judgments. The null result also contrasts with the significant matching obtained with unedited transcripts by the original SRI judges.

It seems highly unlikely that the original SRI judges could have missed seeing or ignored the available cues. Judging remote viewing transcripts, many of which are highly similar, is not an easy task, and the presence of any cues or hints, however obscure they may seem at first glance, helps the judge rationalize and organize the large quantity of ambiguous information before him. If in the transcript the experimenter states "Nothing like having three successes behind you" (Price, transcript 4), it would be irrational to place it earlier than fourth in the series and, very probably, it would actually belong in fourth position. How the experimenters could have overlooked such distinct major cues and how the judges could genuinely consider themselves "blind" is a problem we consider later (chapter 12). To quote our own conclusion from our report in *Nature:*

> Our investigation of the SRI remote viewing experiment with Pat Price forces the conclusion that the successful identification of target sites by judges is impossible unless multiple extraneous cues which were available in the original unedited transcripts are utilized. Investigators of remote viewing should take much more care to ensure that such cues are not available. Furthermore, the listing of targets given to judges should be randomized and not presented in the same sequence as that which occurred in the experiments.

The Hammid Series

It could be argued that the above explanation of the Targ-Puthoff effect would not be valid for later series of experiments. Perhaps the rather sloppy procedures of the Price series were eradicated from later series and replaced by properly controlled procedures in which all cues were removed from transcripts and the target information was properly randomized. Regrettably, this does not appear to have been the case.

Unfortunately, we were unable to obtain copies of the complete set of Hammid transcripts from Targ and Puthoff. Even Arthur Hastings admitted he felt "paranoid" about showing us the whole series, but he did let us see six of the nine transcripts at his home in Mountain View, California, on 19 June 1977. Of these six transcripts, *four were dated.* Transcripts for Experiments 1 and 3 in the series were dated 18 September and those for Experiments 8 and 9 were dated 11 October 1974.

Whether or not the three remaining transcripts were dated is an open question. The fact that Hastings wouldn't let us examine them indicates there must have been something to hide. One can only speculate what that something might have been, as it is hard to think of a cue more useful than a specific date,* assuming the correct sequence of targets was available, which it was.

Hastings stated that he received the list of Hammid targets in the order in which the experiments were conducted (letter dated 26 May 1977). Hastings also wrote, "Being naturally a cautious type, when I wrote down the target locations on my worksheet, I re-ordered them myself.... That, incidentally, was always my procedure—to randomize my own procedures, and to read transcripts in varying orders each time I went through them. I don't know if it helped substantially, but I did it *to avoid getting biases.*" It seems incredibly lax of the experimenters to have left the randomization of target lists to the judge. It defeats the whole purpose of employing a "blind" judge in the first place! The quoted statements by Hastings force the conclusion that Hastings must have realized the targets were listed in the correct sequence. Why else would he claim to have re-ordered the targets to avoid bias?

Apart from dates, other cues in the Hammid transcripts were similar to those available in the Price transcripts. Consider this example. The target list shows a Pumpkin Patch as the eighth target, and a Pedestrian Overpass as the ninth. Now the judge comes across a transcript in which Hammid refers to previously visiting the "pumpkin field." Sure enough, this *is* the transcript for target 9, the Pedestrian Overpass. Next, the judge finds another transcript with the same date (11 October) as transcript 9. Sure enough, this *is* the correct transcript for target 8, the Pumpkin Patch.

The Hammid series also brought to light a whole new dimension to the

---

* The only "cue" we can think that would be, is the *name of the target written on the transcript.* Hastings told us that an instance of this did occur (series unspecified), but he returned the transcript to the experimenters.

problem that we had not detected in the Price transcripts. *This is the problem of selecting good data and discarding bad!* Such a procedure completely invalidates the judging exercise because fairly good matches, occurring by chance, have been saved. Let us consider the circumstantial evidence.

A number of drawings were missing from the original Hammid series of transcripts. We wonder whether some drawings were not deemed accurate enough for inclusion in the judging process. Hammid, we are told, was particularly good at drawing the targets, in which case we wonder why no drawings were included in three of the six transcripts we examined (transcripts numbered "3," "7," and "8").

Evidence of *selection* of experiments included in the statistical analysis also comes to light. There is reference to a drawing purportedly done by Hammid that never appeared in the materials given to the judge. The transcript for the Parking Garage (target 4) begins with a statement from Targ as follows: *"Hella has made a drawing of Hal's first location. And we'll see where he is for the next fifteen minutes."* This is clearly a reference to the preceding experiment, which had just finished, in which Hal Puthoff had visited the target site. No drawing was available for either the Parking Garage or the preceding target listed in the series, the Merry-go-round. In fact, it was *Targ* who visited the Merry-go-round, not Puthoff. *This means that there must have been another target between the Merry-go-round and the Parking Garage, visited by Puthoff, drawn by Hammid, and monitored by Targ, that was excluded from the series of experiments.*

Further evidence of selection occurs in the transcript for the ninth target, the Pedestrian Overpass. Despite the fact that the target is listed as the *final* target in the series, the transcript clearly states: "HAL HAS GONE OFF TO THE FIRST OF THREE REMOTE SITES THAT HE WILL VISIT IN THE EXPERIMENT." How come there are *three* sites in the experiment? What happened to the data from the other two?

Again in the transcript for the first target in the official series of experiments, *there is a reference to another experiment done that day.* Of course, it could be argued that the latter experiment was one of the "half-dozen mock experiments" that preceded the experimental series in which a walkie-talkie link was provided to help train Hammid to conduct remote viewing. But this can't be so, as the transcript clearly states that *no feedback was given in this mysterious previous experiment.*

We have, therefore, found evidence that *Targ and Puthoff selected the nine experiments published in the Hammid series from a larger set of experiments.* We have evidence of at least one experiment missing at the beginning, one more missing between the third and fourth targets in the published series, and two more missing from the end of the series, *a total of at least four missing experiments.* Obviously, if experimenters choose which data they publish, their findings become totally meaningless.

Our explanation of the Targ-Puthoff effect would be incomplete without reference to the *quality* of the transcripts of target sites. Close scrutiny of the transcripts made available to us revealed that overall, with one or two exceptions, *the quality of the transcripts as informative, accurate descriptions of target sites was extemely poor.* While it is obviously possible to select for publication a small number of relatively accurate transcripts from the total number available, as Targ and Puthoff have done in *Mind-Reach,* and publish accurate segments of others, the quality of the majority of the descriptions we have seen is poor. Without the available cues, judges are unable to match the transcripts correctly because the information is insufficiently diagnostic.

The Swann-Elgin, Pease-Cole, and Visitor Series

We regret that our efforts to obtain copies of the transcripts and other information given to the judge for these and the remaining series of experiments have not been successful. Neither Targ and Puthoff nor Hastings are willing to make this information publicly available. This fact is sufficient in itself to place the data outside the realm of acceptable science. If scientists are not prepared to allow free and open inspection of their data *after publication of the putative findings,* then the findings themselves are brought under question. One of the goals of science is to let its evidence be known. Science is not a secret society; it is an open forum. If Targ and Puthoff are unwilling to make their data available, their credibility as researchers must fall.

We consider it only reasonable to assume that Targ and Puthoff continued to make the same errors in their later series—errors of transcript cues and errors of data selection for best cases. We believe Targ and Puthoff now claim they removed cues from later experiments, but this amounts to an acknowledgement that the earlier data were invalid, which they have not conceded. Series 3, the Elgin-Swann group of experiments, was still in the period when optimism was high and methodological care was low, and results were very strong. Our guess is that an undoctored presentation of these transcripts would reveal more errors, as we have seen in the Price and Hammid series. But even without this information, yet another kind of error emerges in the three series of experiments included in this section (series 3, 4, and 5).

Note that for each of these three series of experiments, unlike the first two, *experiments from two different subjects have been combined to form the series.* On page 101 of *Mind-Reach* Targ and Puthoff write, "In the process of judging—attempting to match transcripts against targets on the basis of information in the transcripts—some patterns and regularities in the transcript descriptions became evident. Our consultant, Dr. Arthur Hastings, pointed out to us that each person tended to focus on certain aspects of the remote target complex and to exclude others, so that each had an individual pattern of response, like a signature." For example, Swann tended to respond with the topographical and architectural features, while Elgin often described the behavior and actions of the experimenter. In addition to these obvious differences between subjects' styles, transcripts would include the relevant subject's name in the background information always provided at the top of the page.

All that remains is for the judge to determine which subset of places was viewed by each subject. If the judge knows this information, he can easily score well above chance in his rankings. In the Swann-Elgin series, for example, he can rank Elgin's four transcripts against Elgin's four targets and Swann's four transcripts against Swann's four targets. This would divide the odds against accurate rankings in half. This makes nonsense of the statistics used by Targ and Puthoff to evaluate the rankings because *the maximum sum of ranks would now be thirty-two—four less than the chance score of thirty-six when eight transcripts are independently ranked against eight targets.*

This argument depends on our assumption that the judge knew, or could find out, which places were visited by each subject. There are several ways in which this information might have become available: (1) Targ or Puthoff might have told Hastings, the correct orders being an optional extra; (2) cues of the kind available in the transcripts would allow the targets to be grouped and categorized against the subject's name; and (3) communication may have occurred in some cases directly from the subjects to the judge. Hastings admitted that he did meet with some of the subjects and, unwittingly, relevant information could easily have been let slip. Even if *some* of the targets could be tagged by the relevant subject's name by any of the above means, the odds against accurate matching becomes dramatically reduced. These possibilities apply equally well to all three series in which experiments from two subjects were combined. So, in addition to cuing and data selection, we have a third methodological pitfall resulting from an invalid grouping of the subjects.

The Equipment Series

As we are operating on rather incomplete information, we must again ask the reader to excuse us as we must ask questions rather than provide definite answers. These questions relate to yet another possibility emerging in our analysis of these peculiar experiments, particularly to the series involving the selection of visitors as subjects (series 5 and 6). Targ and Puthoff claim: "selection of experiments for reporting did not take place; every experiment was entered on a master log and is included in the statistical evaluations" *(Mind-Reach,* p.101). Close scrutiny of *Mind-Reach,* however, indicates that several kinds of selection must have occurred. We have already reported evidence of selection in the Hammid series. In their reports, Targ and Puthoff refer to "demonstration-type experiments" that were apparently kept separate from experiments entered into the master log and statistical analyses. By what criteria were some trials categorized as "demonstrations" and excluded from the statistical analyses? On page 9-10 of *Mind-Reach,* Targ and Puthoff state that they have carried out "more than one hundred experiments of this type, most of them successful." Why then are we shown the results of only fifty-five (see Table 1)? Where are the remaining forty-five or more experiments, or were these the unsuccessful ones? Targ and Puthoff state that they completed "more than twenty remote viewing experiments with Pat and Ingo" *(Mind-Reach,* p. 69). Why then are only nine with Pat Price and four with Ingo Swann included in their research reports? On what basis were these thirteen trials selected from the twenty-plus Targ and Puthoff say they conducted?

This problem of data selection could become particularly acute in the case of the so-called "Technology" or Equipment series in which from one to five experiments are combined from each of five different subjects. In selecting their experiments for this series, by what criteria was it decided to include *one* experiment from Elgin, *four* from Swann, *five* from Hammid, *one* from Visitor 2, and *one* from Visitor 3? There does seem to be a large degree of variation in the number of experiments each subject was allowed to contribute to this series. Are these differences purely arbitrary? Were these really the *only* experiments ever done with laboratory equipment? Did no other visitors ever try this task; or, when perhaps they did try it, were they counted purely as "demonstrations" and not as "experiments"?

Another area of selection relates to the drawings. In the technology series we note that Swann's drawing for the Drill Press target is missing from the published material included in the information provided to the judge *(Mind-Reach,* Figure 21). Why are drawings sometimes missing, and, at other times, available for judging? Why was only *one* of the two drawings for the Drill Press target submitted to the engineer asked to identify this equipment? Dr. Hastings informed us that the drawing of the Drill Press by Ingo Swann was an excellent rendition of a *typewriter,* another target in the series. Could this be the reason for its exclusion from *Mind-Reach* and from the materials given to the visiting scientist invited to judge the Drill Press equipment?

In the Technology and Visitor series, it seems likely that we have a careful selection of materials collected in haphazard fashion over a period of time. If visitors came to try remote viewing for themselves and the results were good, these were "experiments." If the results were not so good, they were "demonstrations."

The Hammid Precognitive Series

In this series, the subject not only described the invisible, she predicted the future as well, and with 100 percent accuracy, so *Mind-Reach* would have us believe. As we have been unable to obtain the transcripts for these experiments or a copy of the information given to the judge, we can only guess at the explanation of the Targ-Puthoff effect that occurred. There were four targets, ordered as follows: Palo Alto Yacht Harbor; the Fountain in the formal garden at Stanford University Hospital; a children's swing in Burgess Park; and Palo Alto City Hall. Hastings informed us that the target list he received had the positions of the Fountain and City Hall switched. Cuing is therefore unlikely to be the complete explanation.

Selection of these four experiments from a larger set is one possibility.

Evidence of selection in the other series of experiments, including the first Hammid series, means that it could have occurred in this case also. Targ and Puthoff report the presence of an independent observer (David Hurt), however, which means that, presumably, selection would only have occurred with his knowledge and consent.

A third explanation for the excellent matches obtained in this series, and in any of the other series as well, relies on the fact that many of the target areas are so large and encompass so many varied stimuli. This means that the on-site experimenter, usually Puthoff, after returning to the laboratory and seeing the subject's description, can always think of some aspect of the target that the description matches and then write that into the judge's instructions as the relevant part of the target site to pay attention to. This *post hoc* selection need not occur consciously or deliberately. More probably, it occurs quite unwittingly as the returning experimenter finds strong *subjective validation* of the subject's description in some aspect of the multifarious and diverse target site. We experienced the power of this phenomenon for ourselves, as did our subjects, in our own remote viewing experiments (see chapter 2).

As an example of this in Hammid's precognitive series, let's consider the Burgess Park target that happens to include, among a multitude of other things, a child's swing. When Puthoff returns to the laboratory and discovers that Hammid has described a "black iron triangle...bigger than a man," Puthoff automatically thinks of the swing and the experiment is counted as a direct hit. When the subject and, later, the judge visit the site, they too are all impressed at the striking match obtained. To make sure of this, Puthoff actually specifies the swing in the target demarcation instructions that are given to the judge.

Many of the targets used in the Targ-Puthoff experiments are far too diffuse and all-encompassing to allow for satisfactory, objective experiments: parks, marinas, churches, theaters, large buildings, and the like. Within each of these target sites one could match almost any description or drawing.

The problem of target specification is exacerbated still further by another peculiar property attributed to the remote viewing process. When one of us (RK) visited SRI in December 1975, he was told by Puthoff that the results didn't always depend upon the on-site experimenter(s) actually looking at the source of information relayed on to the subject. According to Puthoff, each observer was like a "beacon" relaying information from the target area, *even from parts of the target invisible to the naked eye or not actually observed directly.* As an example of this, there is Hammid's drawing for the Drill Press target, part of which, it is claimed, included the belt drive visible only from above the machine and out of sight from normal eye level.

Taken to its extreme, this property becomes the final *reductio ad absurdum* of remote viewing. The subject receives accurate information transmissions from a sender at a remote location. The distance separating the subject from the sender is not a limiting factor in the subject's ability to perceive the target area. Furthermore, the target area includes stimuli beyond the sender's normal sensory awareness, so he too, in effect, becomes a remote viewer. The target area is indefinite in size—potentially it could become infinite, encompassing the whole universe. Then, finally, we add the property of time travel and we have reached total omniscience. How much closer to God could we earthly mortals hope to be? We wonder if, in the whole history of science, wishful thinking has ever reached such lofty heights as in the wondrous works of Mr. Russell Targ and Dr. Harold Puthoff.

The fact is that any description can be made to match any target. Objective research on remote viewing must guard against all known forms of bias. Independent observers should always accompany the experimenter(s) in the target demarcation team. The targets should be sufficiently discrete and unambiguous to allow objective demarcation of the target area from the surrounding nontarget area. Within the target area, what the experimenter perceives should be strictly monitored and recorded. Film or video recordings of the observer's perceptions should preferably be made during the on-site observation, and the visual record should be available for later judging. Thus, any form of bias on behalf of the returning experimenters to produce accurate matches could be completely avoided. Because Targ and Puthoff have failed to control for these biasing factors, no credence can be placed in their findings.

Summary

We have explained the Targ-Puthoff effect on the basis of a number of methodological flaws and artifacts.

1. There is substantial evidence of *cues,* including dates and references to previous experiments, in the unedited transcripts. These enable the judges to successfully match the transcripts against the list of target sites. Our own

experiments have shown that transcripts can be successfully matched against the target list remotely, that is, without visiting the target sites, by utilizing the cues available. When the cues are removed, matching becomes random.

2. Despite Targ's and Puthoff's claim not to have selected only their successful experiments for publication, there is clear evidence that selection has occurred.

3. In three series of experiments, the statistics and procedures for evaluating the results are invalid as the series were composed of experiments from two different subjects. Cues would have allowed the judge to accurately match the transcripts.

4. Most of the targets were too large and diversified to specify for objective data collection. Biasing through *post hoc* adjustments of the target site following the subject's description was an unavoidable danger, as no objective records (film or videotape) were kept of the movements and perceptions of the on-site experimenters.

Our own attempts to replicate the Targ-Puthoff effect under artifact-free conditions have consistently failed. When all of these considerations are put together, it appears to us that the remote viewing effect is, at present, nothing more than a massive artifact of poor methodology and wishful thinking.

4

KRESKIN'S RIDDLE

I can realize my greatest potential as an entertainer who uses suggestion and ESP.

Kreskin

We now take up a relaxing interlude for two chapters to consider the somewhat ambiguous claims to psychic powers that surround the stage personality of Kreskin, the popular American magician. We may say that the aura of psychism "surrounds" Kreskin, rather than saying he claims to be a psychic, because Kreskin is highly evasive on this point; yet, as much as possible, he encourages the association of the language of parapsychology and the occult with his name.

Kreskin is historically significant in our research because he provided us with our first case study of alleged telepathy and our first exercise in psychological detective work. He was our warm-up for the more challenging study of Uri Geller, which we present in subsequent chapters, and for remote viewing, which we have already reviewed. At one point we considered that Kreskin's claims to psychic status were so vague that he did not require a public refutation, but we have encountered so many advocates and believers in his camp that a brief review of his methods seems worthwhile.

In his book *The Amazing World of Kreskin,* Kreskin recounts the longest on-stage mind-reading demonstration of his career. "Someone here is thinking of her boyfriend," he began. An attractive blond girl of nineteen or twenty stood up. From that point Kreskin ticked off her boyfriend's name, his street address, his telephone number, the names of the girl's two brothers and two sisters, and finally, all their birth dates. By this time both he and the girl were shaking (he writes) and he vowed then and there to limit his "mental adventuring" to a few single thoughts. *(The Amazing World of Kreskin,* New York: Random House, 1973, pp.1-2.)

Does Kreskin have ESP or not? This is the riddle that the stage and TV star poses with puckish charm and wit, a riddle that has produced a sharp division of public opinion. In a random telephone survey, we found that 23 percent believed that Kreskin uses ESP, 34 percent were uncertain, and 41 percent thought not. Only 2 percent of the sample had not heard of Kreskin. So, almost a quarter of the population thinks he is a psychic, and another third thinks he might be. But when we did a survey of people who had actually seen a Kreskin show, the percentage of believers jumped to 59 percent. We cannot say, as yet, how much of this increase is due to the fact that believers are more likely to buy a ticket to see Kreskin, and how much is due to Kreskin's ability to convert people into believers through his stage demonstrations.

Throughout Kreskin's entire book, *The Amazing World of Kreskin,* and throughout everything he says or writes, Kreskin retains his secret behind a barrage of double talk and verbal flip-flops. In fact, he contradicts himself so freely that finding the truth from him is like finding your way out of a hall of mirrors.

...and if he can't find [his paycheck] through ESP he forfeits payment. (Stage Program.)

Kreskin is the enemy of all professed psychics, mind-readers, mediums and charlatans, who attempt to guide people's lives. (Stage Program.)

Kreskin has been successful in applying his special abilities to help dentists, doctors, expectant mothers, golfers and the police. (Stage Program.)

The name Kreskin has become synonymous with all that is fascinating in the worlds of auto-suggestion, hypnosis, telepathy, and parapsychology. (frontispiece, *The Amazing World of Kreskin.*)

I am not a psychic. (ibid., p.14.)

Perhaps some of what I do fits into the category of the "psychic," so-called, under certain conditions. (ibid., p.15.)

I do pick up information through a kind of telepathy.... (ibid., p.16.)

In using ESP as a form of communication, I receive information in images... (ibid., p.17.)

Millions have seen [Kreskin] perform his astounding extrasensory feats on the Johnny Carson Show, Mike Douglas, and his own national program. (Advertisement for Kreskin's "Institute for ESP Research.")

Now—the amazing mentalist Kreskin shows you how to harness the enormous hidden powers of your mind. (Advertisement for *Kreskin's Mind Power Book* in the *New York Times.*)

I'm not a fortune teller, and I'm the last person who would want to be associated with occultism. It's taboo in Catholicism, you know. (Interview in *Twin-Circle,* a Roman Catholic weekly magazine in California.) In the same news story, *The Church fully accepts the existence of Kreskin's main meal ticket—extrasensory perception.*

Much of the book *The Amazing World of Kreskin* is devoted to anecdotes of mind-reading events for which Kreskin offers no explanation at all. Indeed, he comes across as being baffled and bewildered by it all himself. Surely, if he were merely a stage magician, he would know what he is doing, would he not?

To spare the reader any further confusion, we shall state clearly and simply that Kreskin does NOT have ESP.

In our view, he can be called a very skilled magician, conjuror, illusionist, and/or entertainer, but in no reasonable sense of the word could he be called a "psychic." The term Kreskin uses—*mentalist*—is just another semantic inkblot. According to *Webster's Third New International Dictionary Unabridged,* a mentalist is "a mind reader or fortune teller," but among magicians, *mentalism* is a brand of conjuring that creates illusions of thought transference. (Will the real Kreskin please stand up?)

Some people reading our articles on Kreskin have suggested that we, as psychologists, just couldn't swallow the idea of psychic powers and so we set out to disprove Kreskin. Nothing could be more incorrect. In fact, we began our studies on ESP after numerous students had suggested we "wake up" to psychic reality. At the same time eminent scientists like Carl Rogers, Charles Tart, Harold Puthoff, Russell Targ, and John Taylor were reporting on successful psychic experiments. So, we considered it entirely possible that the psychology of perception was about to go through a psychic revolution, and if so, we wanted to be included. But over the next three years of research, when we examined each dazzling claim of ESP, or psychokinesis (PK), we discovered that a simple, natural explanation was far more credible than a supernatural or paranormal one.

In the remainder of this chapter we present a complete description of the first Kreskin stage show we attended. While this show happened to take place in Dunedin, New Zealand (12 March 1974), the subsequent Kreskin performances we have seen in America follow almost exactly the pattern of that first show, except for nightclub or casino performances, which are considerably shortened. In fact, in none of our psychic researches have we found any significant differences in a "psychic" performance or an audience response between the United States and New Zealand, which is not surprising given their common heritage of English language and Western technological culture.

However, here we report a New Zealand show rather than an American show because it is the case for which we have the most complete and accurate records. Since we did not know whether we were going to see a psychic happening or just a good magic act, we (independently) took as many detailed notes as we could for each "telepathic" event. In the days immediately following this show, we reviewed these notes step by step and were able to reconstruct the entire stage show in every essential respect.

It may be admitted that we were generally as baffled as anybody else in the audience as the Kreskin show whizzed along from one startling event to another, and it was only during our *post mortem* discussions that a pattern of conjuring techniques began to dawn on us.

We present these explanations and our follow-up studies that supported them in the next chapter. Here we present the Kreskin show with very little comment of our own, in an effort to recapture at least a shadow of the uncanny and usually mystifying effects that Kreskin produces.

Kreskin's Stage Show

After having taken our seats in the theater and browsing through the Stage Program, we got the edgy feeling that we were about to witness something almost mystical, something that cognitive psychologists wouldn't be able to explain. One of us (RK) wrote the following account shortly after.

To tell the truth, I went into a temporary state of intellectual paranoia. My first hypothesis was that maybe there were girls standing behind the back railings watching us all. (That girl looks suspicious.) Next, I peered at the edges of the stage curtains to see if there was a telescope peeking out. (I couldn't decide.) I studied the chandeliers on the ceiling, imagining I could make out telephoto lenses or hidden microphones. I glowered at the

stranger on my right (knowing a spy when I met one). Pretending to tie my
shoestring, I looked under my seat for electronic bugs.

Kreskin finally breezed onto the stage and warmed up the audience with
a mixture of prepared jokes and witty commentary on his recent travels.
We got a precognition, so to speak, of Kreskin's mind-reading ability when
he taunted those of us who had been looking for hidden microphones,
telescopes, and accomplices in the audience! Kreskin's patter includes a
series of misleading mini-lectures on psychology. The magician happens to
be a voracious reader in some areas of psychology, but, as usual, he
purveys quarter-truths to foster an aura of occultism. For example, in his
first mini-lecture, he stated that people have more than five senses, in fact
they have eleven, or by Margaret Mead's reckoning, twenty-two. What
Kreskin did *not* reveal is that these senses are perfectly ordinary ones that
are listed in most textbooks of introductory psychology. For example, one
of us (RK) has listed eleven bodily senses in addition to seeing, hearing,
smelling, and tasting for a total of fifteen. *(Workbook for General*
Psychology, Englewood Cliffs, N.J.: Prentice-Hall, 1970, pp. 80-81.) It is
easily possible to get a higher number—tasting can be divided into four
basic types—seeing can be divided into two categories (rod vision and cone
vision), and so on. These senses are all used by every normally equipped
human being every day. None of them is psychic or paranormal.

We now report all of Kreskin's mind reading events in the order they
took place. The dialogues are not truly verbatim, of course, because we had
to reconstruct them over the following few days, using our independently
written notes. Most of what is missing is irrelevant stage patter; there were
three occasions on which neither of us could hear the participant's reply to
Kreskin and these are shown as "inaudible." Nothing that we could
observe has been left out.

In retrospect, the telepathy effects fell into four definable phases, as
follows:
1. Kreskin broadcasts his own thoughts.
2. Kreskin reads thoughts in the audience.
3. Kreskin perceives written messages.
4. Kreskin finds his hidden paycheck.

Phase 1. Kreskin broadcasts his own thoughts.

Kreskin opens his mind reading with a brilliant gambit for getting the audience maximally involved. Instead of reading the thoughts of single individuals in the crowd, he mentally transmits two or three thoughts of his own—the majority of spectators will get at least one of them correct. (As the psychic boosters say, we *all* have ESP!)

Event 1

Kreskin said he was thinking of *two very simple geometric forms,* one inside the other; he was "projecting" them onto his "mental screen." "Just open your minds," he said, "and see what appears on your mental screen." (The reader may wish to stop and try to receive these two shapes right now.) "Okay, I am thinking of a triangle inside a circle— did any one get that?" Hundreds of hands go up amidst great hubbub. "Or a circle inside a triangle," he beamed. More hands go up. It seemed that perhaps a third of the audience had gotten it. (Applause.)

Event 2

Kreskin said that the audience was very good and he would try to send them a number this time, say a *number between one and fifty.* "I'll make both digits odd," he continues, "but not the same odd digit. For example, fifteen would be okay, but eleven wouldn't do because the two odd digits are the same. I'm projecting it on my mental screen." (Pause) (The reader is invited to stop and choose a number now.) "How many got thirty-seven?" Again, there were gasps and cries as a forest of hands appeared in the air. "I started to think thirty-five, but... " (More hands go up.) "Did you get the thirty-five—that's what came to me first." (Applause.)

Phase 2. Kreskin reads thoughts in the audience.

In Phase 2, Kreskin usually asks the audience to write down any thoughts or messages they want to on slips of paper. At this point he bounds around the aisles of the theater giving out slips of paper, dashes back up on stage to get pencils or envelopes, and back into the crowd, sporadically calling out instructions or witty banter.

One of the points we want to make about the psychology of the "psychic" magician is that he exploits people's natural habits of thought. As Kreskin dashes about the room, you will be concentrating on unusual messages with highly personal meanings, messages that Kreskin could not get right by guessing. This is exactly what Kreskin wants you to do. In particular, he does not want you watching *him* too closely as he moves along the aisles—but that gets ahead of the story.

Finally, the messages are all folded up and passed along to people seated by the aisles who have been given empty envelopes. (Aha, you might say, these are his accomplices.) Now, it is an interesting fact that Kreskin does not use these written messages until Phase 3 of the show. The audience may assume that the mind-reading stunts that follow here are based on the written messages, but that is merely an assumption. (In our analysis, probably only three of the messages received in Phase 2 of our show had been written down—you might try to guess which three they were.)

We continue with the show.

Event 3

Kreskin: Who is planning to make a long-distance phone call to your mother, or perhaps your mother-in-law? *(Pause)* No one, a phone call to your mother, or somebody...
Woman: Yes.
Kreskin: Is it your mother?
Woman: No, my daughter.
Kreskin: Do you belong to some kind of group studying plants? *(Pause)* Do you do something with plants?
Woman: *(Pause)* No.
Kreskin: Thank you.
(Applause)

Event 4

Kreskin: Somebody's watch is broken...or out of time...something, I'm not quite...

Woman: *(Stands up)*
Kreskin: Do you have it on?
Woman: Yes.
Kreskin: What is wrong with...
Woman: *(Inaudible)*
Kreskin: *(Smiling)* Oh, you were too lazy to wind it. Who is William... *(Pause)* or Bill...?
Woman: No one.
Kreskin: Thank you.
(Applause)

Event 5

Kreskin: Who here is thinking about someone in England...or about England?
Person: I am.
Kreskin: Do *you* know a Bill or William?
Person: Yes.
Kreskin: Is it your father?
Person: *(Inaudible)*
(Scattered applause)

Event 6

Kreskin: Some one has been scolded...or is it scalded...not themselves...possibly in the kitchen.
Woman: Yes.
Kreskin: Your mother?
Woman: No, my daughter was scalded.
Kreskin: Do you have a crack in your kitchen door?
Woman: Umm, no. *(Pause)* It's in my bedroom door.
(Applause)

Event 7

Kreskin: I am getting a name, or word, with M-I-D... or D-D...

Man: *(Stands up)*
Kreskin: Is it a place?
Man: Yes.
Kreskin: Is it two words?
Man: Yes.
Kreskin: How many letters in the first word?
Man: Six.
Kreskin: I only get five. Are any letters doubled?
Man: Yes.
Kreskin: I get Middle...Middle Marca...no that's not quite...it's Middle March!
Man: Right.
(Applause)

Event 8

Kreskin: I am receiving a number with 551 in it.
Woman: *(Stands up)*
Kreskin: What does the number mean to you?
Woman: It's my bankbook number.
Kreskin: How many digits are in the number?
Woman: Six.
Kreskin: Is it 551026?!
Woman: Yes.
(Great applause)

Event 9

Kreskin: Someone is thinking of work...shop work... *(Pause)* No one? Something about shop work.
Woman: *(Stands up)*
Kreskin: Do you work in a shop?
Woman: A milk bar.
Kreskin: You're married, right?
Woman: *(Inaudible)*
Kreskin: What does August 10 mean to you?
Woman: *(Pause)* Nothing.

Kreskin: Thank you.
(Applause)

Event 10

Kreskin: I get the letters A.M. ...is there an A.M.?
(Pause) Perhaps A. Michael.
1st Woman: Yes, Michael.
Kreskin: Is there an A before Michael?
1st Woman: No.
Kreskin: Then it's not you. It's not her thought. I can't get it, perhaps...Armene or A. Michael. There's more but I don't know what they are. *(Pause)* Aren't you going to own up? A. M. or A. Michael. *(Pause)* And I get Christchurch.
2nd Woman: Yes.
Kreskin: What does A. Michael mean to you?
2nd Woman: It's my baby's name. And my husband's.
Kreskin: What does Christchurch mean to you?
2nd Woman: We took my baby to Christchurch.
Kreskin: 1973. What does that mean?
2nd Woman: The year my baby was born.
Kreskin: Was he born in May?
2nd Woman: Yes.
Kreskin: On the 5?
2nd Woman: Yes.
(Applause)

Phase 3: Kreskin perceives written messages.

One of the principles we have developed after watching stage "psychics" is that everything they do has a meaning or a purpose. Even the most trivial and innocent movements or comments can create a key distraction, if not to keep the eyes from looking, then to keep the brain from thinking.

Consider this example. In Phase 1 of a stage show, Kreskin holds up a fancy looking clipboard with flaps on it and casually mentions that it is only his writing pad. Then, he jots down his geometrical figures and the number between one and fifty. But, it will become obvious in the next chapter that there is no way in the world that Kreskin could forget these messages, so writing them down is completely unnecessary. According to our rule, this action must serve some other purpose. As we shall see, the writing board now reappears in Phase 3. Back to the show.

Kreskin came into the audience and asked that some of the folded written messages be placed on his writing board (to show that he wasn't touching them). With the flaps up, the board served adequately as a tray. "Okay, enough," he called out, and went back up on stage, putting the writing board down by the stage steps. Here he gave another nonsense lecture on parapsychology. (Remember, everything he does is significant.) He then retrieved the tray and asked four or five people in the front rows to take one slip of paper each, to remain standing, and to concentrate on the message. Back at stage center, Kreskin tried to receive these chosen messages, as follows:

Event 11

Kreskin: I get something about a book.
 Person: Yes.
Kreskin: Is it a title?
 Person: No.
Kreskin: Not an author, no.
 Person: No.
Kreskin: Is it a rare book?
 Person: Yes.
Kreskin: It's "a rare book on witchcraft"?
 Person: Yes.
          (Applause)

Event 12

Kreskin: Is there a slip with a name on it...Sherry or Sharon or
          Cherry...
    Man: Yes.
Kreskin: And another name. Theresa?
    Man: Yes.
Kreskin: And their ages. Is it Sherry, age six?

Man: Yes.
Kreskin: And Theresa, she's eight!
Man: Yes.
> *(Applause)*

Event 13

Kreskin: Are there any numbers, or perhaps just one number?
Man: Yes.
Kreskin: What kind of a number is it?
Man: It's a date.
Kreskin: I see a six...no, that's not from anyone standing. All right, I need a volunteer from the audience. Will some one down there come up here? You, come on up. I won't hurt you. Good, come right up here. *(A woman walked uncertainly over to stage center)*
Kreskin: Now you are going to receive this message for me. Don't worry. I know you can do it. It's a date, we're going to get the month first. Just face me and close your eyes and concentrate as I call off the months. *(He places his hands on her folded arms)* All right *(rolling his head in rapid circles he chanted)*, January, February, March, April, May, June, July, August, September, October, November, December. Yes. I think she got a really strong impression. What was it?
Woman: June?
Kreskin: *(Turning his head to man standing)* Is it June?
Man: Yes. *(Ripple of applause)*
Kreskin: Now, let's see if you can get the day. Are you ready? Okay, *(again rolling his head)* 1, 2, 3, 4, 5, 6, 7, 8, 9, 10, 11, 12, 13, 14, 15, 16, 17, 18, 19, 20, 21, 22, 23, 24, 25, 26, 27, 28, 29, 30. Did you get it? What day?
Woman: 18?
Man: *(Holding the message)* Yes.
> *(Long applause)*

Phase 4: Kreskin finds his hidden paycheck

Kreskin offers twenty thousand dollars to anybody who can prove he uses accomplices or paid confederates. For many people, this is proof itself. Some have said to us, "If you psychologists really know how Kreskin does it, how come you haven't collected twenty thousand dollars?" But alas, poor us, Kreskin doesn't offer the money if we can prove he is cheating, or if we can explain his tricks, but only if we prove he uses stooges in the audience, and that is a different matter.

We now consider one of Kreskin's most famous and dramatic effects, the finding of his paycheck. First, he usually calls onto stage some local official, like the mayor or the chief of police. Kreskin hands over his paycheck and asks for it to be hidden anywhere in the theater. Two volunteers go backstage with Kreskin to make sure he cannot peek. When Kreskin finally returns, he must locate the paycheck, or else he gives it over to the charity of his choice, which he has had to do only three times. But we can return to our first psychic show for more details.

It was the mayor who hid Kreskin's paycheck in the pocketbook of a woman about halfway back in the theater. Coming out and down from the stage, Kreskin asked the mayor to take hold of one end of a handkerchief while Kreskin held the other end. "Just follow me," Kreskin said and started off quickly to his left. "Don't lead me!" he said sharply and then turned to his right, going up the (correct) aisle with the mayor in tow.

The audience was still and hushed. Kreskin walked far past the paycheck and searched around the walkway at the side of the room. Then suddenly, he reversed himself and came back down the (correct) aisle. He stopped by the correct row, went forward a step, then back two steps. He asked a man and (the correct) woman to come out and stand in the aisle. He let the mayor off the hank while he walked around each of them and then asked the man to sit down. He took the woman up on stage with him. She was very good, not showing the slightest sign of "guilty knowledge" that we could see. But then Kreskin asked her to open her purse, and as he pulled out his paycheck, there was a deafening round of applause.

A Demonstration of Non-Hypnotism

After intermission, Kreskin shifts his shows from mind reading to stage hypnotism, wnicn ne says is *not* hypnotism. A simplified version of the mini-lecture goes something like this:

There is no such thing as a hypnotic trance. For example, if you hypnotize a person and hook him up to a lie detector, and then you speak his name, his nervous system will go "boing" and the lie detector will go "blippity-bloop," just like it would for any normal person. And, if you hook your victim up to an EEG machine, you will find his brain waves humming away just like any person who is wide awake, not a person who is asleep.

Therefore I, Kreskin, offer twenty thousand dollars to anybody who can prove the existence of a hypnotic trance. Although hypnotism doesn't exist, I have rediscovered something called suggestion, which I shall do now. Then Kreskin does his stage hypnotism. (We offer Kreskin twenty thousand dollars if he can prove it is *not* hypnotism.)

But, let us return to the show we were describing above to see what Kreskin did with about seventy-five volunteers from the audience. When the group was assembled on stage, he began with the simple exercise of having them clasp their hands together tightly for a while, with fingers interlocked. "You are pulling them, squeeze them, tighten them," he ordered. "Keep going, you can't pull them apart. You are not able to pull them apart, they are locked together! They are stuck." His voice was now practically shouting in triumph. When several people pulled their hands apart, Kreskin deftly waved them off stage while the remainder struggled and writhed to free themselves from severe cases of lockpaw. "One, two, three," a snap of Kreskin's fingers, and all hands came unglued.

Kreskin slipped smoothly and progressively up the steps of his hypnotic ladder, chattering wittily as he told the victims what they would experience next. They couldn't uncross their legs; then, they couldn't get out of their chairs. When Kreskin told of a cold wave coming through the room, they shivered and pulled up their collars. When a heat wave followed, they opened their collars, threw off their jackets, and then mopped their brows. While all this proceeded, Kreskin periodically gave a shotlike point of his finger and a flick of his wrist, and another victim disappeared off stage like a duck in a shooting gallery—Kreskin was weeding out the uncommitted and unsuggestible.

Eventually Kreskin began to work with individuals. A man couldn't lights his cigarette; (snap) he then lit it, but the taste was so revolting he was in danger of puking. (Snap.) When he tried vigorously to throw the cigarette away, it would not leave his fingers. Two men, wearing their jackets inside out, went up and down the line asking the others why *they* all had *their* clothes on inside out. As Kreskin said it, so it happened, until three or four different people were simultaneously caught up in their own ludicrous, imaginary predicaments. Kreskin was dashing about, enjoying himself. "Did you ever hear about the man who forgot his own name," he chided a young fellow. "Isn't that ridiculous? You couldn't forget your own name, could you? By the way, what *is* your name?" The chap stood there looking off into space (as in a trance), trying to think of his name. Another tidal wave of laughter broke over the theater.

Our notes showed that the number of people on stage had dwindled steadily—fifty-seven, fifty-two, forty-five, thirty-eight, thirty, twenty-four, until only twenty-one performing clowns were left. Then Kreskin waved them all away and bowed out to a thundering applause that we joined ourselves.

Although hypnotic comedy is not classed as a psychic effect, it rounds out our picture of Kreskin as the jovial showman, a picture that clashes against the subdued seriousness of a Uri Geller performance.

In recounting Kreskin's mind-reading feats in this chapter, we have tried to include just enough hints to make it theoretically possible for readers to solve them—at least in a general way—for themselves. So, you have the easy option of reading our explanations in the next chapter, or the more challenging option of going back over the episodes in this chapter and testing your wits against Kreskin's tricks.

5

SOLVING KRESKIN'S RIDDLE

I would say that I do manifest some of what we call ESP. But I don't do it under just any conditions; I have to control my conditions.

Kreskin

On a warm spring day in 1949 in a Philadelphia junior high school, a normally quiet lad of fourteen suddenly interrupted his teacher's geography lesson. Staring off into space, he urgently announced that a classmate, Jimmy Wright, had just fallen off a brick wall, badly injuring his right shoulder and right leg. When he could not say how he knew this, the teacher took the lad to the principal's office, while the boy kept giving a running account of things happening in his imagination. About twenty minutes later he calmed down, saying that Jimmy Wright was on his way to the hospital in an ambulance but, nevertheless, the principal delivered him home and advised the family to take the boy to a doctor.

That same afternoon, however, Jimmy Wright's mother phoned to say that her son had fallen off a high brick wall two miles away from school, hurt his right shoulder and right leg, and was taken away in an ambulance. A check on the timing revealed that these events were occurring in exact synchrony with the unusual behavior observed in the classroom that day.

In the three years following, 147 episodes of clairvoyance and telepathy were documented on the psychic prodigy by parents, teachers, and visiting scientists. Until recently, FBI security has prevented disclosure of the boy's faultless solution of the baffling Penlot family murder, as recorded by the eminent criminal pathologist, Professor J.B. Watson, from his tape recordings of the sensitive interviews conducted on the boy by Chief Detective Warlock Holmes.

But, we must interrupt this tall yarn to say that it has nothing to do with Kreskin or anybody else in real life. It is the kind of biography that would give credit to a true psychic, and thus, the kind of history that a proper psychic fraud would try to create *ex post facto*. But Kreskin, unlike some psychics, is not the man for the Big Lie.

In actuality, Kreskin was born with the name George Kresge in West Caldwell, New Jersey. At the age of five he became fascinated with magic, at age nine he was performing half-hour shows around the country "as a traveling magician" (Stage Program), and at age eleven he incorporated hypnotism in his act.

At Seton Hall University (New Jersey), George Kresge obtained a bachelor's degree in psychology, apparently taking in Psychology Professor Frank Murphy who is quoted as saying, "Kreskin has developed a striking and unique method of communication which may take more than fifty years to be common" (Stage Program).

The adopted stage name KRESKIN was taken from KRESge plus K from Harry Kellar, one of America's early great magicians, plus IN from the French conjuror, HoudIN. (Houdin is not to be confused with the great magician, escape artist, and life-long exposer of psychic frauds, Harry Houdini, whom Kreskin publicly detests.) The name KRESKIN itself symbolizes stage magic! Furthermore, Kreskin is well versed in all the traditional arts of conjuring and often warms up his audience with a sophisticated card trick, or by taking three men's rings from the audience and interlocking them without breaking them. (He doesn't even pretend this is psychokinesis.)

Not only is Kreskin a well-practiced magician, but his mentalism is anything but original, being very closely copied from the Great Dunninger's routine, which was heard weekly on American radio in the 1940s, including the offer of a large reward for proof of confederates in the audience. Indeed, Kreskin owns all the original kinescopes of Dunninger's TV appearances in the early 1950s before the older magician developed Parkinson's disease and retired not long before his death.

We now take up the events of the Kreskin show described in the preceding chapter to see how the illusion of mind reading is created by conjuring techniques. In some cases there is more than one possible method of deception, but we also report follow-up studies that give us extra confidence in the explanation we provide.

As in the remote viewing studies, we include the method of the *delayed control group* as one type of follow-up. This means that we have reproduced a "psychic" result by going through the same procedures (as Kreskin), except that paranormal processes are essentially ruled out. If we predict and then get the same result by perfectly normal modes of communication, then the conjuring method is supported and the psychic hypothesis is superfluous.

Many Minds on the Same Track

Kreskin starts out in Phase 1 by reaching as many people as he can in two quick tricks. He thinks of a circle and a triangle, and immediately a third of the audience thinks the same; he thinks of the number 37, and again, a third of the audience "gets it." The only hitch is that Kreskin could have thought of anything—including wooden boots without a zipper—and the audience would still have produced the circle-triangle and the number 37. The reason is that they are not responding to Kreskin's thoughts, but to the previous *instructions* about what (he says) he will think about.

Most people imagine that they could think of a large number of simple geometrical shapes, but in reality only three will come to mind quickly—a circle, a triangle, and a square. Try to think of anything else and you are likely to draw a blank. Now with only three shapes to work with, there are only three possible pairs: circle-triangle, circle-square, square-triangle. Thus, by chance alone, about one person in three should get the correct answer. (Although Kreskin first suggests that one figure must be inside the other, he later gives credit for either arrangement.)

More generally, Kreskin knows from previous tests of his own that certain instructions will cause a certain association to occur in a sizable percentage of any audience, and he simply chooses this one as his "thought." No psychic vibes need apply.

Likewise, 37 is merely the most common association to Kreskin's complicated definition of the number he (says he) is thinking of. Again, the illusion depends on the untested assumption that people *could* think of a wide range of numbers. But could they? Try this simple problem. By defining both digits as odd, how many numbers are left between 1 and 50? Would you say about half as many, about 25? The correct answer is only ten. Furthermore, Kreskin uses up two of these numbers, 11 and 15, as examples, and eliminates 33 because the two odd digits are the same. This leaves only seven numbers, 13, 17, 19, 31, 35, 37, and 39; so, the chance probability is already up to one in seven.

But there may also be a statistical tendency to prefer some numbers over others. After Kreskin mentions the numbers 11 and 15 in his examples, perhaps most people try to think of a number that is away from, rather than close to, the examples, numbers such as 35 or 37 rather than 13 or 17. This may sound far-fetched, but such response preferences are well known in psychological experiments, where they are known technically as *population stereotypes,* which we sometimes refer to casually as *pop-types.*

For our delayed control group test, we conducted a simple free association experiment. Some helpful college instructors went to their introductory psychology classes and asked the students to write down the first word that came to mind in response to each stimulus. Then the instructors read the following instructions.

All right, we will begin. The first stimulus is as follows. Think of two very simple geometric forms, one inside the other. (Pause) *Has everybody written down his response? Okay, the second stimulus goes like this. A number between 1 and 50. Both digits are odd, but they are not the same digit. For example, it could be 15—the odd digits are not alike—but it could not be 11 because the two odd digits are the same.*

ᵥ To make sure that the instructors were not sending out real psychic vibes, we told them to concentrate on false targets, like an oval-in-a-trapezoid or the number 31—we did *not* tell them that we were predicting a circle-triangle or number 37. Following the stimulus presentations, the instructors collected the student answers and handed them over to us for analysis, giving us a total of 202 students' reponses.

As can be seen in Table 5, 36 percent of the students chose the circle-triangle and 35 percent chose the number 37. As predicted, over one-third of the audience could get Kreskin's thoughts by chance. By some simple probability calculations (omitted here), we can also estimate that 58 percent of the audience will get *at least one* of the two targets correct. Furthermore, 13 percent of the audience will get *both* answers correct, and, after this double-whammy, will probably believe they are just as psychic as Kreskin is (which would be correct).

Of course, this nonpsychic explanation would collapse if Kreskin chose unpredictable targets, but over several such shows in the United States, he

TABLE 5

Associative Responses to the Geometric Forms and the Number Tasks
(N = 202)

Geometric Forms		Number	
Shapes Selected	Percent Selecting	Number Selected	Percent Selecting
circle, triangle	36	39	10
circle, square	25	37	35
square, triangle	15	35	23
circle, circle square, square triangle, triangle } 10		31	5
		19	9
		17	10
		13	5
all others	14	all others	3
	100%		100%

always chose the circle and triangle as his geometric shapes, and the number 37 for the two odd digits. When he does a repeat show in the same place, the shapes are omitted, while the number is defined as being between 50 and 100, for which Kreskin's choice is 86 (or, as he says, it could also be 68).

This type of thought transmission can be used in living room demonstrations of "ESP." Everybody is asked to write down what they receive. On the first task the sender draws a circle overlapping a triangle. For those who get the wrong answer, the sender says, "Now try harder this time—open your mind—don't be skeptical." On the second trial, the sender writes down 35, crosses it out, and writes down 37 next to it. Later he claims that he started out thinking of 35 but it didn't feel right, so he quickly changed to 37; those choosing 35 will be just as impressed as those who produce 37.

How to Find a Straw in a Haystack

It is widely claimed that once Kreskin starts working on a subject, he is always able to get more and more information. In Phase 2 of the show, we find that this claim is usually not true, and when it is true, we find that Kreskin has cheated.

To make this clear, we must divide the mind readings of Phase 2 into two different conjuring methods. First we take up those more trivial cases in which Kreskin throws out commonplace ideas that have a good chance of connecting with somebody's past or present thoughts. This method, which we call making *probability matches* (or finding a straw in a haystack), seems to account adequately for events 3-6 and event 9. In these cases Kreskin "received" a phone call to a daughter, a stopped watch, thinking about England, somebody who was scolded or scalded, and shop work.

If you read the script carefully, you will notice that Kreskin actually throws out very vague ideas—for example, "somebody is thinking of a mother or a mother-in-law or..." (expectant pause). Now in an audience of over five hundred people, perhaps several thousand in some shows, there is bound to be somebody who is (or has been) thinking about a mother or a mother-in-law or...(?). Note that the eager woman who jumped up was thinking of her *daughter,* which is two generations off. Thus, the victim may actually make the match for Kreskin, while emotionally expressing a sense of great astonishment.

This combination of vagueness by Kreskin and people jumping up with answers applies to the other events as well. In event 4 Kreskin was thinking that somebody's watch was broken, or out of time, or "something...." A woman who forgot to wind her watch imagined that Kreskin was speaking directly to her and stood up in amazement. Events 5, 6, and 9 fit the same pattern.

The diagnosis as probability matches is confirmed by Kreskin's failure to get much new information on the follow-ups. On event 3 the woman denies that she has anything to do with plants, and on event 4 the subject doesn't recognize William or Bill, which Kreskin whimsically tries out on the next customer with better luck. On event 6 he suggests that there is a crack in the kitchen door, to which the woman replies, "No...it's in the bedroom door." By referring to "it," she assumes that the crack in *her* head is the same as the crack in *Kreskin's* head. Actually, her long hesitation strongly suggests that she had not been thinking of any crack at all, but remembered one to meet Kreskin's expectations. (Psychologists call this pressure of social expectations the *demand characteristics* of the situation.) On event 9 Kreskin tosses out August 10, but it doesn't work for his subject. So all in all, Kreskin produced only three failures and two weak probability matches on his follow-ups, a far cry from his reputed success rate.

Having solved these cases to our satisfaction, we were subsequently surprised to learn from professional and amateur magicians that there is another common device to achieve the same kinds of fragmentary mind reading. This is the method we call *foyer reconnaisance,* although it may include the parking lot as well as the foyer of the theater. In this technique, the performer or an accomplice hangs about in the foyer to overhear snippets of conversation, or to look into purses when they are opened, or hangs about in the parking lot noting license plate numbers. These bits of information are then used to produce more "mind reading" on stage.

In a subsequent casino show in the United States, Kreskin did in fact, describe a man's car and the state he came from, and then read off the man's license plate number, which amazed him and amused us.

We also took note that Kreskin does not rely on simple probability matches when he has a small audience, since the chances of drawing a blank become too high. In these situations, more direct methods of cheating are required to guarantee successes.

The Mysterious Disappearance of "551026"

But, it is the other three events in Phase 2 (events 7, 8, and 10) that are the glory makers. Here the pattern is somewhat different—Kreskin first gets only a fragment of the message and then proceeds to "home in" on the whole thought. With messages as specific as Middlemarch, 551026, and A. Michael, Christchurch, May 5, any theory based on chance is obviously ruled out. Even more puzzling is how Kreskin can proceed progressively from part to whole—unless, of course, he actually knows the whole message before he begins on it! We have good reason to believe he does.

In the beginning, we had no clear hypothesis to cover these three cases and had not made up our minds about Kreskin, until we did some follow-ups of our own. We ran a large ad in both local newspapers asking for people who had been involved in any of the mind-reading events in Kreskin's show to call us by telephone at the number given. To make the ad more effective, we listed all eight of the individual mind-reading messages which occurred in Phase 2 (events 3-10).

The very first ad produced calls from the people involved in events 5, 7,

8, 9, and 10, giving us five of the eight victims. Luckily, our net included the three cases that had puzzled us the most, events 7, 8, and 10. In all three cases, the caller gave us a personal interview at home, which turned out to have certain consistent patterns.

Mr. Newsome (the name is fictional) was the author of Middlemarch; he told us he was *seated next to the aisle* and, after writing MIDDLEMARCH (in capital letters), he received several other slips which were passed down the row to him. He then recalled that "somebody" came down the aisle to collect the slips of paper into an envelope. He couldn't recall if this was Kreskin or not, but we were pretty sure it was because Kreskin had made the point, as he dashed up and down the aisles, that he didn't have any helpers. So it appeared that Kreskin had the chance to palm Newsome's slip into his pocket.

There were other points of interest as well. Written in capital letters, the name MIDDLEMARCH could look like two words, whereas in lower case letters this mistake is unlikely. When Kreskin asked, "Is it two words?" Mr. Newsome was suddenly unsure so he said "Yes."

But the most telling point was that just as Newsome stood up to take Kreskin's bait ("I am getting a name, or word, with M—I—D...or D-D..."), he saw that a woman had already stood up about ten rows ahead and off to one side (oops, Kreskin gets an unplanned probability match); so, he started to sit back down. However, Kreskin ignored the woman and directed his questions directly to Newsome, as if he knew which person was his subject. This could be ESP, but then, if he had stolen the message, he would have a good idea of where it came from.

In event 8, Kreskin's opening cue was a number with 551 in it, which turned out to be 551026. The author, a Mrs. Martin, told us that she was seated among members of her family *only one seat away from the center aisle.* Seated on the aisle next to her was her niece, while one row forward, also on the aisle, was her nephew. As Kreskin ran up and down the aisles, he stopped by Mrs. Martin's row, took the envelope with the messages in it from the niece, and passed it forward to the nephew.

We interrupted Mrs. Martin to ask if we could interview the nephew as well—since he lived close by, he appeared within the next few minutes. Here is what the nephew told us. He couldn't recall just who gave him the envelope, but he had taken it home as a souvenir of the show in which Kreskin had read the mind of his aunt. As the family discussion got more excited, he dumped out the contents of the envelope onto a coffee table. The slip of paper with 551026 was no longer there! (Kreskin had struck again.)

Event 10 gave us further confirmation that Kreskin was cheating. Mrs. Edwards explained that the message she had written was:

Graeme Michael

Christchurch

May 5, 1973

At that time, she was seated next to her husband in the front section of the theater. We pulled out a seating plan of the theater and asked her where this was; she pointed to *two seats that backed on a cross-aisle,* giving Kreskin every opportunity to peek over her shoulder as he passed behind, which we know he did.

On stage, Kreskin threw out the cues "A.M." or "A. Michael" but Mrs. Edwards remained quiet. A woman in the balcony then stood up and said, "Yes, Michael," whereupon Kreskin impatiently asked if it had an "A" before it, and then said, "Then it's not you, it's not her thought. I can't get it, perhaps...Armene or A. Michael. There's more but I don't know what they are...(Pause). Aren't you going to own up? A.M. or A. Michael. (Pause). And I get Christchurch."

Kreskin's rapid dismissal of the first candidate and his persistence in looking for the right subject well fits the theory that he had peeked and knew exactly who and what he was after. Unfortunately, he had not read "Graeme" correctly, and had to use some of his extra ammunition ("Christchurch") to get a reply. Mrs. Edwards also told us she kept thinking over and over, "Graeme, Graeme, does he mean *Graeme* Michael," but for all her concentration on it, this psychic vibe never got through to Kreskin. Of course, some people will say that psychic things work like that—very mysteriously!

When we look over events 7, 8, and 10, the pattern seemed clear. In all three cases the person was sitting near the aisle, and in all cases it is known that Kreskin came by. In two of these three cases, he handled the slips of paper or the envelope, and in one of these cases the message was later shown to be missing. In two cases he passed over the wrong volunteer, and in another two cases his "mind reading" appeared to be stuck on an error of misreading the message as it had been written down. The simplest conclusion, especially given Kreskin's background as a magician, is that he either stole the message or peeked over a shoulder.

After we caught on to this gross method of deception we were able, in subsequent stage shows, to observe Kreskin actually slipping messages into his pocket. And after one nightclub performance, we interviewed three of Kreskin's mind-reading victims, and found that they had all completely lost track of their written messages, but they were still impressed that Kreskin had "received" the very same thoughts they had written down. As we have found so often in our psychic researches, the desire to believe in miracles causes many people to become careless observers who do not wish to consider any evidence that they might have been duped.

Kreskin Reads His Own Mind

In Phase 3 we encounter three more specific messages that could not be based on probability matching. The messages were:

a rare book on witchcraft

Sherry, age 6, and Theresa, age 8

June 18 [received by a volunteer]

Admittedly, June 18 could find an accidental match in the whole audience of nearly eighteen hundred people, but we must remember that these three messages were among the five or six messages that had been distributed to as many people in the front rows. These people did not write the messages, but their job was to remain standing and act as psychic senders. Since Kreskin was about to "read" from these particular messages and no others, it would be nearly impossible to get anywhere by probability matching against only five or six target messages.

The actual significance of June 18 was its suitability as a message that could be received—not by Kreskin—but by a volunteer from the audience. But first, we must consider how Kreskin got the first two messages, although properly we should say, how he got all three messages, since it will become clear that he must have known June 18 as well.

The detective-minded reader may have noted that Kreskin collected these slips on his writing board, set it down, picked it up again, and gave the messages out to people in the front rows. Recalling our principle that "everything is significant," we are left with much to explain. Why does he use the writing board? Why does he put it down by the stage to give us a short lecture? Finally, why does he give the messages back to people in the front rows—why not let the people who wrote them just keep them? And if you think about it, how come Kreskin never asked who wrote each of these messages?

Now if we rotate our mental kaleidoscope just slightly, all of these facts suddenly click into a new pattern. The so-called writing board is actually a magician's tray with two compartments. When he sets the tray down it flops shut, and when he picks it up after his mini-lecture he opens it to the second compartment where—violas!—he has placed his own written messages. Now these papers are given out to "new" people in the audience, which is necessary because there aren't any "old" people who actually wrote any of them. But after all the mind reading in Phase 1 and Phase 2, who is thinking of that old magic technique, *simple substitution?*

When we first came to this conclusion, it made sense of all the facts, but we wanted to test it further. We reasoned that if Kreskin were the author, then no amount of local newspaper advertising should be able to locate any other authors.

In our first ad (the same ad which located five of the eight people from Phase 2), we got a response from all three people who were *holding* the Phase 3 messages, but nobody came forth as the *author* of any one of them. Now, it should be noted that this first ad had reached a total of eight out of the eleven individuals who had visibly participated in the stage show. For contacting these real people, our ad had an instant success of 73 percent, but the three missing authors were still missing.

Not yet convinced, we carried out a series of ads for these authors only. We advertised on five different dates over four months in both the morning and evening newspapers and once in a national magazine, but we never got a caller. Since these ads had a steady success rate of 00 percent, we became even more confident that the authors of the Phase 3 messages were only figments of Kreskin's magicianation. He had merely read his own mind.

We also asked holders of the three messages if they had kept them—which led to another interesting bit of information. Kreskin had personally instructed them to memorize the messages and then tear them up "into many little bits" and throw these on the floor. Thus, our hope of comparing the handwriting from one slip to the next was neatly foiled by the magician himself. But even this tactic gave us minor supporting evidence.

We have yet to explain how a volunteer from the audience was able to "receive" the message June 18. We must recall here that Kreskin placed his hands on the woman's folded arms while he called off the months, and then the possible days from 1 to 30. In this stunt, he only needs to deliver a quick squeeze as he calls out the correct month or day.

Such a simple method seems outlandish at first, because the woman should realize how she had been cued. But note that Kreskin only asks her to name a month and then a number. With the whole audience watching her, she is under pressure to come up with the answer. On the other hand, it would take a very assertive person to say "Hey, wait a minute Kreskin, you squeezed me!" And furthermore, since the magician is holding the hand microphone, he can pull it away if the subject starts to talk out of turn. Our bet is simply that Kreskin cannot do this effect without his hands-on rigamarole and calling off the months and the days. As usual, every trivial action is significant for locating the loophole.

Did Clever Hans Have ESP too?

For sheer breath-taking drama, Kreskin's hidden check demonstration was the highlight of his show. As Kreskin wandered about the aisles with the mayor trailing on the end of a handkerchief, our heartbeats waxed and waned as he drew closer to and farther away from the target location. The rest of the audience, especially those near the secreted envelope, and most especially the mayor himself, must have had the same involuntary feelings. This is the first clue. If Kreskin has sensitized himself to the reactions of people around him, their restlessness when he is off the scent, and their attentive silence as he draws closer, he could home-in on the check. He could also sense the involuntary muscular reactions of the mayor on the end of the handkerchief.

But is it feasible that people will involuntarily reveal their expectations through posture, muscle tension, movement, and so forth? And is it feasible that Kreskin is sensitive enough to these cues to count on them to find his own paycheck?

There is good evidence that people do unwittingly communicate their expectancies. The most classic case involves the famous horse Clever Hans, who was renowned for his mathematical and reading abilities in Germany near the turn of the century. Clever Hans normally reported his answers by tapping the correct number with his right front foot. Special commissions of scientists and animal experts investigated Hans and his master, Herr von Osten, and concluded that there was no trickery involved, which was correct.

The case was finally solved by Oskar Pfungst, a psychologist who spent many months working with von Osten and the horse. Eventually Pfungst discovered that when von Osten asked a question, his head and shoulders dropped just slightly towards Hans's counting foot. And, von Osten was so sure of Clever Hans's intelligence that he slightly raised his head and shoulders confidently when Hans had reached the correct number of taps, whereupon Hans executed a backstep to put his foot down. In short, von Osten was unconsciously signaling the horse to start and stop tapping. Once Pfungst picked up this cuing system, he was able to make the horse give any absurd answer he chose simply by holding his head down until Hans got to the selected number. If Pfungst bent his head farther forward, the horse tapped faster. If the questioner stood behind the horse, the animal struggled to twist around and look at the man. If the questioner asked a question to which he did not know the answer himself, the horse would fail even the simplest problem.

It could be argued that this study only proves that Herr von Osten had a peculiar nervous twitch. However, Pfungst also showed that such slight involuntary movements can be found in most people. Using a sample of twenty-five subjects of "every age and sex (including children of five and six years)," Pfungst asked each one to think of a number between 1 and 10, or sometimes 1 and 100. While the subject concentrated on the number, Pfungst (taking the role of the horse) started tapping with his right hand, while looking at the subject for the expected head-jerk, which was so slight it was often on the order of one millimeter. He found some sort of consistent head movements in all of the subjects except two, whom he described as "scientific men whose mode of thought was always the most abstract." (He took one of them to see Clever Hans; as expected, the horse was unable to answer this man's questions.) In another series of tests, six other subjects, taken one at a time, had to concentrate on one of five sheets of paper arranged in a small arc in front of them. By watching their heads and eyes, Pfungst was able to divine the correct sheet on 82 percent of the trials and, like Hans, when he was wrong, he was usually off by only one position.

If Pfungst could so quickly learn to read people's minds by nonverbal cues, so could Kreskin. An excerpt from Kreskin's theater program confirms this strongly.

> As early as eight (Kreskin) began "fooling around" with ESP when he thought it would be a good trick to be able to pick up on the thoughts, instead of the spoken words, of his playmates in the game " Hot and Cold." (In this game an object is hidden from one of the

players and the others direct him to it by saying "hot" or "cold.")
Kreskin practiced on his younger brother for over three months
before getting what he considered were encouraging results. It was
from this childhood game that his "check test" feat emerged, in which
he invites anyone to hide his fee for his performance, and if he can't
find it through ESP, he forfeits payment.

Stage Program

Here we see the missing link, the extensive practice beginning at an early
age, which would be required to develop an unusual perceptual ability,
much as an art connoisseur must learn gradually to distinguish an original
painting from an imitation, or a wine connoisseur, one vintage from
another.

True, Kreskin claims that all this practice enhanced his "ESP" rather
than his sensitivity to audience reactions, but there is no reason to purchase
any psychic proposition when a nonpsychic one is so clearly available.

It has been pointed out to us that the check feat could be most easily and
reliably accomplished by use of a confederate who gives hot-and-cold
signs (or directional signals) as Kreskin moves about. This is entirely
possible, as we have been told that Kreskin usually travels with one or two
male companions (who have been described to us as "bodyguards"). We
have no direct confirmation of this, and we would be very disappointed to
learn that what appears to us to be a very exceptional and psychologically
significant skill is based on such a crude form of deception.

Final Reflections

There are those who argue that, no matter how many psychic effects can
be explained by trickery, if there is even one left over, then the man must be
a psychic after all. Although we don't share this Alice-in-Wonderland
logic, we have taken pains to study every one of the feats presented to us in
the Kreskin stage show and have uncovered a very plausible nonpsychic
explanation for each one. These are summarized in Table 6.

It should not be imagined that the four Phases of the show were obvious
to anybody in the audience, including us. Rather the events popped up
unexpectedly in the flow of Kreskin's jokes and mini-lectures and his

TABLE 6
Explanations of Kreskin's "Psychic" Feats

Event No.	Message (abbr.)	Explanation	Supporting Evidence
KRESKIN SENDS HIS THOUGHTS			
1	Circle-triangle	population stereotype	duplicated by us
2	37	population stereotype	duplicated by us
KRESKIN READS THOUGHTS OF AUDIENCE			
3	Mother (daughter)	probability match	vague cues; doesn't progress
4	Stopped watch	probability match	vague cues; doesn't progress
5	England	probability match	vague cues; doesn't progress
6	Scalded in the kitchen	probability match	vague cues; doesn't progress
7	Middlemarch	Kreskin stole the message	interview, Mr. N
8	551026	Kreskin stole the message	interview, Mrs. M
9	Shop work	probability match	vague cues; doesn't progress
10	A. Michael	Kreskin peeked	interview, Mrs. E
KRESKIN READS WRITTEN MESSAGES			
11	Witchcraft	substitution of messsages	magic tray, no author found, duplicated by us
12	Sherry, Theresa	substitution of messages	magic tray, no author found; duplicated by us
13	June 18	substitution of messages	magic tray, no author found; duplicated by us
KRESKIN FINDS HIS CHECK			
14	Check found	reading cues from people's reactions	possible with practice, and Kreskin had much practice

forays into the audience. The magician relies on confusion.

In retrospect, we can see a steady progression from the least to the most spectacular effects, while the underlying method is changed through five different conjuring techniques: (1) use of population stereotypes; (2) making probability matches; (3) reporting a message which had been stolen or overseen; (4) substitution of own messages; (5) reading audience reactions to locate the paycheck.

The use of five different methods is consistent with a basic principle of stage magic—vary the technique as rapidly as possible. Ideally, the magician avoids any repetition of the same magic trick in the same show because it gives the audience more opportunity to notice the pattern and more time to reflect on the possibilities. Thus, in the Phase 3 substitution of messages, Kreskin changes the protocol by having a volunteer from the audience read the third message for him.

According to magician and statistician, Dr. Persi Diaconis, a mix of tricks makes a bundle of sticks (Diaconis, 1978). By a "bundle of sticks," Diaconis indicates that a magic effect (or a psychic effect) becomes more impressive if it is accomplished by several different methods so that any weakness in one approach is ruled out by another approach. That is, the "bundle of sticks" is stronger than any individual stick. (Diaconis's article also provides several other cogent observations on self-professed psychics and the pitfalls of parapsychological research.)

People may ask, "But what about all those spectacular things Kreskin describes in his book or his Stage Program, such as getting ESP messages during a long distance phone call or while flying in an airplane?" But wait a minute, this is what *Kreskin* has written, or what *his writers* have written for him, and how could we or anybody else refute such claims? It only takes a bit of judicious editing to convert a conjuring feat into a psychic miracle, and Kreskin *is*, after all, a master of the white lie.

Kreskin does not really want to be tested as a psychic. If he did, he could present himself to any of a number of psychological or parapsychological laboratories around the country, and demonstrate his powers under controlled conditions. Even better, he could present himself to the Committee for the Scientific Investigation of Claims of the Paranormal.

6

URI GELLER: SUPERPSYCHIC OF THE SEVENTIES

I don't think this power is coming from me but that it's being channeled through me. What I am able to do is maybe part of a much greater plan which concerns more than the earth and mankind.
Uri Geller

In the early 1970s, a young Israeli hit the limelight with some amazing powers. Apparently, he could make metal melt by mental concentration and know your thoughts merely by thinking. After a successful television appearance in London in November 1973, the whole of Britain seemed to be buzzing with talk of Geller's miracles of metal bending and ESP.

URI SENDS BRITAIN ON A BIG BENDER, declared a *Sun* headline, while the *News of the World* ran an exclusive, front-page story entitled URI'S MIRACLE PICTURES, which revealed Uri's ability to take photos of himself with the lens cap still on the camera, with "no signs of trickery." And not only were the newspapers clearly persuaded about Uri's psychic powers, but a number of distinguished scientists and writers were publicly claiming that the "Geller effect" was authentic and scientifically verified.

On the other hand, a number of articles appeared that expressed considerable ambivalence and even outright skepticism about Uri Geller's claims. Barbara Smoker entitled her article, published in the February 1974 issue of the *New Humanist*, "Uri Geller, the Joke's Over!" Smoker took the position that Geller was simply a clever magician. In the June 1974 issue of *Popular Photography*, Yale Joel and Charles Reynolds offered the theory that Uri Geller's psychic photographs were produced by simple trickery. The June and July 1974 issues of *Psychology Today* contained an interesting account of Geller's abilities by Andrew Weil. Weil was initially convinced by Geller and then disillusioned when Randi (the "Amazing"), a highly talented professional stage magician and escape artist from New Jersey, duplicated all of Geller's effects and more. Andrew Weil ended his two-part article (entitled "The Letdown") with the conclusion that questions like, "Is Uri Geller a fraud?" or "Do psychic phenomena exist?" are unanswerable. "The answer is always yes and no," says Weil, "depending on who is looking and from what point of view."

This skeptical approach to Geller, however, was clearly a minority viewpoint. October 18, 1974 marked the occasion of a unique event in the history of psychic research. One of the world's most respected scientific journals, *Nature,* published an article by Russell Targ and Harold Puthoff of the Stanford Research Institute claiming verification of Geller's ESP ability. Targ and Puthoff describe how Geller reproduced pictures drawn by the experimenters at remote locations around the laboratory. According to the report, Geller was physically separated "from both the target material and anyone knowledgeable of the material." Only following Geller's isolation, usually in a double-walled steel room, was a target chosen and drawn, and Geller was not told who would select the target drawing or the method of selection to be used. For ten out of thirteen experiments, Geller was able to produce a drawing, and many of these were highly similar to the corresponding targets. When Geller's responses were matched against the target drawings, two independent judges both matched responses to targets without error. *The probability of this happening purely by chance is one in three million.*

A second investigation by Targ and Puthoff in which Uri performed well was an example of highly accurate clairvoyance. A 3/4″ die was placed in a 3″ × 4″ × 5″ steel box. The box was shaken and placed on the table. Nobody knew which die face was uppermost—except Uri. In ten trials he passed twice, but gave a correct response on the remaining eight. *This result has a probability of occurring by chance of about one in a million.*

Targ and Puthoff concluded their scientific report with the conclusion that "a channel exists whereby information about a remote location can be obtained by means of an as yet unidentified perceptual modality"—in other words, that ESP is a scientifically proven reality. Our interpretation of these experiments is presented in chapter nine.

Although Geller's most widely publicized ability is to bend spoons, forks, keys, and other metal objects by nonphysical means, Geller's metal bending was not reported in detail by Targ and Puthoff. This was because they were not able "to combine such observations with adequately controlled experiments to obtain data sufficient to support the paranormal hypothesis."

The difference between a stage performance and a scientific experiment boils down to one of control and who has it. On stage the performer has (or should have) control over what the audience sees and hears. In the laboratory the experimenter has (or should have) control over what the performer sees and hears. In practice, some compromise is almost bound to occur. But for a meaningful test of psychic powers the experimenter can never afford to allow the performer to set all the conditions—he already knows peculiar effects are possible when the performer has complete control and nothing new or of any consequence would be discovered. Russell Targ and Harold Puthoff's investigation appeared to have used some pretty impressive controls and, nevertheless, obtained results indicating that Uri Geller had some means of access to the target material. This single paper threw the world of science into a hornet's nest of controversy. If the phenomena described by Targ and Puthoff were real, nothing short of a revolution in science would be needed to find an explanation.

In the same week the *Nature* article appeared, another reputable British journal, *New Scientist,* published a sixteen-page report on Uri Geller by Dr. Joseph Hanlon. Hanlon's thesis was that Geller is a fraud—that he cheats, uses tricks, substitution, distraction, sleight-of-hand, and all the other tools of the magician's repertoire. Unfortunately, Geller failed to cooperate with a research committee set up by the *New Scientist,* and so Hanlon's account of Geller's abilities, in stark contrast to the Targ-Puthoff approach, was based largely on hearsay or anecdotal reports from a variety of sources.

The real crunch in Hanlon's attack on the SRI study is his explanation for the significant results. Hanlon brings to light the fact that Dr. Andrija Puharich, the man who brought Geller from Israel, is a medical electronics expert who has developed a radio receiver that can be hidden in a tooth. Hanlon argues that Puharich could easily have had one of these miniature devices fitted to Uri, allowing the possibility of signals sent by an accomplice. According to Hanlon, an old friend of Geller's, Shipi Shtrang, "was constantly under foot during the tests—at least sometimes accompanying the experimenters during actual experiments. Shipi could easily have signaled Uri in code with a transmitter hidden in his pocket."

Hanlon extended his radio transmission hypothesis to account for Geller's successful performance in the SRI die experiments. Hanlon suggested that Geller could have substituted a special "radio die," obtainable from magic shops, that radioes which face is up.

Targ and Puthoff made a very speedy reply to Hanlon's attack in the November 7 (1974) issue of *New Scientist:* "Throughout our work with Geller we took precautions against the very form of trickery suggested by your author (Hanlon), first, by excluding everyone other than the experimenter or experimenters from the target area, and second, by maintaining silence about the target until after the experiment was completed and Geller's response was collected." And further they stated: "The die we used was marked with an SRI code and was of the transparent variety to preclude the use of any internal electronics to indicate die position."

Who to believe? On the one hand, a scientific report published in *Nature* verifying Geller's psychic abilities under supposedly cheat-proof conditions, and on the other, a highly speculative but critical attack published simultaneously in *New Scientist.* While Targ and Puthoff's reply to Hanlon would seem to invalidate his explanations of their significant results, it is difficult to disregard the doubts Hanlon has raised about the "circus atmosphere" that he believes surrounded the SRI experiments. Frankly, at the end of 1974, we were puzzled and confused. Weighing all the evidence available at that time, it seemed impossible to decide whether Geller was a genuine psychic or an ingenious and highly skilled hoaxer. Clearly, the Geller effect had to be taken seriously as, in either case, there would be much of interest to learn about the mechanics of psychic performance. Clearly, what was needed was more experimentation.

Our first live encounter with Geller was accidental. On 23 March 1975 Geller arrived in New Zealand from Australia to begin a series of four "lecture-demonstrations" of his psychic powers. To facilitate communications, I (David Marks) checked into the same hotel as Geller in the Dominion capital, Wellington. Hopefully we could obtain a sufficient level of cooperation to complete a series of laboratory tests. I left a letter for Geller at the hotel reception inviting his participation in some experiments.

I had been told by Geller's local agent, Bruce Warwick, that Geller was due to arrive on the ten o'clock plane, and so an arrangement was made to talk with Geller the next morning after a press conference. At eight o'clock on the evening of the 23, I went down to dinner in the almost empty hotel restaurant. At about nine o'clock a party of noisy, flamboyant people sat down at the table next to me in the quiet dining room. From their accents, some were obviously Americans, others Australians, and others sounded like Americanized Israelis. Suddenly, as I idly scanned their faces, to my utter amazement, I saw Uri Geller. Apparently, he had materialized himself into New Zealand prior to the aircraft's arrival! He was sitting with his back to me, not more than ten feet away, opposite a woman with blond hair who spoke loudly and clearly with a distinct American accent.

Although I was dying to meet Geller, my first reaction was to leave, as the last thing I wanted to do was invade Geller's privacy. However, it was I who had been there first, and they had sat next to me, not *vice versa,* so I decided to finish my dinner and then leave.

To this day I can still hardly believe what took place in the next few moments. The American woman (whom I knew later to be Miss Solveig Clark, one of Geller's personal assistants) asked Geller in a clear and distinctive voice whether he had "read the letter from Dr. Marks." Like most other people, I find it hard not to tune in to a conversation when my name is mentioned. *I heard Geller reply: "Keep that guy away from me; he'll pick up the signals (sic)."*

No words can describe how I felt at that moment. What signals? Could these be the signals described in the *New Scientist?* Who was Geller's female confidante? Was Puharich there, or Shipi Shtrang? Although I couldn't answer all these questions, Geller had already told me more than I ever imagined would be possible. Yet Geller was blissfully ignorant of this major faux pas. I couldn't help feeling that if Geller were truly psychic, he'd certainly have sensed my presence and avoided giving away trade secrets!

In preparation for my interview with Geller the next morning (March 24), I copied a drawing of a sailing ship, Captain Cook's barque *Endeavour,* folded it, and placed it inside a single white envelope from the hotel stationery (see Fig. 6a). I didn't realize at the time that sailing ships (along with flowers and houses) are a popular target in ESP tests (a population stereotype, see chapter five). If I had known, I would have been more creative and tried Geller on something more unusual. A second informal test would be to see if Geller could use his ESP powers and describe an object hidden in my desk drawer (a bus ticket).

Before my interview with Geller I attended a press conference, which was the normal kind of promotional exercise accompanying tours by show biz personalities. I arrived early to obtain a good position, as I planned to film Geller bending a key. I sat at one end of the front row. As proved to be his norm, Geller arrived about ten minutes late. He talked smoothly and with considerable charm for about an hour. Finally, he agreed to bend a key. I switched on my movie camera. At this point, Geller looked disturbed and told me he didn't allow movie cameras and that I was not to use the film for "commercial purposes." I assured him the film was for research purposes only, and, reluctantly, he agreed to let me continue. He looked distinctly uncomfortable and nervous—I wondered why. I stood in a corner, at the front of the room, trying to film Geller as he took the key and began to work on it. Eventually, Geller, who at first had his back to me, turned to face me and stated that "it would be much easier to bend near metal as this gives me energy." He pointed across to the central heating vent in the wall right next to me on my left and asked me to check that it was made of metal. Anybody could tell that it was, but social pressure necessitated that I go through the motions of checking it. The last thing I wanted was to stop filming and tap the metal ventilator, but suddenly everybody in the room was staring expectantly at me, so I reached down and tapped the vent with my left hand while continuing to film Geller with the camera in my right. I confirmed the obvious; the vent was metal.

Then Geller asked me yet again, was the ventilator made of metal? He seemed impatient and annoyed. It was almost as though I had ignored his original request. So I panned my camera slowly away from Geller towards the wall on my left, switched off the camera, tapped the vent loudly, and confirmed that it was quite definitely metal.

By the time I looked back up, Geller had hurriedly moved halfway across the room towards me. He came all the way across the room, crouched down beside the ventilator, and held the key beside it.

An attractive lady reporter was asked to hold the other end of the key. Although I resumed filming immediately, Geller arrived next to me. *Geller obscured the key from view by positioning himself between it and the camera. I moved over slightly to allow for this maneuver but, as the key was now hidden by Uri's hand, I could no longer be sure Geller had not already bent the key while I was distracted.*

A frame-by-frame analysis of my film confirms that Geller had undoubtedly bent the key on his way across the room. Immediately before the move, the film shows Geller firmly clenching the key in both hands in a good position for bending (see Fig. 4A). I have subsequently bent many keys myself holding them in this same position, and with practice anybody can do it. The film immediately following Geller's move over to the ventilator clearly shows that *the key had already been bent* (see Fig. 4B). *It is important to note that by this stage, Geller had not started his "psychic" bending procedure, which involves stroking the key and thinking aloud, "Bend, bend, bend."*

I'm not the only one to have reached this conclusion. An American journalist with a Wellington newspaper, the *Dominion,* Frederick Szydlik, put his suspicions into these words:

> Uri Geller bent a key yesterday. So what?...All you need is the technique and the ability to divert your audience's attention. Ask them to leave their seats and gather round closer (give the key a little tweak with two hands). Make them look at the air vent in the wall over there (another tweak). So that when you're ready to start rubbing, the key still APPEARS straight, but is already on its way. Conceal this slight bend with the thumb and forefinger and start rubbing. Now, to convince the onlookers that the key will continue to bend, divert their attention some more. Say something like: "Shall I stand over there by the window for photographs?" (Meanwhile, more of the two-handed tweak.) In the end a well-bent key. Applause. (Quoted from the *Dominion,* 25 March 1975.)

After the press conference, Geller and I went up to my room. Uri was friendly and seemed to be in good spirits. With the exception of Szydlik, whom ironically Geller described as a "foreigner," and who obviously had been a skeptic, he was pleased with how the press conference had gone and talked with enthusiasm about his New Zealand tour.

To maximize our chances of gaining Geller's cooperation for properly controlled tests in the lab, I planned not to impose rigid controls on his demonstrations during this initial interview, allowing Geller plenty of scope to produce his "paranormal" phenomena. I invited another psychologist along, however, as a second observer. Geller called Shtrang to tell him where he was in the building. When Geller asked me what my room number was, I showed Geller my key. *I actually threw my key on to the bed near the telephone, so he could read the room number from the tag.* He picked up the key at this stage and held it—which is interesting, considering that I later found this key had been bent.

Geller agreed to try and receive a drawing using telepathy. While Geller looked away, I drew a horselike figure, folded it, and placed it under my chair. Geller told me to visualize a screen and to draw it over and over in my head. He then told me to show the drawing to my fellow psychologist, Tony Egan, while he looked away again, and then to hide the drawing. At this point I felt that Geller looked back too quickly, before I'd had enough time to conceal the drawing properly. Geller produced a pretty good rendition of my original drawing and signed it with a flourish.

Geller then said he'd draw something and try to send it to me. He wrote something down and stared intensely into my eyes for a few seconds, apparently to transfer the thought. There was a penetrating, almost hypnotic, quality to Geller's stare. He told me to write any number from 1 to 10. I wrote "3". He then continued to do another drawing—I wondered why on earth he'd asked me to write down a number and then failed to confirm it against his. Later, I discovered that he'd written "8" and got it wrong, but didn't want me to know it.

Next, while I kept my eyes shut, Geller did a drawing and showed it to Tony. He then asked me to draw whatever I felt. I drew a pair of dumb-bells, one much bigger than the other. Maybe this merely reflected the way Geller was treating Tony and me! As Geller had drawn a yacht and a sun, I had obviously failed to read Uri's mind.

Again I was puzzled when for some reason Geller asked Tony if seeing the drawing had bothered him. Geller seemed unperturbed by this ESP failure and passed smartly on, saying that we'd try it again. Geller then motioned as if making another drawing and told me to draw whatever I felt, as he was "thinking of it very, very hard." By concentrating on my pencil as I did my drawing, Geller said he'd be able to help me get it right. I started to draw a plane, but I changed my mind and drew a tree. Geller then produced a similar drawing, which at the time, I must confess, I found more than a little astonishing. (See Fig. 5.)

As I looked back over this sequence of events and listened to my tape recording, I became aware of a simple explanation for what otherwise seemed an impressive paranormal feat. First, Geller's strange question about whether Tony had been bothered by seeing the first (yacht) drawing could have been designed purely to draw our attention to the fact that, in this instance, Tony had seen Geller's drawing, proving Geller had done his drawing first. Second is the fact that Tony did *not* see Geller's second (tree) drawing until *after* I had done mine. Afterwards, it seemed easily possible that Geller simply copied my tree drawing as he watched me draw it.

As the photo shows, the last two lines of my drawing were actually missing from his, which supports this hypothesis, and his drawing looks hurried in comparison to mine. "Drawing-after-looking" is something we later found to be a conjuring trick recognized by magicians, and one Geller has been suspected of using many times. I have since performed this trick dozens of times myself and never got caught once.

I asked Geller to apply his ESP to the object hidden in my drawer (a bus ticket). He concentrated for a while and wrote down the word "watch." I next asked Geller if he would like to try and apply his ESP to the envelope I had prepared. He accepted the envelope and *asked me to sign across both flaps so that "you'll see I'm not opening it."* This seemed strange, as I didn't think until then that he would. He continued to talk as he handled the envelope. Geller said it was easier if he held the envelope because many times he would use clairvoyance rather than telepathy. "I put my mind into the envelope" he said, *"I go into it."* I failed to realize at the time that Geller probably meant this quite literally! He had been suspected of opening envelopes in such tests before.

After Geller had been holding the envelope for eight minutes, he actually told me to whisper into Tony's ear what was in the envelope. At this point, we couldn't contain our laughter. I said to Uri, "Look, if I whisper it, you might accidentally overhear it." Uri, nonplussed by this skeptical response, asked me to go into the bathroom and to do the drawing again. He told me to close the door and to let him know when I'd finished the drawing. When I'd finished, he asked me to repeat it again, and then one more time, but slowly. So I attempted to redraw the *Endeavour* a total of three times, with its three masts and eight sails, all the time wondering what Geller was doing while I was out of the room. Then I heard Geller tell Tony also to draw what he could pick up. Geller asked Tony to fetch him another pen, and so Tony got one from his jacket on the bed beside him. *This was a quite unnecessary distraction because Geller already had a pen that he'd placed on the floor.* As a result of this maneuver, Geller was left completely unobserved for at least twenty seconds, probably more.

Then the telephone rang, and Uri told me to come back in and answer it. I had been out of the room for three minutes. It was Shipi Shtrang. While Shtrang waited at the other end of the line, Geller quickly sketched a drawing of a sailing ship. He seemed genuinely thrilled when we told him he had got it more or less right.

What happened next seemed inexplicable at the time. *Geller ripped open the envelope, or more precisely, he gave the impression that he ripped it open.* I was puzzled by this lapse in procedure on Geller's part, as he had especially asked me to sign my name across both flaps as some kind of evidence that the envelope had not been tampered with. Before leaving, Geller explained how he'd seen the drawing, as follows:

> Now let me tell you what I did. I didn't even look (who said he had?!)... I looked out and tried to see what I see in the clouds—your drawing in there—and suddenly I saw water. And suddenly I saw, not white sails, but orange sails, for some reason. Orange sails, and I said, well, if it's not a pirate boat then it's nothing....And he (Tony) was here to control, you know, that's why I didn't want him to pick up the phone or go away. *So you can say that I didn't open the envelope or whatever.*

Again, a reference by Geller to the notion that the envelope could have been opened. Methinks he doth protest too much!

Finally, Geller suggested we throw away pieces of paper "we didn't need," and began to sort the papers into two piles: "his" and "mine." He screwed up "his" pile immediately, but told me to keep all of those in "my" pile. This struck me as more than a little presumptuous, as all the papers were relevant as far as I was concerned. As he left, he threw "his" scrunched-up papers into the wastepaper basket. Pity, he didn't take them with him.

Although we had a few hunches about how Uri may have done it, Tony and I were baffled and confused about much of what we had seen. Overall, it had been a fairly impressive demonstration, although there were many strange aspects to the performance, suggesting that either he was a phony or that psychics, like God, work in mysterious ways. Geller had accurately reproduced two drawings (horse and sailing boat) and somehow transmitted one to me (tree) or so it seemed at the time. On the other hand, he'd failed to transmit another drawing to me (yacht vs. my dumbells) and he failed also to describe what was concealed in a drawer (a bus ticket, not a watch).

Above all else, one or two aspects of the envelope test had made me decidedly suspicious. On the assumption that the pile of papers Geller had designated "his" would be at least as interesting as those designated "mine," I recovered them from the waste basket.

I wasn't wrong. There were three items: a piece of paper containing the number "8", another piece of paper with the word "watch" written on it, and the envelope that had contained my drawing of the *Endeavour.*

It takes no imagination to understand the "8" and "watch." Both of these were testimony to failures of Geller's powers. Presumably Geller hoped I'd forget about these if he threw them away. But if he'd read my mind accurately, he'd surely have realized that, as a psychologist, I'd be as much interested in his failures as in his successes.

But what of the envelope? Why had it been included in the pile of rejected materials? Careful inspection soon gave the answer. Although Geller had seemingly ripped open the envelope with a very loud tearing sound, *the only rip on the envelope was down the side seam.* Both flaps were intact, although both showed evidence that *they had been peeled off from the envelope. It now seemed highly possible that Geller had thumbed open the envelope while I was out of the room and peeked at the drawing when Tony was distracted.* His own spontaneous and unsolicited remarks indicated his awareness of this technique for generating mentalistic effects.

At noon, Geller called me about a radio interview that was to be on the air that lunchtime. He seemed pleased with the way the interview had gone, and suggested enthusiastically that I should visit people at their homes after the program as he anticipated many "paranormal" events would take place. He told me that broken watches and clocks would start, and many keys, forks, and spoons would become bent during the program. Geller seemed to believe that enquiries such as these might satisfy our thirst for scientific data on his abilities. I thanked him for calling but didn't take up his suggestion. I didn't doubt for a second that people would discover and report these events, but their information value for the investigation of the paranormal is zero. It's quite obvious that virtually anybody could find a bent fork in their house if they made a thorough search through their cutlery any time, night or day. Geller's presence is quite irrelevant and purely coincidental.

The next little Geller incident occurred after lunch. I took my room key from my pocket to discover that it was so bent I couldn't get it in the keyhole. I couldn't help smiling as I thought back over the interview and tried to figure out when he had bent it. I remembered how I'd shown the key to Geller when he wanted the room number.

I was halfway up the hall on my way back to the reception desk to ask for another key, wondering how I'd explain my little "accident," when I thought I'd test my own skill at bending it back. Although quite a thick key, by giving it a firm tweak in both hands, I easily bent it straight again. Was this how Uri bends his keys? Is it really that simple? I, like most people, assumed that keys are impossible to bend in the hands, but this assumption turns out to be false. This is an example of an important principle in the psychology of the psychic: people carry around many untested, false assumptions about everyday life, which a psychic can capitalize on in his performance. Only if we test some of these assumptions can we gain a true picture of reality against which to compare the psychic's performance. A performance can only be deemed "paranormal" when we have a true impression of what is normally possible under the prevailing conditions. It is amazing how few people, scientists included, take this principle properly into account when observing so-called psychic phenomena.

At three o'clock I received a call from Dr. Brian Edwards, a New Zealand TV and radio personality. Dr. Edwards hosted a daily talk-in program on a local radio station, and invited me to participate in a three-hour program with Geller the next morning. As this provided a further opportunity to try to gain Geller's cooperation for the planned experiments, I was pleased to accept.

I felt that Geller was beginning to trust me as a friend, while at the same time I was beginning to have doubts about his psychic powers. Psychologists often have to face the fact that some deception may be necessary to gain a full understanding of certain aspects of human behavior. Through my reading and thinking about the ethics of deception, I had adopted a policy of avoiding deception in my research. But this was the dilemma I now faced: either I could mislead Geller, as he was possibly misleading me (and thousands of others), and pretend that I fully believed his psychic claims, or I could avoid deception and tell him the truth about the doubts I was having. I had given this issue some hard thought during the afternoon and decided that I should let Uri know that I did have serious doubts about his claims to being psychic.

That evening, Uri telephoned me to ask if I would be participating in the Edwards talk-in the next morning. I confirmed that I would be and decided to take the plunge and let him know how I was feeling. I started by expressing skepticism about the envelope. Why had he opened it at the end, instead of me? Geller first denied opening it, then admitted it. He referred to this as a stupid "mistake" and sounded upset. I lightened the conversation a little by telling Uri how amused I had been to discover my bent key after lunch. Uri sounded surprised and said he hadn't seen it. "Yes you did," I replied, "I showed it to you when you phoned to say which room you were in." "Oh yes!" said Uri, "But I didn't touch it. Honestly, *you know keys only bend in your pocket (sic)."* Geller had obviously said a very strange thing. Only that morning, as he well knew, I had watched a key become bent *in his hand!*

Uri then became very angry. *"There will always be skeptics. I don't care about them. You can tell them from me they can go to hell!"* He went on to point out that if he didn't want me on the Edwards program, then I wouldn't be there. Somehow I managed to calm him down from his tantrum, but it was obvious that irreparable damage had been done and that our scientific experiments were now in jeopardy. Clearly, Geller didn't like skeptics and wouldn't work with them.

As I reviewed the day's events, I couldn't help wondering about Geller's strange behavior. The chief puzzles can be summarized as follows:

1. Why did Geller distract my attention during the first key bending and effectively prevent me from filming at a critical stage of the procedure?

2. Why did he ask me to show Tony Egan my drawing and to whisper to him what I had drawn?

3. In the ESP test with the *Endeavour* drawing, why did Geller open the envelope and not allow me to inspect it before he opened it, and why was the envelope in such a strange condition afterwards?

4. Why did he require me to leave the room for approximately three minutes while he attempted to perceive the drawing by clairvoyance?

5. Why did he ask Tony Egan to fetch him another pen when he already had a perfectly functional pen in his possession?

6. Why did he try to select only his successful records for me to keep and throw away all evidence of his failures?

7. Why did he first deny and then admit that he had opened the envelope?

8. Why did he first deny he had seen my key and then admit that he had seen it?

9. Why did he state that "keys only bend in your pocket"?

10. Why did Geller react so angrily at the mere suggestion of doubt on my part, or to minor corrections of his memory?

These and many other puzzles didn't seem to add up to a picture of a genuinely honest-to-goodness psychic. On the other hand, could these be idiosyncracies of a hypersensitive psychic, the signs and symptoms of a paranormal personality adjusting to a normal world? Or were they evidence that Geller is a sleight-of-hand artist completely lacking in psychic powers? Only following many further observations would it be possible to decide between these hypotheses. It wasn't very long, the next morning in fact, before some crucial observations were made.

7

THE GELLER EFFECT OBSERVED

Seeing is believing.

Anon.

For the first hour of the radio show the next morning, host Edwards and I (DM) warmed up the audience with some off-the-cuff analyses of callers' stories about talking seagulls, visitations from dead relatives, epileptic auras, psychically foreseen telephone calls, and other assorted mysteries I was challenged to explain. Geller, Shipi Shtrang, and Solveig Clark appeared promptly at ten o'clock. I wondered if Uri had heard my part of the program, which must have sounded a little skeptical for his liking, and I was curious to see how he would react when he saw me in the studio. His threats to exclude me had clearly led to nothing, and I wondered if his anger of the previous evening might recur. Surprisingly, he greeted me with a friendly smile. Edwards asked Geller if he had any objection to my being present in the studio. Geller said that he had not. I wish Geller had said he did object—it would have been an interesting program, as Edwards isn't known for pulling punches—one of his programs was banned from a television series after taking a pretty heavy line with the then Prime Minister.

From this point on, I shall report the main events of the Edwards talk-back program in chronological order. This is not a format designed to produce the easiest reading, because we'll switch back and forth from one psychic task to another as we describe Geller's chaotic meanderings from one thing to another. The normal journalistic procedure would be to reorganize the whirlpool of dialogue and happenings into a few neatly defined psychic feats, which is what happens in most of the press reports on Uri Geller's miracles. However, apart from the fact that I'm a psychologist and not a journalist, the chronological record and its details help to illustrate Geller's style. His "paranormal" feats do not occur as tidy, brief, unified tasks that can be closely and accurately observed but pop up at unpredictable moments, during a chaotic stream of discussion topics taken up and dropped at Geller's whim. This is what Joseph Hanlon described as the "Geller tornado."

Although at the time I couldn't clearly understand what was happening, I have added a few observations to give some idea of explanations that may have occurred at the time or were developed and verified soon afterwards. It also helps to know in advance that in this sequence Geller (*a*) "fixed" Brian Edwards's broken watch and those of several callers; (*b*) "read Brian Edwards's mind" about a little white animal with brown spots in a surrounding of green and brown tapestry; (*c*) bent a key; (*d*) reproduced a drawing of a flower sealed in two envelopes; (*e*) predicted correctly that one caller was wearing some clothes containing a flower design; (*f*) predicted that another caller had a large family with unusual children in it (twins); and (*g*) correctly received a drawing done by me, on the spot, in the studio. But now let's see what really happened.

First, Edwards gave Uri a watch of his own that hadn't been going for six months. Edwards said he'd taken it to a watchmaker to have it cleaned. It had gone for about a week and then stopped. Geller asked Edwards if the watch had any parts missing and seemed satisfied when Edwards replied that it did not.

Edwards then gave Geller an ordinary house key and two envelopes. One envelope contained a drawing of a flower done by Edwards's daughter, Rebecca (see Fig. 6b). The other envelope contained an unknown drawing (which turned out to be a goblet), done by his wife, Susie (see Fig. 6c). In answer to a question by Geller, Brian Edwards said he knew what was in the first envelope (i.e., a flower) but he did not know what was in the second envelope (a wine goblet).

Geller asked Edwards if I had told him to do the drawings, and Edwards replied that I had not. Was Geller trying to avoid any drawing prepared in advance by me? Although Edwards didn't mention it, I *had* advised him that any drawings should be placed inside *two envelopes* and that we make quite sure that Geller didn't open them before submitting his final drawing.

Edwards followed both suggestions. Finally, Geller wanted to know whether the drawings were "simple," but, since Edwards only knew what was in his daughter Rebecca's envelope, he could only say that the one marked "R" was simple. This drawing, the one that was "simple" and was known to Edwards, is the drawing that Geller later chose to work on first.

The dialogue on the air began with some questions by Edwards on the way-out book *Uri* written by Dr. Andrija Puharich, the man who brought Geller to live with him in New York.

"Uri," Edwards inquired first, "how true is this book?" Geller stated that the book was factually correct. Cassettes had dematerialized and voices had mysteriously appeared on tapes, but Geller was noncommittal on where his psychic energy came from, although he said he believed the energy came from "an outside source." When he demonstrated his powers, he said he believed they were "triggered" by some external intelligence that he and Puharich knew as "Spectra." Although Puharich's book is claimed by the publisher to be authorized by Geller, Geller denied giving his authorization.

Edwards asked Geller if his powers could be used for healing, as Puharich had claimed. Geller replied that healing a person was a "delicate situation.... You are handling a human soul, a person, and I don't believe I'm entitled to heal. Maybe one day I will heal. What I do on stage today, by the way, is not just performing or making money or whatever. I'm working with scientists and they're proving it's real." I silently wondered, in that case, why he'd threatened to have me excluded from the program.

He went on to say, "Yes, there is a lot of controversy, there will always be. People will always say there are chemicals, laser beams, and bugs in his teeth, but that I accept. There will always be controversy. But I know that in the long run, very slowly, science will prove that it's real. If I start healing without being experimented on healing first, I don't think that's fair of me, because.... Maybe I can't heal, I don't know. When I mean experimenting, if they prove that I do telepathy under scientifically controlled conditions, I think that it should be proven also that I can heal under medically controlled conditions. That's why I don't heal now."

Geller then described an early experience in which he claims a beam of light struck him in a Tel Aviv garden. Geller described this incident as follows: "A sort of beam hit me, light, I would say light.... It wasn't the sun's light... it was something definitely stronger. I didn't feel any pain. On the contrary, I felt really nothing. I was hit backwards, and I fell backwards, and that's it...it is a mystery to me, I don't know what it was. I asked people, hundreds of people, if they experienced these things. Well you know, strangely enough, if people catcall, I'm not the only one who's had such an experience. There are many people who did experience very strange beams when they were children...so I don't believe that was the moment when I had a contact with an outside energy, I believe I was born with this, ummm, more born with this power than given it at that stage, but I don't know. I really don't know what to believe."

This version of the story took me by surprise. In his autobiography *My Story*, Geller reports how he felt "a sharp pain" in his forehead and lost consciousness after experiencing the brilliant light. One would imagine that, if such a powerful experience had really happened, it wouldn't change too radically in the telling: Was there pain, or wasn't there, Uri?

Geller went on to describe his childhood experiences of a psychic nature. At about the age of five, he claimed, he had the ability to predict the outcome of card games played by his mother. Also, he noticed that spoons and forks would bend while he was eating. He reported that the bending phenomena had occurred more frequently in recent times, without the necessity for physical contact on his part. At school his exam papers seemed identical to those of classmates sitting nearby. Teachers thought he copied. Uri says he used ESP. As he also claims he never reads, ESP would come in pretty handy at exam time. Classmates also reported that, while sitting near Geller, watches would move forwards or backwards about an hour. Only in recent years was it possible for him to will these events to take place, especially telepathy and metal bending. As Geller talked on, innocently and modestly recounting things he couldn't explain himself, his credibility to the listeners at home as a sincere and honest person must have climbed steadily.

He stated that in the laboratory he couldn't command unusual things to happen, but had to "sit there for hours until it happens." I wonder why Geller can command his powers on schedule before thousands of viewers in stage and television shows, but needs so much more time in the presence of a few scientists?

During the commercial break we had an important conversation. Geller tried to establish when I believed he had opened the envelope containing the *Endeavour* drawing. Here is an exact transcription (from a tape recording of the show) of what was said:

Geller: Tell me, when you described on the radio, were you negative before or not?

Marks: No.

Geller: I'm so sorry that all of this...you thought of all those...that the envelope...that I tore it...are you sure that I opened it?

Marks: No.

Geller: Are you sure that I opened it?

Marks: No, I didn't say you had.

Geller: No, you didn't understand, are you sure I opened it in the end? Was it I that opened it?

Marks: Yes, you did.

Geller: You haven't made a mistake?

Marks: No.

Geller really seemed worried about the envelope test!

The next part of the program was a demonstration of the most famous of Geller's effects, the "fixing" of broken watches and clocks. Geller, who by now had had Edwards's watch for over fifteen minutes, started by clasping the watch tightly in his left hand for about thirty seconds.

Here's an exact transcription of what then took place:

Geller: Yes, now, hold your watches in your hands, broken watches, and start stroking them very gently, very, very gently. Just want the watches to start working. Say "work, work" in your head...*(turning to Edwards)* this is your broken watch and what I'm doing is just putting power and energy into it, and I'm sure that hundreds of watches will start ticking. You see what I'm doing.

I'm holding it like this in my hand...like this... Now let's see if it starts working... It's working you see... Now what happens is that I put energy into the watch... Could you explain what...

Edwards: *(Flabbergasted)* Well...David Marks might...I'm completely taken aback...I have a watch in my hand. It is my own watch. It stopped working six months ago. I put the watch in a drawer. I haven't worn the watch for six months. I tried it this morning. It was fully wound. Shaking it, bumping it, doing anything to it, wouldn't make it go. The watch is now going!!!

Geller: Now what's happened is that I put an energy into it. I don't know what kind of energy it is, but apparently it fixes the watch. I don't think it'll ever stop again. Maybe it will, but it's working because I'm around now. Now, you people at home whose watches didn't work again just put your hands over the watches, in a fist and your other hand over your fist and just...how do you say?...what I'm doing now?...scrunch it...and want the watches to work...Now if you're skeptical and you don't believe and all that, forget being skeptical now and really believe you can see the watch and really believe that even if the springs are broken, parts are missing, the watch will start ticking. If you really believe that you can do it. Please call into the studio and please tell us what happened.

Edwards: If anyone had a watch that did start working that hasn't been working, I'd like them to ring us and tell us about it, and I repeat that a watch I had that was broken, which I've had in a drawer for about six months is now going, that the second hand is going around; David Marks is in the studio. Come closer to the microphone. You've seen it, would you like to confirm what has happened. *(Edwards is now an enthusiastic believer.)*

Marks: Yes, I'll confirm it is now going.

Geller: I'm glad you shook it and all that, because some people say "Ah, dirt and all that," but look at Stanford Research Institute—they've taken a watch apart. They took the spring out of the watch and they put it in another place in the watch where there's no place for the spring and they sealed the watch again. And this was all filmed under cameras and all that and I worked on it the same way and the watch started ticking and they opened the watch up and the spring was back in its place under...there's no way for the spring to get back there.

Recall that Geller had made sure earlier that Edwards's watch had no missing parts. It is also true that *among the many miracles reported by Targ and Puthoff of SRI, they have never reported the fixing of any watch with missing parts.* As frequently appears to be the case, Geller was evidently claiming a nonexistent success. The fact is that Targ and Puthoff's report in *Nature* contains a report of ESP abilities and excludes any paranormal effects with metal bending, fixed watches, or other so-called "Geller effects." There is absolutely zero scientific evidence that any of the watch or metal-bending effects take place *unless Geller physically handles the target object.* All reports to the contrary came from unskilled, untrained observers who are mostly already strongly committed believers in any case.

After several listeners had called about their watches and clocks that had started at home, Geller returned to the first sealed drawing (the flower).

> Geller: Look while I'm sitting here what I'm trying to do is to get the drawing clairvoyantly. Now something is disturbing me here. I'm getting something that you *(David Marks)* drew to me yesterday in a concealed envelope. Now, are you thinking of yesterday?
>
> Marks: No.
>
> Geller: You're not thinking of it?
>
> Marks: No.
>
> Edwards: Would you like me to go out for a little while?
>
> Geller: No, no, no, no, no. You see what I'm doing is...this envelope is yours, right?
>
> Edwards: That's my envelope.
>
> Geller: You know what's in here. So what I'm trying to do is, I'm trying to draw what I'm receiving from it clairvoyantly. So I'll keep working on it, and if it doesn't work, this one should.
>
> Edwards: That is to say for the people listening, you're not trying to read my mind.
>
> Geller: No, no, no. I'm trying to go into the envelope with clairvoyance, whatever it's called, see what's in here and put it on my...ah...so...
>
> Edwards: Yes.
>
> Geller: So, you know, I can talk meanwhile. It doesn't really bother me.

Edwards then described the envelopes again for the listeners, and Geller asked me, "But what I would like, David, from you is try not to think about what we did yesterday. I get drawings and I don't know which drawing I'm getting." Another commercial break occurred during which Geller talked further about how he tries to pick up the information in the envelope by clairvoyance. "You see what I'm trying to do, when I put my hand like this (holds envelopes prayer-fashion) I always bring the drawing up to my head and feel it here (touches head with drawing) and put it into my head...It's very interesting."

Geller continued to work on the drawing, while Edwards talked to listeners about their watches and clocks. Geller held the envelope in both hands and seemed to be pressing down firmly on it using his thumbs. Geller suddenly interrupted one of the conversations Edwards was having with a listener to attempt a bit of telepathy.

> Geller: Very interesting, just a second. When this woman started talking...Do you have a sort of little white animal?
> Lady: No.
> Geller: That's very interesting. O.K. (A clear failure, but Geller implies that it is not, leaving his options open for subsequent callers to ring in with a positive report.)
> Edwards: You're quite sure. *(To Geller:)* You mean a living animal or a toy?
> Geller: No, I mean a living animal. I got a little white animal with brown spots in a surrounding of green and brown tapestry.
> Lady: A living animal did you say? No, I haven't a living animal.
> Edwards: Have you a statue like that? (Like the victims in the Kreskin show, Edwards was extending the definition to a broader range to get a match.)
> Geller: No. You see what happens here when somebody starts talking, I suddenly feel these things and I don't know where I get them from. Do you understand how difficult it is to know? You see when people are far...if this was at home I would know where I got it from.
> Edwards: There are five people on the line now, all of whom are in some sort of line communication with you; so I'll ask each of the five, if you like. (Edwards increases the chances for a probability match still further.)
> Geller: What I really got is a white animal, sort of brown spots, it could be a dog and then I got a brown and green tapestry with a sort of a green carpet on the floor. That's what I saw in

my mind when this woman started talking so I was sure it's her.

Edwards: The fact that I've got an animal like that wouldn't be significant would it?

Geller: No! You *do* have an animal like that?

Edwards: We have a cat which would more or less *(sic)* fit that description.

Geller: *(Titters)* No I don't know, I don't know. Is this cat kept in a room, by any chance, where the tapestry is sort of light green?

Edwards: The walls are green.

Geller: Really??? (He sounded genuinely pleased and surprised.)

Edwards: The walls in our room are green. They are a shade of green called deep thyr. The walls are green, the ceiling is white, the carpet is a sort of browny-green.

Geller: Well, that's very interesting, because the carpet is brown.

Edwards: The carpet is a light brown, the walls are green. It's unusual because very few houses have green walls *(sic)*. (Edwards has now created the match himself by ignoring many details of Geller's original statement.)

Geller: Of course, I thought it's tapestry because it's green but let me tell you...I got this, but I don't know. This is a difficult thing I cannot know from whom it is coming. But maybe you subconsciously did think of that without even you knowing it, or maybe your people at home or your children or your wife was thinking at that instant, and I picked it up.

Edwards: Well, we do have a room with green walls. It's a matter of comment among our neighbors, and we do have a cat which more or less *(sic)* fits that description.

Geller: What's the name of the cat?

Edwards: Well you tell me.

Geller: I couldn't do that. It would take a long time.

Edwards: If I were to concentrate on the name of the cat...

Geller: Yes...but then...I would have to get the letters, the same way I'm doing the envelopes. I have to see it, I don't feel it...I have to see it in my head. That's why it takes that long. Yesterday with David I did some drawings and they were incredibly fast. I was on the TV and it worked very fast...But you see today I'm not in the exact mood to do it, so it takes longer.

(The thought-of name of a specific cat is too difficult. But it also cannot be gotten by a probability match nor by a magician's trick.)

Edwards said goodbye to the lady caller and about one minute later another listener rang in to report that he was playing with a white cat "out on the carpet...uhrrr...grass...is that the thing?" Edwards replied: "I think that's a little further away from my own situation where he describes green tapestry. Well, we have green walls in our livingroom." (It now seems Edwards wanted *his* mind to be read, more than one of his listener's!)

During the next commercial break, Geller again returned to concentrate on the envelope:

> Geller: Now, its hard you know, I'm only getting sort of triangular things and so on... *(To Edwards)* now you concentrate on this...All I'm getting from these...it's only triangular shapes with lines inside.

(Had Geller asked me not to think of yesterday's drawing because the triangular lines suggested another sail boat? Was he fishing for "clues"?)

> Geller: Now you've got to start concentrating on what it is because if it's got a name also say the name, O.K.?

(I wondered why Geller was now asking Edwards to concentrate on the drawing. Previously, he stated he would use clairvoyance and not telepathy. Was clairvoyance failing, or was this a method for keeping Edwards's eyes off Geller as he palmed and squeezed the envelope?)

After the break there were more callers reporting watches and clocks that had started to tick. Geller seemed to be having great difficulty with the first envelope—a whole hour had gone by and he hadn't yet reproduced the drawing.

While the news was being read, Geller again displayed a dismal failure of his ESP ability in an everyday situation. A photographer had come into the studio and started a conversation with Geller who made a number of negative comments about the article by Szydlik that had appeared that morning in the *Dominion*. Geller was highly embarrassed to discover that the photographer was himself from the *Dominion* and was actually a friend of Szydlik!

A diversion was provided for the next fifteen minutes, as Geller bent a key and talked about his metal-bending abilities. I'm not sure how Geller bent this key—as usual, he did it when nobody was looking. We never actually *saw* any keys bend the whole time Geller was in New Zealand. We saw them *before* they were bent, while Geller handled them, and *after* they were bent, but not once did we see keys, or any other metal objects, actually in the process of bending.

Then came another break. Geller was still struggling with the first drawing, and he'd produced many attempts, mostly triangular in shape. He verbalized his difficulties and said he "just wasn't getting it." At this point Edwards told him not to give up. This clearly indicated to Geller that he was on the right track and encouraged Geller, who now seemed pleased that he was getting somewhere at last.

The double triangular figures Geller was now sketching were the basis for the stem and lower leaves of the flower, but the flower top itself, and a faint yellow sun were both missing. Uri then told Edwards to make another copy of the drawing from memory. Edwards did so and passed this copy to me so that I, too, could concentrate on it. Shortly thereafter, Geller's sketch included a new cometlike blob with raylike sun-spokes attached, and the idea of a flower began to emerge.

The extra drawing by Edwards gives Geller three possible supplementary clues: *(a)* a peek out of the corner of his eyes at Edwards's pencil movements—pencil reading is a very simple skill that anybody can do with a little practice; *(b)* the sounds of the pencil strokes; *(c)* a chance to glance at the drawing directly or through the back of the sheet as it is being handled and passed to me.

Geller justified his slow progress on the drawing by saying that it could take him "days" in a laboratory, that he'd already expended so much energy that he felt tired, not only physically but in some other way that made him feel very hungry. He likened himself to an athlete in training.

Geller again digressed from the ESP task and boosted his image by relating a couple of stories about *teleportation*, including one about a camera that was supposedly left on the moon by Captain Edgar Mitchell, the astronaut. Geller claimed that one day he would bring the camera back to earth. He then diverted our attention completely to a totally different psychic feat. This involved Edwards writing down a number, much hurried by Geller. As he had done the previous day, Geller claimed he'd try to "send" a number. Once again, Geller wrote down "8" and once again it was wrong, because Edwards wrote "4" and then added that he had also thought of "6", again wrong.

Unperturbed, Geller simply screwed up the paper with the "8" on it, as he'd done with me the day before. Edwards asked whether Geller had succeeded the previous day with me and Geller replied that he had. Since I'd retrieved the paper containing Geller's "8" from the wastepaper basket where Geller had conveniently thrown it, I knew perfectly well that Geller had *not* succeeded. I promptly asked Geller which number he had written, pointing out that I had written a "3". Smartly, he corrected himself and made out that it was the *drawings* he was talking about, not the number! As slippery as an eel and as cunning as a fox, but, oh, so phony!

Stalling for more time, Geller then asked Edwards if there'd been any calls on metal bending in listeners' homes. After two more calls, Geller finally produced his version of the first drawing. *It had taken him no less than eighty-five minutes and thirty preliminary attempted drawings.* Geller's final drawing was partially correct—it contained the two leaves and the stem of the flowers, the two leaves being at the base of the stem pointing downwards. The grass was missing, the petals of the flower were missing, and the sun was missing, although the curious comet-shaped blob with sun-spikes occurs at the top of the stem. Two lines also occurred at the top of the stem (see Fig. 7B). He made quite sure that Edwards opened the envelope ensuring that it was still sealed. Geller was obviously very pleased at his performance, and he made a point of commenting on the fact that the sun was drawn in a light yellow. We agreed that it was a semi-accurate success and Geller explained that the sun had "misled" him and acknowledged that he saw "the outline of the object rather than the object itself." Geller then stated that the fewer the number of people that know the drawing, the harder it was for him. (Finally it's clear. Geller had shifted from clairvoyance to telepathy.)

During the next commercial break Geller further justified his half-accurate rendition and complained about the writing on one of the envelopes (a signature) and the interference it caused. He also claimed the drawing lacked clarity. Actually, only the sun was drawn lightly. *The flower itself was done in dark, heavy crayon.*

Geller took the second of Edwards's envelopes and established that Edwards did not know its contents. (Oops. Back to clairvoyance.)

Edwards informed Geller that he knew only that it was drawn clearly in a single color, blue. Geller asked me if I knew what it was. When I said I didn't, he remarked, "Oh no, that is bad." (Oops, again. Back to telepathy.)

More calls came in from listeners reporting successes with their watches. One lady reported that she had a watch that had been broken for ten years. Geller chipped in with a little more off-the-cuff telepathy. "What was she wearing?" he enquired, "something with little flowers on it?" "Actually I'm in bed, I'm not very well," she said. She said she was wearing a pink nightgown. He asked if there was anything on it, and the lady replied, "No, it was all in one shade." However, Edwards persisted and asked again whether it had flowers on it. Under this strong pressure to comply, the lady then discovered something or other and said, "Yes, it's got little flowers on it." Geller and Edwards both seemed ecstatic at this amazing piece of ESP. (Another forced probability match. A large percentage of female listeners would have flowers or flowerlike designs on their clothing, and if this caller didn't, surely the next one would.)

While another lady was describing a watch success story, Geller chipped in with more feats of ESP:

Geller: Are you a big family?
Lady: Yes.
Geller: How many children do you have?
Lady: Five.
Geller: Five. Are any three of those children very unusual, because I've got three children that are very unusual. Are they in some way? (Cue for an easy probability match!)
Lady: Well, I've got twin boys.
Geller: I got something very unusual from three children, strangely enough...Now if two of them are twins and one, what's with one? There is something unusual about him. (Pursuing a revised probability match.)
Lady: *(Silence)*...ummm.
Geller: Well, O.K. that's it, but it's a good thing that I felt there was something unusual. (The failure is now a "success.")

The next event was probably one of the biggest and most revealing blunders that Geller has made in his whole checkered career. After handling the second of Edwards's envelopes for the past three to four minutes, Geller now offered his version of the drawing inside. What he drew was a shaded-in rectangle with a superimposed circle in the middle. When the two envelopes were opened *and* the drawing was unfolded, it turned out to be a wine goblet (see Fig. 7C). The blunder was not that Geller had missed the drawing, but that the particular shape of his error immediately suggested his primary technique for reading drawings in envelopes. *Geller's drawing was almost an exact copy of the way the drawing appears when it is folded and placed inside the envelope!*

Geller complained bitterly that the drawing was not done clearly. "It doesn't matter if it's folded twenty-five times," he said, "and placed inside ten envelopes or inside tinfoil," but all he got was a "dark blob" filled with "hundreds of lines." He protested that it was difficult because it was "not clear" and stated that he could have gotten it right if it wasn't shaded inside. Geller complained that he could see "all the lines" in his head. When I pointed out that the drawing had a very clear outline, he stated irrelevantly that none of the drawings he did at Stanford were shaded in. He said he could never get drawings if they were shaded in. Once again, Geller had talked his way out of a failure.

Geller then abruptly asked me to do a drawing on the spot. Geller turned his back and faced the window between the studio and the operations room where I knew Shipi was standing. Geller rushed me and I hurriedly drew two circles, one inside the other. I couldn't be sure that he didn't see my drawing or reflection of it in the window, or even if Shipi could see it through the window. I felt exhausted at the end of this three-hour program with so much to concentrate on, and with practically more "psychic" phenomena than I had eaten hot dinners. Somehow I just knew Geller would get it right, and he did.

I had reached saturation point. If the whole radio station had suddenly dematerialized and rematerialized again on the surface of the moon, I think I would have felt very little emotion. Geller drew his two circles, and I felt nothing except relief that one more episode of Gellerized chaos was over at last.

When Edwards finally asked me to publicly confirm that Geller had bent a key, started a watch, reproduced two drawings, and that dozens of listeners had reported watches starting and metal bending in their homes, I could easily and honestly confirm that all these things had indeed taken place. *Whether anything paranormal had occurred was another question and one that Edwards never raised.*

Following this radio program, we again asked Geller if he would be prepared to undergo tests of his powers in our university laboratory. He was vague and evasive and said that he might if he had time. Frankly, we weren't very optimistic and we agreed that it was now Dick's turn to find out what Geller was up to. This involved a move to another city. Christchurch, and another opportunity to study Geller at close quarters. Dick quickly managed to arrange a personal audience with the psychic superstar. Geller agreed to arrive at noon on the appointed day. He actually arrived seven hours late! Uri was very apologetic, saying that he got tired of cameras and tape recorders and interviews and so on. He suddenly announced he would do some drawings but without the tape recorder on. He pulled his chair away and turned his head toward a far corner with his eyes unnecessarily covered by his hands. Dick was sure he couldn't peek, but he kept his tablet tilted up so high that nobody in his location could possibly see the top of his pencil moving. To eliminate auditory cues, Dick drew his pictures in a series of disconnected parts, starting from different corners alternatively and joining it all up afterwards. These drawings had to be done quickly as Uri asked every few seconds if he was done yet. Uri didn't get the first one, nor the next, nor the next. With a touch of annoyance he proposed to drop it, but with honest enthusiasm Dick urged him to keep trying, hoping he would have a true psychic success. By this time, it is worth noting that Uri had swung around and pulled up his chair directly across from Dick, a mere few feet away, no longer averting his eyes, but merely closing them very lightly with his head upright and rocking slightly. On the sixth trial, Dick deliberately tipped his writing tablet forward so that most of his pencil could be seen, and drew a boot. Then, keeping his pencil point off the paper, Dick "drew" in some holes and bootstraps along the front of the boot, making a series of curlicue movements, using his fingernail to produce the appropriate sounds on the paper. "Look," Uri said, "I think I've got something this time." He drew two vertical lines corresponding to the sides of the high boot top, and added some holes and a vertical curlicue! Dick gulped, somewhat embarrassed by his own trick, and said, "No, that's not it," showing him his boot, which had no laces. Again he suggested we drop it, but Dick urged him to try just another trial or two, and finally after ten failures, Dick deliberately lowered his tablet again to reveal his pencil movements as he drew a commonplace figure in an orthodox manner. "I've got it," he said, and produced an excellent match.

Even though his technique for getting visual cues had become fairly obvious, Dick felt relieved he had finally gotten a "success" so that he and Uri could chuckle about it together and reestablish their tenuous friendship. He must have thought Dick would never get around to relaxing his guard, as he steadily improved his position for peeking through the slits of his eyes.

Pursuing our goal of proper laboratory experiments, Dick again asked Uri if he would come to our laboratory for a few hours. Again, Uri was vague and said that he might. In fact, he never did participate in our planned experiments.

Certainly, over our several encounters with Geller we had witnessed an amazing and confusing sequence of events, many of which lacked an immediate rational explanation. Geller certainly liked switching from one task to another, making it difficult to follow any one of them through in a logical manner. And yet, while one had the feeling of being rushed most of the time, some effects took a long time to complete, such as the flower drawing. Geller's patter was full of contradictions and seeming fictions, such as the story of the SRI watch with the missing parts, autobiographical confusions, and rationalizations. He used probability matches just like Kreskin and seemed to show a lack of ESP ability for everyday events where it should have come in useful. On the other hand, somehow he had started a watch, reproduced a drawing of a flower sealed inside two envelopes, and also a drawing of two circles. Dick's clever personal experiment with Uri's ESP drawing ability indicated pretty clearly that, on that occasion, Uri's ability rested more on pencil reading than ESP. The goblet drawing was a peculiar and significant failure, and it provided us with an interesting hypothesis for further research.

8

GELLER EXPOSED

Populus vult decipi: People want to be deceived.
                                                    Roman Saying

A professional magician will rarely do the same trick twice in a row, and, if possible, he'll not do it twice at all before the same audience. Even if he appears to do similar stunts, as Kreskin appears to "read the minds" of several people, *he will vary the underlying technique as often as his repertoire permits* (see chapter five). The obvious reason for avoiding repetition is that repeats give the audience a chance to notice which features of the routine are constant and, thus, provide clues as to the technique being used. Therefore, if one wishes to entertain the open-minded hypothesis that a man claiming to be a psychic might only be a magician, it is important to observe him performing the same type of act several times in a row, which may mean following him from city to city. Obviously, very few people will have the time or money or motivation to do this.

Receptive media people, whom Geller consistently flatters by his personal attention, are often totally convinced by a few one-time only demonstrations and publish their astonished conclusions on the basis of these inadequate observations. As the media generate a cumulatively favorable interpretation, the public and other media people become all the more predisposed to believe in Geller's psychic powers on the basis of very scanty personal experience. One of the responsibilities of scientific investigation is to suspend judgment until enough systematic data have been collected to permit a carefully reasoned conclusion. It is never the scientist's own conclusion that is important but the quality of his evidence. While careful data collection is necessary for scientific work in general, it is all the more vital when one must observe "in the field," rather than in the laboratory, and will be more crucial when one is studying psychic phenomena that *could be* the illusory product of a deliberate deceiver.

We present now the follow-up research that leads to our conclusion that *Uri Geller is a conjuror.* We shall then offer a comprehensive expose[1] of the full range of his magic menu. A truly decisive study of Uri Geller's claims is made the more difficult by his avoidance of controlled laboratory studies. He has participated in only one scientifically acceptable laboratory study. This was the well-known project at the Stanford Research Institute to which we have devoted chapter nine.

The purpose of the laboratory set-up is to isolate the one factor that is being studied, partly by the use of appropriate rooms, apparatus, and procedures for observations, and partly by the use of a control group of subjects. While Geller has generally evaded such conditions of study, we have been able to develop a new research strategy to bring our field observations one step closer to the controlled conditions of the laboratory. We call this the *method of the delayed control group.* For each of Geller's effects we argue that, if the same detailed pattern of results can be obtained using ordinary sensori-motor functions, then there is no reason to hypothesize paranormal, supernormal, psychic, or otherwise extraordinary powers. If a group of normal, nonpsychic people can produce the same results as Geller, in the same situations where Geller produces his claimed psychic effects, we can safely assume Geller uses the same normal methods, whatever they turn out to be. Scientists normally find that the simplest, most parsimonious explanation of their observations is the one that best reflects natural events, and there is no good reason for departing from this principle in the area of parapsychology. In the light of the results we have obtained using our delayed control groups, Geller's claims to special powers become null and void of any truth or basis in reality.

Perceiving Drawings Inside Envelopes

The first application of our new method occurs in our study of Uri Geller's ability to perceive and reproduce drawings or other graphic material sealed in opaque or semi-opaque envelopes, of which we observed three cases. These were the drawings of the *Endeavour,* the flower, and the goblet previously seen in figure 6. In the left column of figure 7 we have traced in black ink the appearance of these drawings *when folded* and ready to be put into their envelopes. It is useful to consider how the folded targets differ from the originals. Note the disappearance of the sun from the folded drawing B that was drawn in light yellow crayon and was therefore invisible through the paper. Note also the complete transformation in shape for drawing C when it was folded. Placed inside the envelopes, all three drawings appear on casual inspection to be *totally invisible.* How then could a nonpsychic magician succeed?

We consider, first, the fact that on all three occasions, Uri Geller handled each of the envelopes continuously during periods that ranged from 11.5 minutes for the ship up to 85 minutes for the flower. His handling included massaging the envelope, stretching it, pressing it between thumb and fingers, and holding it prayerlike against his forehead. The question is whether or not, under similar conditions, normal people can repeat Geller's performance by simple inspection. We retained all of the original target drawings and their envelopes, as well as all of Geller's attempts at them. So, all we needed was a set of attempts from normal, nonpsychic subjects against which Geller's efforts could be evaluated.

We asked a group of forty-eight näive students to study the three envelopes under indoor lighting to see what they could pick up without peeking inside. When we say the subjects were näive, we are using the standard psychologist's way of saying that they had no knowledge of the experimenters' theories or hypotheses, or whose drawing they were looking at, or why. Since we didn't know how long Geller might have effectively had to study the envelopes, while all observers were distracted, we randomly divided forty-eight subjects into four groups and gave each group a different, but brief inspection time of five, ten, twenty, or fifty seconds. Also, we gave them two other envelopes to try first so they could get a little practice. Here are the instructions we gave our subjects:

This is an experiment on visual perception. I'm going to give you five envelopes. Inside each one there is a drawing which has been done on note paper. The paper will be folded and it may be inside another envelope. I would like you to copy the drawing inside exactly as you see it. You may hold the envelope up to the light or use any method you like, but you cannot open the envelope. We want you simply to draw an outline of what you see. It's not complicated. There may be a few details in the drawing but they're not important. Just draw the main idea. No guesswork—just draw exactly what you see.

In the second phase of the experiment, we had six naive students judge the accuracy of each set of forty-eight student attempts along with Geller's final drawing. Geller's final drawing was faithfully copied on to a 3" x 5" card, so that his drawing would be indistinguishable from the others in the series. Accuracy was rated by comparing each of the forty-nine responses with the original target drawings in both its folded and unfolded states. The scale of accuracy ranged from 0 for "no drawing submitted" up to 7 for "almost perfectly accurate."

The results showed that Geller did slightly better than the *average* student performance at fifty seconds for both the ship and the goblet drawings and about equalled the twenty-second average for the flower drawing. Geller may have had longer than fifty seconds to effectively examine the envelopes, however, and also he's had years of practice. Geller was also allowed multiple attempts for the flower and goblet targets. It, therefore, seems more reasonable to evaluate Geller's performance against that of the *best* students from each group. As shown visually in figure 7, Geller's accuracy turns out to be no better, and in one case (the flower) *worse,* than the students'. Hence, there is no evidence that Geller's performance exceeds that obtained by normal methods of visual inspection, and these results therefore lead to the conclusion that *Geller perceived the faint outlines of the folded drawings through the envelopes.*

This conclusion is further supported by the observation that Geller's drawings matched more closely against the folded versions of the target. Gellerites will want to argue that Geller's apparent detection of target information by normal sensory perception on these occasions says nothing about his claims to having ESP ability on other occasions. Perhaps, they will argue, he only employs ESP when ordinary perception fails.

At this point the goblet drawing is particularly enlightening. Owing to the heavy shading and the position of the folds, the folded drawing bears little resemblance to the unfolded target that Geller was supposed to reproduce. This was the only case in which the true nature of the target was invisible to normal visual sensory perception. Uri failed. He simply drew a rectangular blob like everybody else (see *folded* target) and was thus completely inaccurate despite his claim that he used ESP. Geller's performance did not differ from that of subjects using normal visual perception and therefore there is no support to his claims of special powers. Uri's got the same sensory powers as any other normal human being—he's just trickier than most of us in the way he uses them.

Fixing Watches and Clocks

So far, we have not accounted for Uri's famous ability to fix broken watches and clocks by mental concentration (he says). Surely, this can not be trickery because even watches and clocks in people's homes fix themselves while Uri is on radio or TV. Nor can these results be considered accidental flukes, since the studio switchboard may be jammed with hundreds of callers reporting success after Uri has done his "work, work, work" routine.

As we had no hypothesis for the Geller watch effect, we canvassed some jewelers for their opinions and ideas. They told us about half the watches and clocks that come in for repairs are only jammed with dust and gummy oil—such pieces are given the familiar "cleaning and overhaul." But some of the jewelers pointed out that, *if a watch or clock is held in the hand for a few minutes, body heat could warm and thin the oil, thus freeing the mechanism.* Of course, the mild bumps and shakings that accompany the handling of the watch or clock would contribute, too. Notice that Geller instructs his audience to hold the timepieces in their hands before starting to concentrate.

While this was an interesting theory, it was still just speculation. And, it could be argued that perhaps jewelers were exaggerating to preserve their own public image. So, we challenged seven jewelers to see how many customers' watches they could start by holding and handling procedures before opening the watch case. One week later, they had started 60 out of 106 watches attempted, for a 57 percent success rate!

It was time to employ the *method of the delayed control group* to see if we could match Geller's "psychic" success rate with the purely physical effects of holding and handling. We asked a class of first-year students to conduct a survey on a volunteer basis. They were given detailed written instructions to approach people and ask them if they had tried to fix a watch or clock with Uri Geller's help, and if so, with what results. This would give us a baseline for the Geller effect. The instructions emphasized that the students were not to go after any cases that had come to their attention by hearsay, but that they must approach each person "blind." This point was important, because people whose watches had been Gellerized into life were very likely to talk about it with friends and relatives, whereas people who had failed would tend to remain silent. So if they followed up on hearsay reports, they would naturally track down many more successes than failures, for a misleading result.

If the person interviewed had *not* tried the Geller effect, he or she became a candidate for the physical-procedures control group. The student then asked if the respondent happened to have a broken watch, in which case the student himself went through five minutes of prescribed holding and handling procedures and recorded the results.

In a second telephone survey we asked the same two basic questions: had the respondent tried the Geller effect, and with what result? If the answer was "no attempt made," the respondent was asked if he or she had a broken watch, and, if so, to bring it to the telephone. We gave exact instructions for holding the watch firmly in one hand, while we kept them talking by asking a number of irrelevant questions about it. Twice during this trial, we instructed the subject to gently shake and rotate the watch as directed. After three minutes had lapsed, we recorded whether or not the watch had started ticking.

The results of both surveys are shown in Table 7. In total we found forty-three people who had tried the Geller effect at home with a 48.8 percent success rate. But we also located sixty-one broken watches, and like the jewelers, were able to start 57.4 percent of them by purely physical procedures. Although the physical-only success rate is actually higher than Geller's success rate, the difference is not statistically reliable. *We can conclude that the amazing Geller effect on timepieces can be attributed entirely to perfectly natural mechanics.*

Geller's Stage Performances

We believe that we have now amassed sufficient evidence, collected over

TABLE 7
Watches Started by Geller's Instructions
and by Physical Procedures

Survey	Geller		Physical only	
	N watches tried	% Success	N watches tried	% Success
Students	13	38.4	32	68.9
Telephone	30	53.3	29	44.8
Combined	43	48.8	61	57.4

more than a dozen different exposures to Geller at close quarters, to permit our conclusion that Geller is not psychic. Among this evidence are our own observations of Geller's stage performances, which we'll now describe. Our exposé of Geller is based in part on clear-cut examples of cheating. This has been witnessed not only by us, but by other Geller-watchers, and his stage trickery has been confirmed by at least two of his close associates who both worked as his manager for considerable periods of time (Messrs. D. Pelz and Y. Katz, and also by an ex-girlfriend, Miss H. Shtrang).

The several stage shows we have seen followed exactly the same format, and so we shall describe one typical show on a step-by-step basis. As we review this typical show, we will comment on some of the effects as they occurred, but the reader must keep in mind that *no* conclusions were actually reached during the performance itself. In most cases, the initial effect was mystifying, but then we reflected back on the events, saw another show, reflected again, and so on, until the complete *modus operandi* had been revealed.

The first demonstration involves the reading of a color name written on a board on Geller's stage, behind Geller, but visible to the audience. Geller obtains two volunteers from the audience and takes great pains to ensure that the two ladies he selects are known to other members of the audience, thus establishing that the women are unlikely to be accomplices. He instructs his audience not to whisper the color so there would be "no way" he can cheat. One lady writes up a color and erases it. Geller stands at the front of the stage with one hand on his forehead. His whole body sways back and forth as he counts "One...two...three." It is as if Geller is a kind of human aerial, trying to tune into the right wavelength of psychic radiation sent out by the audience in front of him. It is a dramatic routine that he repeats three or four times. Finally the signals get through (we use this phrase advisedly!) and Geller successfully reads out the color name (e.g., green). He receives a loud applause. He may then say he was getting two colors, e.g., the other one may be yellow. He asks if anyone in the audience has been thinking of "yellow." Yes, *somebody has been thinking of "yellow"* and he gains a second round of applause.

For his next piece of "telepathy," Geller sits on the right-hand side of the stage at the front and holds a piece of board in his hands. The board is about 2′ × 3′ and Geller states that its purpose is to *disprove skeptics who claimed somebody is signaling to him from the audience.* Geller asks another lady to write up the name of a city and also to do a drawing, but not a house or a flower because "everybody does those." Geller sits with the board in front of his face and says he has his eyes shut. Nobody is in a position to confirm this, as Geller's eyes are hidden by the board, and people are much more interested in the lady's attempts to think of a capital city and to do a drawing with her right hand, while making random chalk marks with her left hand to cover the writing sounds—a task as difficult as simultaneously rubbing circles on your stomach while patting your head. When the city name (e.g., Dublin) and the drawing (e.g., cat) are finally completed and erased (this usually takes several minutes), Geller goes through his "One, two, three" routine and gives the city name correctly. He then may claim to pick up a second name, e.g., "Moscow," and ask if anybody has been thinking of this. Sure enough, one man in the audience of perhaps one thousand or more will probably state that he had! Then, after a painfully long time, Geller correctly reports the drawing.

Next he chooses two more volunteers. Let's call them Jenny and Bill. Geller asks Bill to write another color name on the blackboard while Geller and Jenny both sit at the front of the stage with their eyes closed. The idea is that Geller will receive the color from the audience and then transmit it to the lady using ESP. Geller stands next to Jenny, holding her shoulders at arms length, and tells her to close her eyes. He tries to reassure Jenny with the words that there is "nothing wrong in being wrong," and tells her: "Listen, listen in your ears. I'm going to shout it in my head. I won't open my mouth or anything, but you might hear it."

We have to admit that although we didn't know how Geller picked up the color when we first saw this, we believed he might try to whisper it to

Jenny without moving his lips, rather as a ventriloquist might throw his voice into a dummy. Jenny resists answering and then finally writes "blue," which is wrong: Geller says he'd tried to pass her "black" (which itself is the correct color written on the board).

The final effect before the intermission involves the use of a blindfold and more lady volunteers. The first lady ties a scarf around Geller's head and is then asked to choose the second lady from the audience. When the second one comes up onto the stage, Geller asks her first to stand beside him, and then to move behind him towards the back of the stage. Geller, supposedly by ESP, has to try and see what she is wearing. Everybody is told to look at this lady. Always suspicious of blindfolds, the fact that Geller first asked the lady to stand right beside him increases our suspicions that he sees the clothing under or through the blindfold. He correctly describes the clothing, e.g., dark blue trousers, red shoes, blue top and jacket.

The second half of Geller's lecture-demonstration begins by a request for a five- or six-year-old child to go up on to the stage. When a little girl has been found. Geller asks for a thin, man's wrist watch. He collects a watch and places it *face down* on the little girl's open hand. He scrunches his fist a few times over the watch, turns it over, and announces it has advanced one hour. Although it doesn't take much imagination to figure out how this effect is done, we'll return to it again later.

Next, Geller says he'll try to fix some watches. A large number of enthusiasts rush towards the stage carrying "broken" or "stopped" watches, like a group of crippled pilgrims on their way to Lourdes. Geller shuffles through these sick watches and sorts them into two piles. Then Geller counts "One, two, three" and the audience all shout "Work." Now the whole audience are budding psychics because, lo and behold, watches actually start to tick. This faith-healing ceremony is repeated a further three times to "repair" watches that have not responded the first time, and again a few more start ticking, so Geller says. Also, a few people in the audience report that their watches have started too.

The final and slowest phase of this display of psychic strength is a demonstration of metal-bending power. Many different keys are brought up to Uri, who shuffles through them selecting a suitable case for treatment. Another volunteer from Uri's endless supply of willing ladies holds one end, while he strokes it and holds the other end, everybody thinking "Bend, bend, bend." The key is eventually revealed to be bent, and, once again, we have a very amazed audience. Opportunities for substitution could hardly be more obvious, but nobody seems bothered by this possibility, as Geller has by now built up a high level of belief within his audience. Charisma and boyish charm get a lot of mileage in this mind bender's masterful performance.

Summary of Geller's Methods

In summary, Geller's stage effects consist of seven definable events:

1. Geller receives a color name from the audience.
2. Geller receives a color name from the audience and attempts (but rarely succeeds) to transmit it to an individual from the audience.
3. Geller perceives a city name and a drawing from a blackboard apparently hidden from Geller's view.
4. Geller describes the clothing of an audience member standing behind him while he is wearing a blindfold.
5. Geller moves the hands of a watch onwards one hour.
6. Watches that are supposedly broken start ticking again.
7. Geller bends a key.

Each and every one of these allegedly "paranormal" events is produced by using a childishly simple conjuring trick. The following event-by-event analysis provides a complete exposure of each of these so-called "Geller effects." The numbering of the events follows that of the above list.

Events 1 and 2: Geller receives signals

For events 1 and 2, Geller receives coded information from accomplices stationed in the audience. We have witnessed hand signals used by Clark on several occasions during this early part of the performance. On the first occasion we saw Solveig Clark sitting in a vacant block of seats so she would be in full view not only of Geller on stage, but also of Dave, who was with a friend, Linda Addis. When the telepathy routine began, Dave asked Linda to sit with her eyes glued to Clark while he kept his glued to Geller.

The color "blue" was written on the blackboard and erased. Geller repeated the "One, two, three" routine and then glanced up at Clark. Dave muttered "Now!" and *Linda clearly saw Clark move both hands up and down in front of her. It was a highly visible signal in which both hands were raised and lowered about the wrists that rested on the vacant seat in front of her.*

The second color reading served only to confirm what had already been observed. Geller again looked up to Clark, Dave said "Now," but Clark was so busy staring at Dave and Linda she missed her cue. As a result of this Geller had to repeat "One, two, three" and look up for the signal a second time. Again Linda saw Clark make a distinct hand movement. Clark's arms were folded across her chest, and she moved her right hand in a patting motion on the upper part of her left arm. Geller received the correct color, which happened to be purple, to a round of applause. *So now we finally knew what Geller had meant when he said we'd pick up the signals!*

Hannah Shtrang, Shipi Shtrang, and Solveig Clark have all been used for this purpose. In addition, two different ex-managers of Geller have, on separate occasions, described this simple technique: on the first occasion in Israel, Danny Pelz told an audience of five hundred how Geller reads the colors through signs transmitted to him by a "secret coworker" in the audience; on the second occasion, as reported by Randi in the *New Scientist,* Geller's ex-manager in New York, Yasha Katz, has confirmed that signaling does take place. Geller may have also used this technique at SRI (see chapter nine).

Once he has received the hand signal from Shtrang or Clark, he can then attempt to pass on the information by subtle whispers to an innocent victim on stage (Event 2). We have never observed this done successfully, and obviously this is too difficult to do without being detected.

Event 3: Geller peeks at the blackboard

Yes folks, it really is that simple. For this feat you may recall, Geller states that he shields his face from the audience "to prove to skeptics that signaling from accomplices is impossible." *He actually reads the city name and drawing directly from the blackboard while hiding his face from the audience's view.* Unfortunately for Uri, a few people, including the authors, have sat close enough to the stage, in direct line with Uri and the blackboard, to see this peeking take place.

Event 4: Geller peeks under the blindfold

Only by trying this for yourself can you determine just how easy it is to see through, under, or around a blindfold. This is a standard magician's trick that anybody with normal vision can duplicate. After he's seen the relevant details, Geller moves the lady behind him to help convince the audience he couldn't have used normal, everyday perception.

Event 5: Geller moves the hands of a watch onwards using the winder

While handling a watch borrowed from the audience member, Geller moves the hands around, using the winder in the normal manner. He then places it face down in the hand of a small child, too nervous to turn over the watch and check that the time is still true. Distractions galore, and a good delay between the physical wind-on and the final time check, make this an easy but effective feat of mind power. Try it yourself on unsuspecting friends, and see how easy it really is to convince them you are psychic. But remember to make sure they don't notice you sneakily using the winder. Like Uri, it's far better to fail completely than to get caught cheating—after all, you can always say you're not in the right mood to do it, or that there are too many "bad vibrations."

Event 6: Geller starts watches by warming, shaking holding, and handling them

As the evidence we have presented in the last section indicates, Uri, or anybody else for that matter, can get about 50 percent of stopped watches to start ticking by physical holding and handling. These watches are not broken in the first place, and merely require warming or shaking or moving to start them again. Probably they do not tick for very long as, in most cases, they need cleaning and lubricating. But that doesn't matter, as most people accept the sound of the ticking as a miracle of psychic power. But why does the watch that Geller works directly on always start going? As he sorts through the pile of watches brought onto the stage, there are two possibilities: (1) Geller selects a watch that is ticking, which he or an accomplice previously dropped into the pile, or (2) he selects a watch that starts ticking after its journey to the stage and any handling and holding, which Geller can quickly perform as he sifts through the pile, commenting on the watches as he does so. In the latter case he can then identify that watch with its owner in the audience and place that watch in the hands of a child. Hence, it is to his credit that *that* watch starts ticking. If one isn't found already ticking, the substitute watch will do.

Event 7: Geller bends keys using physical techniques, not psychic power

There are many ways of making small objects bend: (1) Distract everybody, bend the object manually, conceal the bend, and then reveal the bend to the now attentive onlookers. This is his usual method. The bend is made either by a two-handed tweak, or by levering it in something tough like a belt buckle or the head of another key with a hole in the top. (2) Geller (or an accomplice) pre-stresses the object by bending it many times until it's nearly at breaking point. Later it can be used to dazzle unsuspecting audiences as it bends, appears to melt, or even snaps in two pieces following the slightest pressure from Uri's wiry fingers. (3) Quite often collections of metal objects (e.g., a bunch of keys or a drawer of cutlery) contain one or more items that are already bent. Geller tells you he'll bend something and, when you examine the whole set of objects carefully, the bent item is found and Uri takes credit. (4) When an object is already bent, Geller will often say that it will continue to bend. He may move the object slowly to enhance the effect, or place it on a flat surface and push down on one end. But many people will believe they can see an object slowly bending purely as a result of Geller's suggestion that it is doing so. (5) Substitute objects already bent for the ones provided.

Note that Uri's bending powers are confined to *small objects* that can be handled and manipulated silently. Nothing plastic or wooden ever gets bent—imagine Uri's face go red as loudly cracking plastic or wood snapped in his fingers, drawing attention of curious eyes at the wrong moment!

In addition to the stage techniques, Geller's repertoire includes the following methods to produce the illusion of psychic phenomena.

Conjured Telepathy

This is the ability to make people believe you can "read" their thoughts or "send" thoughts to them in the absence of any normal, sensory communication. The first method uses *population stereotypes* in the same manner as Kreskin. Geller writes a target in the form of a number (e.g., 8) or a drawing (e.g., a ship, house, flower, tree, or car) that has a high probability of occurring spontaneously in a group of "receivers" purely by chance. This stunt works best with a large audience, as a large number of people will then choose the right message and believe Geller has transmitted his thoughts to them. In one variation of this technique, Uri makes a guess at some probable occurrence, e.g., he may require of a lady: "Are you wearing anything with little flowers on it?" In another version he'll restrict the subject's choices to something like "Two simple geometric figures," or he'll obtain a false match with a compliant subject using some seductive persuasion.

In a second technique, *Geller pretends to do his drawing first* by making some phony hand movements behind his pad. He then says he'll "direct" the "receiver's" pen or pencil around the paper as he transmits the thought. In actuality, *Geller quickly copies the unsuspecting subject's drawing as it is being drawn.* This is why Geller's drawing often seems scrappy and hurried compared to the other one that, drawn more slowly, appears neater.

A third technique Geller uses is to *peek at the subject's drawing and then copy it.* There are various ways of getting peeks at drawings, which we shall consider in more detail under *conjured clairvoyance.* (Whether Geller pretends to produce telepathy or clairvoyance depends on whether he suggests that he is getting the drawing from a person's thoughts, or directly from the physical record. However, this is often left undefined or is changed from moment to moment).

A fourth method is to *listen* as the subject does his drawing. This is particularly effective when the subject has been told by Geller to keep his drawing simple. Circles, squares, triangles, and the odd digits are especially easy to pick up this way. This technique is known to professional magicians as *sound mentalism.* Try it out yourself and you'll see what we mean.

A fifth method is to *watch the subject's pencil and hand movements* as he does his drawing. *Pencil reading* is a standard skill of practicing mentalists, and in simpler cases an untrained person may succeed as well.

A sixth method is to give the unsuspecting subject a block of paper, let him do his drawing, have him tear off the sheet, and then *copy the drawing from the impression left on the second sheet of paper.*

A seventh method is to have an accomplice send you *signals* to tell you the information (as described above).

An eighth method (if all else fails) is to *pump the subject with questions* about their drawing to get a few clues, or to get them to start all over again with another drawing. After all, nothing has to work the first time.

Conjured Clairvoyance

This is the ability to make people believe you can obtain information without the aid of the senses or of another mind, e.g., that you can see through solid objects. If a drawing is sealed in an envelope (or two), then by *holding it up to the light (e.g., a nearby window), one can often see right through it* and get most of the outline. Only a few seconds are needed to do this, although obviously Uri must wait until observers are distracted, which is why it can sometimes take a long time.

An alternative method is to *press down on the envelope while holding it and stretching it between fingers and thumbs.* The contents may then be visible as envelopes are rarely completely opaque. A third method is to distract observers for a sufficiently long period of time to allow the envelope to be carefully opened and resealed, allowing a good look at the drawing inside. If Geller can't reseal it properly, he'll rip open the envelope after he's submitted his drawing, or he may substitute another envelope while he goes to the bathroom to look at the target.

Another technique good for stage work as we described above, is to *use a "blindfold" and to peak through or under it.* If objects are hidden inside containers, Geller may *open them when nobody is looking* and take a peek, or he may get to the props beforehand and set the lid differently. If one container has objects inside and others don't, Uri can tell you which one by causing them to vibrate slightly as he moves around them, or as they are jostled by a person who removes them one at a time.

As we noted before, any case of conjured telepathy can also be made into conjured clairvoyance by suggesting that the drawing is being received directly without the aid of another person's thoughts; which one the magician suggests will depend on his tactics for patter and distraction, which is why Geller appears to contradict himself so often about which type of psi he is using.

Dematerialization and Related Effects

Another set of techniques relate to the mysterious disappearance (dematerialization) and reappearance (materialization) of objects. These effects are childishly simple and usually involve concealing the object for a period of time (e.g., in your pocket) and then throwing it up in the air when nobody is looking. A technique suitable for convincing scientists in laboratories is to move delicate balances, magnetometers, compasses, or other sensitive electrical or magnetic devices by using concealed magnets or by vibrating or tampering with them when nobody is watching closely. Of course, any normal malfunctions that occur Geller can also attribute to his own doing. The simpler the method, the more it will fool and fox believing scientists looking for more complex explanations for psychic powers, as we shall see in the next chapter.

FIG. 1 (A) VIEW OF TARGET FROM THE ROAD

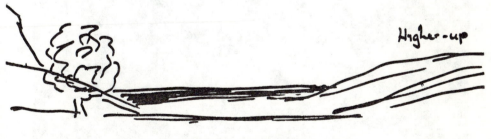

Space

A yellow light.

Higher-up

Green

FIG. 1 (B) SUBJECT'S FINAL DRAWING

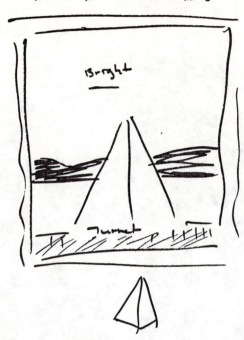

FIG. 1 (C) JUDGE'S FIRST CHOICE

FIG. 1 (D) VIEW FROM STEPS ABOVE HOUSE

FIG. 2 (A) "TRIANGULAR" GRAVE

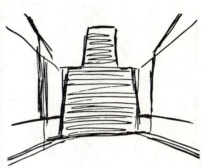

FIG. 2 (B) VIEW FACING AWAY FROM GRAVE

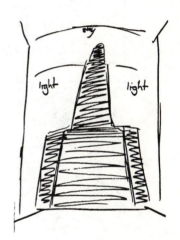

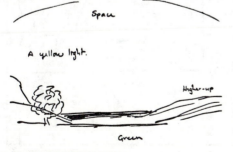

FIG. 2 (C) JUDGE'S FIRST CHOICE

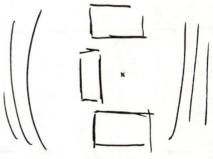

FIG. 2 (D) SUBJECT'S DRAWINGS

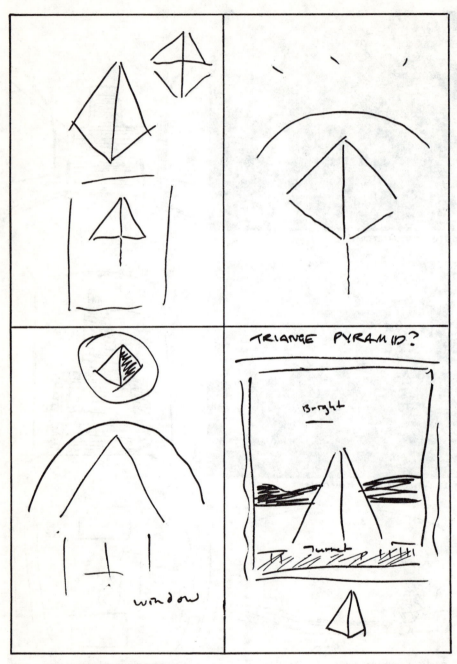

FIG. 3 (C) SUBJECT'S DRAWINGS

FIG. 3 (A) RAILWAY STATION PLATFORM

FIG. 3 (B) VIEW UP RAILWAY LINES

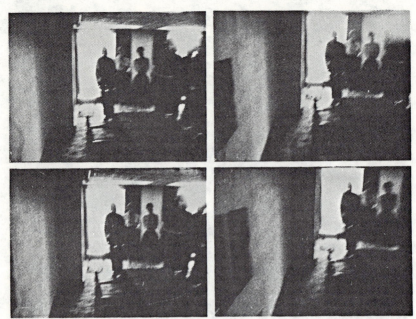

FIG. 4 (A) STILLS FROM THE MOVIE FILM OF GELLER BENDING A KEY.
NOTE POSITION OF GELLER'S HANDS.

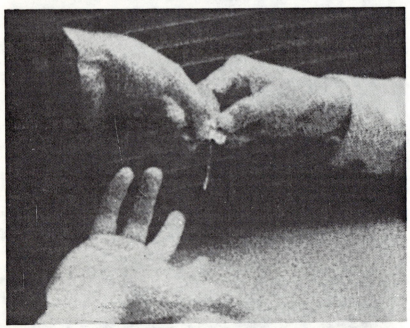

FIG. 4 (B) NOTE BEND IN KEY AFTER GELLER HAD WALKED TO THE
VENTILATOR TO COMMENCE THE "PSYCHIC" BENDING
PROCEDURE.

FIG. 5 THE AUTHOR'S DRAWING (ON THE LEFT) AND GELLER'S. WHICH WAS DONE FIRST?

a   b   c

FIG. 6 THREE TARGET DRAWINGS SUBMITTED TO GELLER IN ENVELOPES.

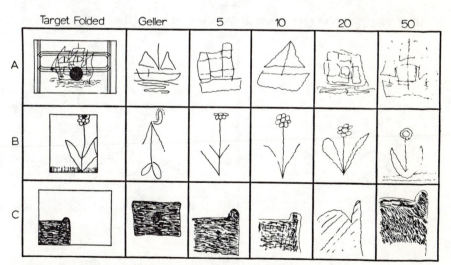

FIG. 7 THE LAY-OUT OF THE TARGET DRAWINGS WHEN FOLDED (LEFT COLUMN); GELLER'S RESPONSES, AND EXAMPLES OF STUDENT RESPONSES TO SEALED DRAWINGS.

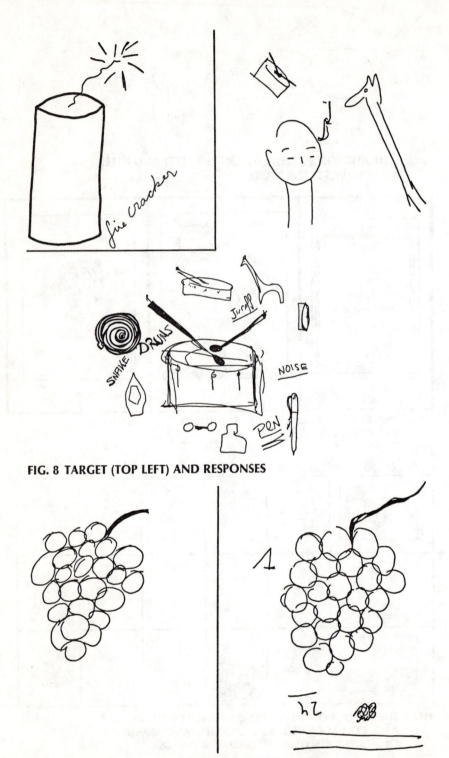

FIG. 8 TARGET (TOP LEFT) AND RESPONSES

FIG. 9 TARGET (AT LEFT) AND GELLER'S RESPONSE

FIG. 10 TARGET (TOP LEFT) AND GELLER'S RESPONSES

FIG. 11 TARGET (LEFT) AND RESPONSE

FIG. 12 TARGET (LEFT) AND RESPONSE

FIG. 13 TARGET (LEFT) AND RESPONSE

FIG. 14 TARGET (AT LEFT) AND RESPONSE

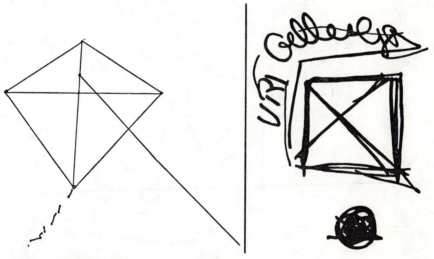

FIG. 15 TARGET (AT LEFT) AND RESPONSE

FIG. 16 TARGET (AT LEFT) AND RESPONSES

FIG. 17 TARGET (AT TOP) AND RESPONSE

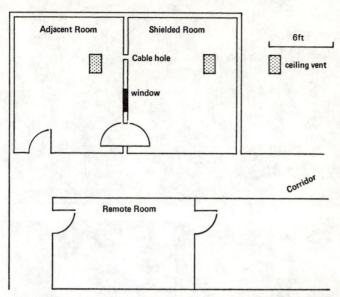

FIG. 18 FLOOR PLAN AND FRONT WALL OF "SHIELDED" ROOM

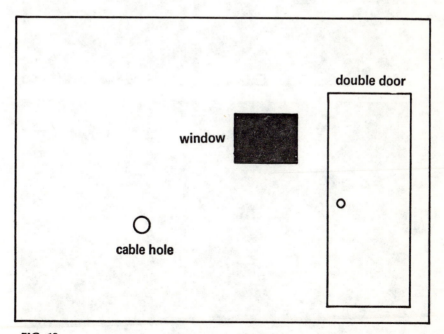

FIG. 19

(A)

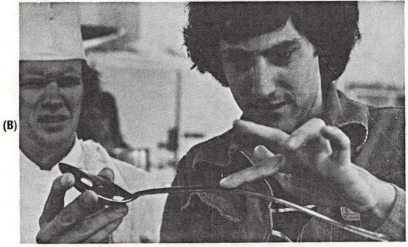

(B)

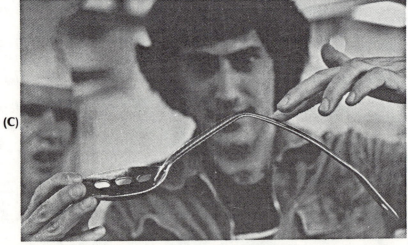

(C)

FIG. 20 A GELLER MIRACLE CREATED BY A NEWSPAPER JOURNALIST.

9

GELLER PERFORMS
AT THE STANFORD
RESEARCH INSTITUTE

When a man's knowledge is not in order, the more of it he has, the greater will be his confusion.

Herbert Spencer

As we followed Geller's act in the field, his psychic powers toppled over like a row of dominoes. But there remained the paradox of SRI. If Geller is only a magician, how did he apparently demonstrate ESP under controlled conditions in one of the most high-powered research labs in the world? In the same *Nature* paper in which Russell Targ and Harold Puthoff presented their remote viewing experiments, they also reported two apparently cheat-proof experiments with Uri Geller reading drawings and calling dice.

Although Targ and Puthoff didn't claim any metal bending, how could we ignore their ESP effects? Could we have gone wrong somewhere? Did Geller have a residuum of psychic ability behind his barrage of deceptions? Or did he bamboozle Targ and Puthoff? If so, would anybody ever know besides Uri Geller and Shipi Shtrang?

Each of us in turn visited Targ and Puthoff at SRI, but, while we were treated cordially, the inside story on Geller's performance remained clouded in generalities. Our first clue came when we finally got a look at the famous double-walled steel room in which Geller received most of the drawings. As we shall soon see, it was not foolproof. Meanwhile, Targ and Puthoff scoffed at Joseph Hanlon's theory *(New Scientist,* October, 1974) that Shipi could have contacted Geller in the steel room by miniature radio. As Puthoff told us, they even checked to see if Geller was using fiber optics to look around corners. No way, they said, could Uri and Shipi have worked out a bug system—but then there was no evidence to back this up, either.

Not long after our personal encounters with Geller, magician James Randi published a scathing review of the miracle man *(The Magic of Uri Geller,* Ballantine Books, 1975). Randi had come to the same conclusions we had. But he also offered a crucially new explanation for the SRI dice-calling experiment—that Geller had simply peeked. It is not as farfetched as it sounds.

Targ and Puthoff palmed off Randi's theories in a privately circulated *Fact Sheet.* But gradually, over the months and then years, little bits of information kept leaking out of SRI, and the methodology in the *Nature* paper began to crumble. One key source of information was John Wilhelm, a former science writer who, on assignment for *Time* Magazine, got to SRI many months before the *Nature* article appeared and plowed through the surface of SRI generalities to get hundreds of details about the Targ-Puthoff research. Wilhelm ended up unconvinced about Geller. (John Wilhelm, *The Search for Superman,* New York: Pocket Books, 1976.)

The second key source of inside information was actually Targ and Puthoff themselves, first in their *Fact Sheet,* and then in an informal article on the drawings experiment titled, *The Record: Eight Days with Uri Geller,* which was published in *The Geller Papers,* edited by Charles Panati (of *Newsweek)* and published by Houghton Mifflin in 1976.

Ten Drawings and Eight Dice Throws

Considering all the excitement and Geller's visits to many scientific laboratories in the United States and England, it is significant that only two experiments have ever been published on Geller's psychic powers. Geller convinced several other scientists personally as well, but then parlor demonstrations don't make good science, as we shall see in the next chapter. But what did Geller really achieve by dice and drawings at SRI?

Let's consider the drawings first. Geller was usually placed in a double-walled steel cubicle while the experimenters stayed in the next room and drew a "target drawing" after selecting a word at random from the dictionary. Geller concentrated anywhere from a few minutes to half an hour, possibly longer, making drawings of the images he was getting. Then he came out and turned over his drawings which were compared with the target.

Thirteen trials were run, but Geller only "attempted" ten of them, we are told. His matches ranged from very poor in one case (devil) to a nearly perfect copy (bunch of grapes). Most drawings were in between these two extremes but were far too good to be passed off as chance. A horse may not be a camel, but it is a lot closer than, say, a sailboat or a flower. (See Figures 8-17.)

To prove that these similarities are not just imaginary, Targ and Puthoff used the method of blind judging. Geller's list of ten drawings was shuffled randomly into one random pile, the ten target drawings into another random pile, and the two outside judges from elsewhere in SRI were asked to guess independently which "Gellers" went with which targets. *Both judges were able to match all ten pairs correctly.* The probability that either judge would do this by chance is only three in ten million (3/10,000,000).

The quick reader might suggest that these matches were based on extraneous cues as in the remote viewing transcripts. This is sharp thinking, but it is not the answer, because the drawings are matchable on their own merits, and extra cues would be hard to hide effectively.

In the dice experiment, a single die was shaken up vigorously in a metal filing box, the type used for storing 3" x 5" filing cards. Before the box was opened, Geller had to write down which face of the die was showing up. This was tried ten times, with Geller passing twice, leaving eight trials. *Geller was right all eight times.* The probability of getting eight out of eight dice calls by chance is about one in one million (1/1,000,000).

Many obvious guesses that might be offered to explain away these results are blocked by the methodology. In the drawings experiment, for example, Targ and Puthoff avoided the use of commonplace drawings by using the dictionary as a random word generator. That Geller could peek seems impossible, since the two steel doors had huge plungerlike door handles that move visibly and emit a noticeable clank when opened. Targ and Puthoff stated, "Geller was at all times visually, acoustically, and electrically shielded from personnel and material in the target location."

Likewise, the SRI team prevented any fast shuffle to substitute a magician's die or a magic box in the dice-calling experiment. They supplied their own materials marked with an SRI code.

So the experiments look foolproof—but all that glitters is not gold.

Two negative results were also given in the *Nature* paper. The first, another drawings-test, was set up by some SRI psychologists (Targ and Puthoff are physicists) in which Geller was presented with twenty drawings on each trial. The drawings were left in sealed envelopes, rather than opened and studied by the experimenters present. The result was that Geller could not do better than chance.

The second negative finding was that Targ and Puthoff couldn't report any psychic metal bending. While they had seen bendings, they couldn't control the experimental conditions to rule out hand power in place of mind power. As they noted in a film on Geller, "It was always necessary for him, in the experimental situation, to have physical contact with the spoon or, for that matter, any other object that he bends." (Now that sounds more like the Uri Geller WE met.)

So we have one dice experiment—challenged by Randi—and one drawings experiment.

Sidling Up to SRI

Some people think that Uri Geller would not have gone into a scientific laboratory if he were not sincere. This overlooks the possibility that it was *he* who was tracked down by eager believers, or that he could have discovered, a step at a time, that most scientists are no better at seeing a sleight-of-hand than the general public. (Why should they be?)

Geller's first visit to America was set up by Dr. Andrija Puharich, medical doctor, electronics inventor, and UFO addict who had been looking for signs of extraterrestrial intelligence for many years before he discovered Uri Geller performing as a popular stage psychic in Israel. Puharich thought he saw some connection between UFOs and Geller's ESP, and brought Geller and Shipi and Hannah Shtrang to his luxurious home in Ossining, New York. Suiting his colors to the foliage, Geller suddenly became the earthly agent for an outer space intelligence called Hoova, and just as suddenly, Puharich was treated to far-out computer voices speaking to him through his tape recorder about Geller's mission on earth. We consider Puharich's story in the next chapter.

After being dazzled by uncanny events happening all over the place,

Puharich persuaded Uri to expose his "powers" to a wider scientific audience. When Geller finally agreed, Puharich held a weekend conference at his home, attended by Edgar Mitchell, the famous ex-astronaut who founded the Institute of Noetic Sciences not far from SRI in California to study psychic and occult effects, and Judy Skutch, a wealthy benefactress of psychic research, from New York City. There were others as well (see Wilhelm, chap. 5). In usual fashion, Geller bent two rings and broke a needle, convincing all present that something extraordinary was happening (as indeed there was). Shortly after, Mitchell and Puharich brought Geller to California to meet Russell Targ, already well known as a parascientist, and, after a blindfold drive and another evening of parlor tricks, Geller was signed on at SRI in November, 1972, with a retainer of one hundred dollars a day.

Any one who imagines that stageman Geller sat down in a chair and nodded his head while Targ and Puthoff set up foolproof experiments has not read the last three chapters. No, we must expect that he used fast talk, charming enthusiasm, and chafing petulance to steer the experiments into his own orbit.

Of course, he could not work without bringing Shipi and Hannah along, for reasons we can guess. For a while Edgar Mitchell sat in as well. Targ and Puthoff also created confusion by letting SRI higher-ups, psi boosters, and miscellaneous other people wander in and out of the proceedings.

Mitchell, who was helping to pay Uri's bills, became exasperated. As he told Joseph Hanlon, "Hal and Russ were so eager to keep Geller around they worked themselves into a box by meeting his every whim. If he threatened to walk off, they would relent and do what he wanted. Of course, they lost control of the situation and it got worse and worse and worse" *(New Scientist,* 17 October 1974). Geller later said, "Sometimes we sat for three or four hours talking, waiting, and then I'd jump up and say, 'Okay, I feel like doing the thing,' and I would do it" *(Psychic,* May/June, 1973). In writing a chapter on Geller's visit, Targ and Puthoff chose the title "Is Chaos Necessary?" *(Mind-Reach,* Delacorte, 1977). In that chapter, they wrote, "The first requirement for having a well-controlled experiment was to get Uri out of the way." (!) They only achieved this (they thought) in the ten drawings experiment eight months later.

It has never been our purpose to debunk the SRI results by showing Russell Targ and Harold Puthoff in a bad light as scientists. We appreciate the many ingenious precautions they devised to avoid the classical pitfalls of psychic research. For one, they took pains to rule out subliminal cuing, and for another they repeatedly assure us they did not run hundreds of trials and then select the best lucky runs as examples of ESP. Their theoretical interest was in finding out how the psi process works, in terms of electromagnetic radiation, so that a first model or theory could be developed.

But the problem was to take the specific precautions needed to prevent *Uri Geller* from cheating. In order to do this, you must have a general idea of Geller's bag of tricks, and you won't find these in *Magic for Beginners.* Professional magicians distinguish themselves not by using old repertoires, but by devising new ones. In that sense, Geller is a master magician, although he has seriously changed the rules of the game.

If Uri Geller simply billed himself as a magician, then his ability to bend spoons, start watches, and guess a color would be considered the dullest routine being offered for money. Geller's originality is to take a collection of simple effects, requiring almost no modern technology and gimmicks, and mold them into a total psychic image. He takes one giant step further by being a psychic both on stage and off, a step that many magicians consider beyond the ethics of their profession. Geller is the only performing magician today whose public image goes UP by failures, because these help convince people that he is NOT a magician. And, he is able to use the mysteries of psychic vibrations to justify his start-stop-switch-talk-reverse-go method of misdirection.

Targ and Puthoff were unprepared for this novel con(juring) game, and thus missed the meaning of the "Geller tornado." Because scientists are in the "truth business," and their mistakes are quickly exposed by other researchers, they are not accustomed to dealing with people in the "illusion business," and come upon them unprepared.

Targ and Puthoff claim that it is nonsense to say they were unaware of Geller's possibilities for deception. To refute this we shall have to consider instances in which they were looking in the wrong direction at the right time. We do not like to do this, but the question is whether or not Uri Geller demonstrated psychic powers in the laboratories of Stanford Research Institute.

Lights, Action, Camera

Some of the general loopholes made available to Geller have been graciously displayed by SRI in a publicity film showing Geller in action. Uri later used this film to kick off his stage shows under a scientific halo. Except for the dice-calling experiment, not one of these tests was ever published in a scientific journal, and the drawings experiment was still eight months away.

Let us look closely at one demonstration called ten-can roulette. Ten small cans, of the type used for rolls of film, are arranged neatly in an open box with their tops screwed on. Inside one of these cans only is a ball bearing, or a magnet, or some water. Nobody left in the room knows which can is the target. Geller walks in. He mystically waves his hands over the ten cans, then he points to one he wants removed, and it is lifted out by an assistant. He waves his hands again, points to another can, and it too is removed. The ritual is repeated until only one can is left, and it is correct.

We can be sure that this experiment was designed by Geller rather than SRI since he has used it on TV. It is a magician's stunt which Randi demonstrated to Andrew Weil *(Psychology Today,* July, 1974). Although we are not magicians, it occurred to us immediately that, when the assistant lifts out each can, he jiggles the box ever so slightly, and one of the remaining cans does not wobble like the others. (Geller failed when the target was a sugar cube or a ball bearing wrapped in paper.) Most of us would not see the difference, but then most of us would not find Kreskin's paycheck in the audience either. It takes practice, although as Weil says, not that much.

We personally asked Targ and Puthoff why Geller eliminated the cans one at a time, that is, why he didn't just come in, wave his hands about, and say, it's that one. They shrugged their shoulders, then Targ said, "Just for dramatic effect." "What, in a scientific experiment?" They nodded yes.

Later we discovered that magicians have many ways to perform this trick. Several of these are described by Uriah Fuller, who must surely be considered as Geller's chief rival at psychic chicanery, in his two revealing books *Confessions of a Psychic* (1975) and *Further Confessions of a Psychic* (1979).

On top of the SRI film, we find still other revelations in Targ and Puthoff's *Mind-Reach.* In one test, Uri's task was to make a ball bearing move under a bell jar.

"Uri came in early that day. Zev and I had just finished setting up the experiment and getting it balanced. He said it was a terrific experiment and was sure he could move the ball. He tried and tried, he huffed and he puffed. The little ball wouldn't move. Finally, in despair, Uri turned his eyes heavenward and in a true psychic's prayer said, 'Dear God, help me move this shit.' Uri placed his fist over the bell jar and the ball jiggled back and forth and then rolled across the table."

In the confusion they forgot to turn on the recording gear so they had to do the experiment over. "Zev was able to observe the ball through the cross hairs of his camera. The video recorder was able to watch the whole table and the rest of the room, and I (Targ) was able to watch Uri, who said, 'Let's pray this works again.' Hal and Uri put their hands over the top of the bell jar and waited quietly. The ball, as before, started a little jiggling dance and then rolled across the table, recorded by film and videotape" (p. 149).

But did anybody think to look in Geller's fist or up his shirtsleeve? Psychologist Barry Singer of the University of California at Davis has devised his own method in which you will find nothing either in his hand or up his shirtsleeve, but we cannot reveal it here. Regrettably, the remarkable scene of Geller, Puthoff, and the dancing ball bearing are not shown for posterity in the SRI film.

The Dice Experiment Craps Out

With this as the background, we move on to the two experiments that made psychic history in *Nature*.

The SRI film shows only one of the dice-calling trials reported in the *Nature* paper. Oddly enough, this was one of the two trials in which Uri passed, although he offered a guess ("4") that was correct. But why show a trial that *didn't* count?

The debate over the dice experiment begins with Randi's suspicion that Targ and Puthoff might have tried lots and lots of throws and selected the best run. In the *Fact Sheet,* Targ and Puthoff immediately replied that there were exactly ten dice throws, no more, no less. Let's keep that in mind.

But Randi showed in great detail how a magician could accomplish this feat as follows. First, he closes his eyes (almost) for "deep concentration," as he places his hands lightly on the top of the box. He kills time waiting for his vibes to tune up and when his eye-slits tell him that the experimenter is looking away, he thumbs open the flip-top lid for a quick peek.

Absurd, you might say, an insult to anybody's powers of observation.

But Randi also describes a budding psychic at the turn of this century who did just this trick—blindfolded in front of a group of watchful spectators—until Houdini exposed the fraud and put him out of business (Randi, *Magic of Uri Geller*, chapter 11).

Since the peek-a-box theory requires that Geller placed his hands on the box, and since all of this was filmed and videotaped, we should get a simple YES or NO answer from SRI, but the *Fact Sheet* replied as follows, "An elaborate hypothesis is put forward (by Randi) as to how Geller might have handled the dice box and cheated. Film and videotape show otherwise, and magicians examining this material have failed to detect a conjuring trick." If that means "no hands" it is certainly a roundabout way of saying it.

Anyway, Wilhelm wrote in *The Search for Superman*, "According to Russell Targ, Geller sometimes placed his hands on the box 'in a dousing fashion,' but he never picked it up during this reported set of dice experiments." But Randi didn't say anything about picking up the box, but only about thumbing the lid. Wilhelm adds, "Targ maintains that the few times that Geller touched the box he passed" (p. 94).

Wait a minute—how could Geller pass the "few times" or "sometimes" he touched the box? We already know that there were only two pass trials and one of these is shown in the SRI film where Geller does not touch the box.

And how did the magicians examining the film and videotape fail to detect a conjuring trick? And who were they? The *Fact Sheet* tells us that one was Targ himself, now a rusty amateur, another was a local magician "who specializes in exposing fraudulent poltergeist cases and a continuing consultant from the beginning of the project," and the third was Milbourne Christopher, "a world renowned magician and critic of psychic phenomena who was brought in to critique videotape and film of the Geller work, and to suggest protocols for further experiments."

Randi demanded to know the name of the poltergeist magician, but Targ and Puthoff did not reply. After several months we also asked Puthoff to reveal his name, and got back the reply that "Randi now knows his name," but he still didn't tell us. It turned out to be Dr. Arthur Hastings, the same one who judged the Pat Price experiments, who is a regularly paid consultant to Targ and Puthoff, and who staunchly believes in psychic phenomena including Uri Geller and remote viewing. To represent Hastings as either a professional magician or a debunker is a case of spitting into the wind.

So that leaves Milbourne Christopher as our one independent

professional conjuror, who said, just a few months after visiting SRI, that Geller is "nothing more than a trickster." And the same news story adds, "Christopher claims that any good magician can duplicate what Geller does and that the SRI researchers were duped" *(Business Week,* 26 January 1974). So, we can reasonably infer that it was only Targ and his friend Hastings who "failed to detect a conjuring trick."

Next we learn from Wilhelm, "On some tests conducted in his motel room, Geller shook the dice himself" (Wilhelm, *Search for Superman,* p. 94). *In his motel room? Geller shook the dice?* Is this on film too? Were these the other trials on which he supposedly did not touch the box? As the evidence comes leaking out, it only seems as if Randi had been there watching all the time.

There are also a couple of minor confusions. In a letter to *New Scientist* (7 November 1974) Targ and Puthoff wrote, "The die we used was marked with an SRI code and was of the transparent variety..." while Wilhelm tells us that several red dice were used, and "at times," they used a transparent die. Targ and Puthoff seem to keep whitewashing the experiment with oversimplifications. And if there were only ten trials with a metal box, as they steadfastly claimed, why did Uri Geller say, "For example, they know I can read the dice better in a metal box than in a plastic one"? *(Psychic,* May/June, 1974.)

When all contradictions are considered, it seems highly likely that Uri Geller defined the dice experiment, defined when he felt like doing it, and then "jumped up" and did it—by cheating. Subsequently, Targ and Puthoff denied the laying-on-of-hands and invoked three disappearing magicians as their witnesses. Of course, if our analysis is incorrect, it can be easily disproved by having the film and videotape reviewed by a competent and independent panel of judges who submit a public report.

The Drawing Test: A Silk Purse or a Sow's Ear?

"Uri creates confusion around himself even when he is not performing. Weeks later, we were able to deal with the problem by obtaining Uri's consent to remain in an electrically shielded, soundproof booth while experiments were in progress outside. That, of course, limited the kind of experiments we could do with him, but scientists have to work with phenomena under controlled conditions"'(Targ in *Mind-Reach,* p. 141).

Details of these thirteen drawings, reported in *Nature,* are shown here in Table 8. We are told that Geller "did not submit a drawing" on trials 5, 6, and 7. On the other ten trials he did submit at least one drawing, and we are assured that, "In those cases in which Geller made more than one drawing as his response to the target, all drawings were combined as a set for judging" *(Nature,* 18 October 1974). Nothing could be clearer—no drawings on trials 5-7, and all other drawings are shown.

TABLE 8
The Drawings Trials at SRI

Trial	Target	Target Location	Geller Location	See Figure
1	firecracker	adjacent room	shielded room	8
2	bunch of grapes	adjacent room	shielded room	9
3	devil	very distant room	shielded room	10
4	solar system	shielded room	adjacent room	11
5	rabbit [a]	shielded room	adjacent room	"passed"
6	tree [a]	adjacent room	shielded room	"passed"
7	envelope [a]	adjacent room	shielded room	"passed"
8	camel	shielded room	"remote" room	12
9	bridge	shielded room	adjacent room	13
10	seagull	shielded room	adjacent room	14
11	kite	Faraday cage	computer room	15
12	church	Faraday cage	computer room	16
13	valentine	Faraday cage	computer room	17

[a] Trials 5-7 were counted as "pass" trials by the experimenters.

This neat picture simply evaporates in a subsequent Targ-Puthoff paper that gives their personal log of the experiments (*The Record: Eight Days with Uri Geller,* in *The Geller Papers*).

According to *The Record* (as we call this paper) Geller *did* make a drawing on trial 5, and also on either trial 6 or 7, if not both. Targ and Puthoff observed that these drawings did not match the target and left them out on the grounds that Geller "passed," because he said he was not getting anything.

This is merely a rationalization because Geller also "passed" on trial 8 (camel), trial 9 (bridge), trial 12 (church) *(The Record)*, and according to Wilhelm *(Search for Superman,* p. 102), also on trial 3 (devil). To put it bluntly, Targ and Puthoff selected the data that best fit the psychic theory. (If a psychology sophomore did that, his lab report would be failed.) Either trials 5-7 should have been included for judging, or trials 3, 8, 9, and 12 should have been dropped.

Furthermore, on trial 8, *The Record* tells us, "He felt unsure and he passed, but his first choice drawing was of a horse." That is, Geller made several drawings, but only the best one was included for judging, in direct contradiction to the claim made in the *Nature* report.

This data polishing does not tell us just how Geller succeeded (when he did), but it reveals a scientific sloppiness that could never be deduced from the well-edited *Nature* article.

Explaining Away the Failures

More evidence of Targ and Puthoff's näivete arises from their mental gyrations when they account for Geller's blank trials and misses.

For example, under the leadership of Charles Rebert, an independent test of Geller's ESP was conducted by SRI's psychologists. Geller was presented with a set of twenty drawings in sealed envelopes. This was repeated with two more sets of twenty on two more days. Although Geller made about twelve drawings a day, he did not surpass chance. Targ and Puthoff reported, "he expressed dissatisfaction with the existence of such a large target pool" (Explanation 1).

On trial 5 in the Targ-Puthoff series, Geller's failure is attributed to the absence of a person-to-person link, because no experimenter knew what the drawing was when it was left alone in the steel room by Rebert (Explanation 2). Thus, Geller could do telepathy (mind-to-mind reading) but not clairvoyance (object-to-mind reading)—which is odd, since the dice experiment clearly required clairvoyance.

On trials 6 and 7, Geller was hooked up to an EEG machine to record his brain waves. Again the drawings were prepared by Rebert's group and apparently Rebert was with Geller or with the experimenters, and Geller may have been unable to leave the EEG hookup. Puthoff wrote, "He found it difficult to hold adequately still for good EEG records, said that he experienced difficulty in getting impressions of the targets, and again submitted no drawings," the last point being entirely false (Explanation 3).

When we get to *The Record*, however, we find their private explanation—Geller didn't like Rebert and the psychologists who prepared the drawings. This is the old "negative vibes" theory which is always available to explain any psychic failures (Explanation 4). So now we have encountered four different rationalizations for Geller's misses: *(a)* too many targets; *(b)* no telepathy available; *(c)* distraction by the EEG equipment; *(d)* negative vibes.

Targ and Puthoff don't point out the striking "coincidence" that on all these failures either the drawings were sealed up, or Geller was constrained by experimenters or equipment, situations that clearly reduce Geller's possibilities for cheating; yet, on all successful trials, the drawing was put on display in one room while Geller was left alone in another room. We seem to be getting a message.

Some Details They Forgot to Mention

But what were Geller's possibilities for cheating? Let us first consider the double-walled steel room which was supposed to be sightproof, soundproof, and radioproof. We personally discovered a hole of 3-4 inches in diameter used for running cables into the steel room. We also know that two cables were in place, the EEG and the intercom, so this would not be an easy hole to cover up effectively. Puthoff told us it had a metal cover over it, but it was no longer around. And although it was supposedly stuffed with cotton, this could easily be removed from the inside, where Geller was.

The second channel was a dark-glass window, commonly called a one-way vision screen, next to the double doors. Apparently, it had been covered over with a bulletin board.

The third possible leak was the intercom itself, described in *Nature* as "a one-way auditory monitor, operating only from the inside to the outside."

This was not honest. It was actually a two-way intercom with a press-to-talk switch for talking also from outside to inside *(The Record)*.

There were also ceiling vents in both the steel room and the adjacent room, but Puthoff has assured us that these do not connect to each other.

In Figure 18 we show the floor plan of the steel room and adjacent spaces as drawn from memory a few days after our first visit. In Figure 19 we show the front wall of the steel room, as seen from the adjacent room, also from memory.

We have not seen the copper-screen Faraday cage that was used for the last three drawings, but we understand that the screen walls are transparent. This room was apparently chosen to test certain theories about the electromagnetic properties of ESP. The targets on these last three trials were located on computer displays in a room about fifty yards away, around the corner, down the hall, and out of Geller's direct sight.

So, not counting the door or the vents, the steel room had three possible channels for normal sensory communication, and the copper-room was wide open to both sight and sound.

Now the most obvious theory is that Geller was signaled by an accomplice, and even in this "chaos-free" experiment there were possibilities. The preeminent candidate is Shipi Shtrang, who was so much involved that on two trials, according to Puthoff, he was actually in the test room with Geller. He was also left sitting at a desk in the not very "remote room" (see Fig. 18) on the other trials. There is a suggestion by Wilhelm *(Search for Superman,* pp. 168-169) that Shipi's sister Hannah was underfoot as well, but this is not clear.

Targ and Puthoff maintain that neither Shipi nor any other potential confederate was allowed "in the target area," which area they have not defined either in their letter to *New Scientist* (7 November 1974) nor during the five times they used the phrase in the *Fact Sheet.* (We might recall the bit of circumlocution in the *Fact Sheet* that implied that Geller never touched the dice box.)

On some trials, a woman named Jean Mayo was also present with the experimenter, her role being described to us as that of an artist. This is very unconvincing, since her attempt to draw a farmer on trial 3 produced an inelegant devil, and her solar system on trial 4 would not require an expensive frame either. The actual reason for her presence was her reputation as a highly tuned psychic who could amplify the telepathic signal sent to Geller (Wilhelm, *Search for Superman,* pp. 101-102). We are not suggesting that Mayo suddenly became a Geller accomplice, but the ever-changing rooms and people in these experiments certainly makes it more difficult to keep an eye on any accomplice.

Our hypothetical sidekick has a number of ways of reaching Geller, depending on the laxity of surveillance. After getting a look at the target drawing, he might flash his personal rendition at the cable hole where Geller is watching. Or, he might lean against the table and press the intercom switch behind his back while mentioning the name of the target object.

The transparent Faraday cage is even less of a problem, since the accomplice only needs to stand outside the cage for a few moments and flash his personal rendition of the target, or else finger-write it slowly against his chest or the wall, while Geller watches through the transparent wall.

In spite of all the confusion, we still find it hard to credit Targ and Puthoff with such gross experimental negligence that they would allow a single accomplice system to work on all ten trials. *For the sake of the argument,* let us suppose that no confederate could operate effectively on all trials, or even on most trials. And let us accept Randi's suggestion that Geller is more likely to use quick wits and bare hands than an elaborate electronics set-up system.

Even with these restrictions, there are usually several ways on each trial in which Geller could have outwitted the unskeptical researchers. To describe all of these would be cumbersome, but we can at least cycle through the ten trials with one script to illustrate what we mean. It must be emphasized that this is only a "demonstration of feasibility" based on the few bits of information that have now leaked out. If more information ever becomes available (other than the inevitable denials), we may get a clearer picture of Geller's proceedings at SRI.

The script we present here is one which gives maximum credibility to Targ and Puthoff's own description of the trials *(The Fact Sheet; The Record).* At the same time, we pay close attention to certain details in the drawings themselves that have, perhaps, not been given the attention they deserve. These drawings vary widely in several respects. Why is the bunch of grapes so perfect? Why is Geller's bridge so different from the target bridge? Why does the word "BRIDGE" appear on that target? Why does the camel become such a nice, tidy horse? Why are there two camels on the target? Why is it that responses to the church show nothing connected with churchness, and yet so many of the line segments in both responses can be matched up with the outline of the church? Our script takes these details into account. (See Figures 8-17 and Table 8.)

Geller On His Own—A Feasible Script

Our scene opens with Uri and Shipi "casing the joint" to determine the possibilities. They immediately note the cable hole, and then look around the room for reflecting surfaces to expand the field of vision. A mirror would be dandy, but the glass on a picture or a piece of equipment would at least help. Most importantly, they now cut a handy peephole into the bulletin board in front of the one-way window, and then leave the cut covered with a poster or graph between trials. Alternatively, they find they can slide the board to one side to create a slice of vision along the edge of the window. In fact there may have been no bulletin board at all, but only curtains or some other by-passable screen.

Furthermore, Uri has other possibilities during and after the trial, based on past experience with the experimenters. And, he can always find a psychic excuse if all systems fail.

It is important for Geller to spend a lot of time talking between trials. This gives him time to help design the next trial, to set up his system, and above all, to keep Targ and Puthoff from noticing any consistencies in his routine. And in fact, it took an entire morning or afternoon to complete each session; it took eight continuous days of work to complete the thirteen trials.

Trial 1 (Firecracker). Geller is in the steel room and Puthoff is alone in the adjacent room. Puthoff opens the dictionary, comes across the word "fuse," and draws a firecracker. (See Fig. 8.)

Through the peephole in the window (or the cable hole) Uri cannot see the drawing, but he can see Puthoff's pencil moving as he draws it. First a circular shape, and then two lines coming downward from each side, maybe an arc at the bottom. Something squiggly added in the upper right area.

First, Geller thinks of a drum, and fishes for information over the intercom by saying he is getting something associated with noise. Puthoff doesn't answer. Geller tries a face and neck, but he still isn't sure how to put the lines together, so he asks Hal if he has written the NAME on the picture? Puthoff obligingly writes "firecracker" but Uri can't see him, so he covers himself with some more cylindrical objects and says he's ready to come out.

Trial 2 (Bunch of Grapes). Same set-up. Puthoff comes across the word "bunch" and draws a bunch of grapes. He told us that he taped this drawing on the wall "right here," pointing to a spot directly across from the covered window. Geller looks through his peephole and copies it perfectly. When the results are shown to Targ and others, everybody gets into gear for an exciting series of trials. (See Fig. 9.)

Trial 3 (Farmer/Devil). The next day, Targ and Jean Mayo do the target drawing in another building nearly five hundred yards away from Geller's steel room. Puthoff is in the adjacent room to communicate with Uri over the intercom and with Targ and Mayo by telephone from the "remote room" just across the hall, the same room where Shipi is sitting at the desk.

The dictionary draw produces the word *farmer,* but Mayo's rendition looks more like a *devil,* so a tail is added to make it definite. Geller hopes Shipi will overhear something useful in the telephone calls between Puthoff and Targ-Mayo, but Shipi gets nothing useful. He kills time drawing doodles around a theme of a circle with patterns of small objects floating around it. He writes "God" in one drawing, identifies the second with the word "apple," while the third sheet shows a globe. He keeps telling Hal Puthoff he isn't getting anything and wants to pass. (See Fig. 10.)

After Targ and Mayo finally return, Geller comes out and offers his first drawing sheet. While everybody is comparing this with the target, Geller quickly stabs two pitchforks onto his third sheet without looking at his hand drawing them, which explains why they are so sloppy. This was also Randi's immediate explanation, and it reminds us of the sketchy tree which Geller produced in his first interview with David Marks.

Later, Targ and Mayo argue that they had been thinking of the Garden of Eden, which persuades Wilhelm that Geller's drawings are "eerily suggestive of the Judeo-Christian concept implied by the devil drawing." Such is the course of "subjective validation" (see chapter 12).

Trial 4 (Solar System). After that frustrating trial, they bring the experiment back to short-distance telepathy. Targ and Mayo go into the steel room, while Puthoff and Geller remain outside in the adjacent room.

Uri's problem is to get Hal out of the room so he can douse the lights and look through his peephole in reverse, or else use the intercom. As a ruse, he goes walking off for a cup of coffee (Wilhelm, *Search for Superman,* p. 104), followed eventually by Hal, and then gets back first. Geller quickly presses the intercom button, saying he is having trouble and suggesting that they write down the name of it. Pretending to turn the intercom off, he glimpses the drawing while Mayo writes in "solar system, sun, moon." Perhaps it is at this time that Targ says, "Why don't you have a rocket ship?" to which artist Mayo replies, "Because it would make it too complicated" (Wilhelm, *Search for Superman,* p. 104). Geller then returns everything to normal, and after Hal returns, he draws a rocketship with a solar system around it. (See Fig. 11.)

Trials 5-7 (Rabbit, Tree, Envelope). With Charles Rebert on hand, Geller has no chances and gets increasingly irritable until this line of experimentation is dropped as three "passes."

Trial 8 (Camel). This trial is made more difficult by preparing the drawing in the "remote room" just across the hall from the adjacent room and out of Geller's line of vision.

Three possibilities come to mind. The first is simply that Uri got no information and "passed" but drew a large number of commonplace drawings. It is significant that Targ and Puthoff did not publish all of Geller's other responses that might have contained useful information. Anyway, they note Uri's horse among them, and Uri obligingly declares that it was his "first choice." (See Fig. 12.)

Another possibility is that Shipi finally got into the act, noting by pencil movements that a horselike animal has been drawn—he mistakes the dip between the two-humped camel for some kind of saddle. He makes up his own drawing of a horse and then flashes this at Uri's peephole as he strolls briefly into the adjacent room.

Alternatively, Shipi signals Uri with a number code designating a horse. In our own "psychic demonstrations" we have used just such a number code, signaled with out fingers, for commonplace drawings—horse is number seven on our list of ten.

It will be noted that the camel is drawn twice, once with two humps, and then a much larger one with a single hump. Possibly, Uri indicated over the intercom that he wasn't getting it and suggested that they draw it again (to increase Shipi's chances). Or, it might reflect a debate between Targ and Puthoff on how many humps for a camel (two) and a dromedary (one), which gives Shipi the name.

Trial 9 (Bridge). The set-up is returned to the one used on trials 1 and 2 with Geller in the steel room and the experimenters in the adjacent room. The target is a bridge, but Uri doesn't see it and reports he has been having difficulty. (See Fig. 13.)

Next, he asks if they have written the NAME of the object, and then he watches the pencil movements while Targ or Puthoff writes the word "bridge" in large capital letters. Since he doesn't actually see the target bridge, his own bridge turns out to be visually very different.

Trial 10 (Seagull). The set-up is the same, and Uri is able to see the drawing of the seagull. He makes his own version in a different orientation so as not to look "too good," as with the bunch of grapes. Part of Geller's patter is that he often gets mirror reversals on telepathy drawings (due to pencil reading or using glass reflections?) (See Fig. 14.)

Trials 11-13 (Kite, Church, Arrow-through-Heart). We were handicapped here because we have not seen the copper-screen Faraday cage in which Geller was seated. It is only by inspecting the scene that one is likely to discover the best loopholes.

With so little information to go on, the best guess is an accomplice theory, which is now more feasible. If Geller has succeeded so far without much help from Shipi, Targ and Puthoff would be more likely to drop their guards on them or other possible confederates.

We understand that Geller can see right through the walls of the cage, so the accomplice needs only to stand outside the cage and hand signal to Geller. Puthoff is supposedly guarding Geller at the cage, but can he also monitor the actions of Shipi or Hannah standing in the background? If necessary he can be distracted—for example, on trial 11, Uri asks Hal to phone the computer room to find out if it's an object or a geometric shape, giving an accomplice a chance to finger draw and pantomime a kite.

On trial 12, Geller's first response looks as if an ally went through the motions of drinking out of an imaginary martini glass and then turned it upside down. Finger jabbing is used to suggest that it was drawn in dots, but Geller puts the dots off to one side. The second response looks as if somebody traced the outline of the church by finger writing against the wall, or across the chest, while Geller copied line by line to produce the large shape. It made no sense, so he drew several other structures as back-ups. (See Fig. 16.)

On trial 13, the arrow can be pantomimed by shooting a bow and arrow. Now the arrow is inside something, but what—perhaps the Israeli team is not familiar with the valentine symbol. So the heart is also traced out by finger writing, but Geller copies in straight lines, producing the squared-off "heart" at the bottom of his response. (See Fig. 17.)

This then is just one feasible script in which Geller succeeds without needing accomplices on any but the last three trials. We are not saying it happened just like this, nor are we saying that confederates could not have helped on moșt or all trials. We are simply going through a role-playing exercise to ask, if I were Uri Geller, how could I produce these particular drawings in these particular conditions.

We would be in a much better position to assess Geller's "psychic" performance if we had been present, or even if there were any videotapes to review these trials. We have seen that every trivial piece of information makes a contribution. The steel room has two possible holes and a two-way intercom, the cage has transparent walls. On trial 1 the word "firecracker" is added to the target, on trial 4 three words are added, and on trial 9 the word "bridge" appears in large capitals. On trial 4 Geller goes off for a cup of coffee; at another point in this trial, Targ suggests that Mayo add a rocket ship. On trial 11, Puthoff telephones the computer room.

How many hundreds of other details have been omitted that might reveal even more specific possibilities for Geller? Let us make our conclusion specific. We have seen that Targ and Puthoff have used lax experimental procedures, that they saw psychic effects occurring where magician's tricks were possible, that they have glossed over the details of the experimental procedures, that they have exaggerated their precautions, that those details which had emerged suggest many possibilities for Geller to succeed by trickery, and that he had more than one line of opportunities to accomplish the drawings test without the use of psychic powers.

After this chapter was drafted and sent to SRI for comment, we received telling new information about the casual conditions surrounding these drawing experiments. A reliable source inside SRI told us that after certain experiments the steel room and adjacent room were littered with "hundreds" of discarded drawings, and among these were examples of the bunch of grapes and other drawings later published in *Nature*. This fact was known to *several* people on the SRI staff.

This evidence strongly suggests Targ and Puthoff ran many casual tests, giving Geller far more chances to succeed than we have already assumed. At the very least, the many discarded drawings strongly underline the pattern of data selection that we have found in the remote viewing experiments (Hammid series, see chapter three) and in the capricious use of Geller's passes noted here.

Final Reflections

It might be argued that we have developed a one-sided interpretation of the SRI research, looking only for flaws and not for psychic perception.

There are two reasons for this, the first being that everything else we know about Geller has pointed to conjuring, and it is simply parsimonious to ask if he did not carry the same methods with him into SRI.

The second reason is that there is no logical way to test the validity of any scientific claim of paranormal ability except to rule out all possibilities of sensory communication. So-called psychic processes have no rules, no laws, no restrictions. As such, they are untestable and unrefutable in their own terms. The working definition of a paranormal event is that something happened that cannot be explained by existing scientific knowledge, and the only test is whether a normal explanation can be found. In both the remote viewing and Geller research at SRI, we find compelling normal explanations for every result that aspires to psychic status.

Another argument that is bound to arise is that our review of the SRI research has been far more exacting than most reviews of most scientific research. We concede this point, but note that it has also been difficult to get any kind of complete and open accounting of the experimental procedures from the SRI team.

But we must consider this "double standard" argument further. It is undoubtedly true that some scientists in orthodox fields will go into print with half-baked findings based on fallacious methods of research. This is not as serious as it sounds. First, in most research it is not likely that the subject of research is a human being whose goal is to outwit the experimenters. Second, most research does not have the revolutionary implications of the psychic hypothesis. Third, a scientific finding that is invalid is very likely to be exposed, as soon as other researchers try to replicate the effect.

This last point brings out the most telling flaw in Uri Geller's claim to psychic powers. The basic safeguard against error in science is that any result can be checked by repeating the experiment in other laboratories.

Uri Geller has now publicly ruled out any chance that he will submit to any more scientific tests. "Now in my anger and frustration I have slammed the door (on scientific tests). I don't want to be a guinea pig for the rest of my days" (American copyrighted article appearing in New Zealand *Sunday Times,* 10 December 1978). But this tantrum is unnecessary—it should only take about two weeks to do the experiments over correctly. We believe that Geller knows that he can't get away with the same tricks any more.

10

"GELLERITIS": A CASE STUDY IN PATHOLOGICAL SCIENCE

> *We entertain a suspicion concerning any matter of fact when the witnesses contradict one another; when they are but few; or of doubtful character: when they have an interest in what they affirm; when they deliver their testimony with hesitation, or on the contrary, with too violent asservations. There are many other particulars of the same kind which may diminish or destroy the force of any argument, derived from human testimony.*
>
> David Hume: *Of Miracles*

Our title, "Gelleritis," refers to an extreme belief of conviction in the claims of Uri Geller, sometimes reaching pathological levels. The sufferers of this affliction, known as "Gellerites," provide a fascinating case study of what Irving Langmuir once called "pathological science," or "the science of things that aren't so." "Gelleritis" is actually an acute form of that widespread human condition, *gullibility*. While this particular case is based on the claims of a single man, and on those of his supporters, we believe the study of "Gelleritis" has much to teach about the psychology not only of the psychic, but of science in general.

Psychic claims have much in common with other claims in science that are surprising, unexpected, or that fly in the face of accepted laws. The social and psychological phenomena of scientists' belief and commitment to radical claims represent extreme forms of normal scientific beliefs and behaviors. By making an in-depth study of single cases of mistaken beliefs, science can try to avoid similar mistakes in the future. There will always be a Geller—"Gelleritis" is therefore an affliction against which scientists should be constantly on guard. This chapter will hopefully serve to strengthen our immunity to false beliefs and conclusions when future miracle workers attempt to enter the scientific arena.

140

1. Geller's Own Story

All claims relating to psychic or paranormal powers begin with *verbal reports* from either the performer himself or from observers. Testimony from the performer should be regarded as nothing more than a signal that something of interest may be occurring. Such testimony should obviously be treated with the full skepticism and caution normally reserved for anecdotal reports by interested parties. The self-attribution of special powers or abilities by a person should be tested by rigorous and properly controlled laboratory tests before any conclusions can be reached. Even then, as we have shown in the last chapter, the experiments must be carefully scrutinized for methodological flaws and, preferably, replicated in other laboratories.

Geller's own claims are fully described in his book *My Story* (1975). While this book may be amusing to read, it has zero value as scientific evidence of the paranormal. Almost anybody can think of imaginative stories on a fantasy-level about remarkable events that might have occurred during their life, and however fantastic those stories might be, somebody, somewhere, will believe them.

We shall not waste space going into Geller's account in any detail. We reserve our comments for one feature only. The interesting aspect of Geller's own strange story is that it is peppered with examples of quite blatant cheating and dishonesty on his part. His schoolteachers, for example, accused the young Geller of copying during examinations and placed him in the corner of the room where he supposedly couldn't see the papers of the other students. He claims to have eavesdropped on his teachers as they discussed his supernatural powers. He learned to spy on guests at his mother's hotel in Cyprus and, as a result, was befriended by an Israeli spy, Joav Shacham. Geller even admits that he cheated in his early stage demonstrations in Israel. He describes how his publicity man faked a photo of Geller with Italian filmstar Sophia Loren. When Loren protested, Geller was discredited in newspaper headlines throughout Israel. These admissions of cheating by Geller provide evidence of a flaw in his character that we believe permeates his every claim. We believe Geller himself, unwittingly, has provided many clues to his techniques in his own verbal reports of his powers. Geller's motive for deception is quite clear—he freely admits his love of fame and fortune. The only tragedy is the fuel to the fire of irrationality provided by scientific endorsement of his fictional claims.

2. The "Conversion" of Dr. Andrija Puharich

If science had never paid attention to Geller's spurious claims, he would have remained a disgraced entertainer in Israel. But this was not to be. Geller was introduced to Western science by a well-known parapsychologist, Dr. Andrija Puharich. When Puharich first went to visit Geller in Tel Aviv in August, 1971, he was a man with a mission. In his bizarre book, *Uri,* published in 1974, Puharich admits that he had "suspected for a very long time that man has been in communication with beings not of this earth for thousands of years" *(Uri,* p. 9). Following studies with Eileen Garrett, Harry Stone, Peter Hurkos, and psychic surgeon Arigo in the 1950s and 60s, Puharich had long since believed that psychic powers were palpable and real. Uri and Puharich developed a close friendship, and, like many other friendships Uri cultivated, Puharich's was useful in promoting Uri's tenuous career.

Puharich retells the story of how Uri gained his special powers. Going beyond Geller's own account of how Geller had seen a brilliant white mass of light in a Tel Aviv garden at the age of four, Puharich states Geller saw "a huge, silent, bowl-shaped object...suddenly between himself and the bowl in the sky there was the shadow of a huge figure like the shadow of a man with a long cape...a blinding ray of light came from its head and struck Uri" *(Uri,* page 39). This allusion to extraterrestrials and flying saucers becomes the very backbone of Puharich's explanation of Uri's powers.

On 1 December 1971 Geller let Puharich hypnotize him in an attempt to develop Geller's awareness of his "soul." In the first ninety-minute session Uri described several early childhood experiences including the strange events in the Tel Aviv garden just after his third birthday. On this occasion Uri described, in Hebrew, a bowl-shaped light and a figure with arms raised over its head holding the sun between its hands. Then the "voice" occurred, speaking in English but monotonic and mechanical, and it stated: "It was us *(sic)* who found Uri in the garden when he was three. He is our helper sent to help man. We programmed him in the garden for many years to come, but he was also programmed not to remember. On this day his work begins. Andrija, you are to take care of him." Unfortunately, the scientific community has no objective evidence of the "voice" from this session or from any of the large number that followed. On each and every occasion, the cassette recording of the "voice" mysteriously disappeared and *in every case, Geller had easy access to the cassette recorder at the time of the disappearance.* Yet, Puharich believed the tapes "dematerialized" by paranormal means, beyond rational explanation.

Puharich and Geller claim that "the voice" recurred many times over the period 1971 to 1973 in various forms. Sometimes it would occur during hypnosis, at other times tape recordings of it would appear (and then disappear), and on other occasions "the voice" would use the telephone or radio. In every case, Geller or his accomplice Shipi Shtrang could not be eliminated as being responsible, and yet, clearly, Puharich was convinced that one or more superintelligent extraterrestrials living on a spaceship called "Spectra" were responsible. Even "the voice's" poor grammar and strange accent didn't seem to bother Puharich. One would have thought beings intelligent enough to communicate via possession of human minds and electronic communications would have at least learned grammatical English. From Puharich's viewpoint, "the voice" was final confirmation of his strong belief in psychic powers and extraterrestrial beings. Reciprocally, Geller was now assured of visits to Europe and the USA, where Puharich would arrange, with a special committee of believers, the famous "validation" by scientists that took place at SRI and in other laboratories during 1972 and 1973. "The voice" commanded, and the deluded Puharich obeyed. There will always be a Geller, and for every Geller there will always be a Puharich.

3. Other Gellerites

It would certainly be wrong if we gave the impression that poor Puharich was alone in staking his reputation on the wily ways of one Uri Geller. We have recounted already the "validation" of Geller's powers by SRI physicists Russell Targ and Harold Puthoff. In addition, physical scientists all over North America and Europe attempted to study Uri in their laboratories. A large number of these studies are reported in an ambitious book with a misleading title, *The Geller Papers: Scientific Observations on the Paranormal Powers of Uri Geller* (1976), edited by Charles Panati. Panati, a physicist/journalist on the staff of *Newsweek,* collected together the best scientific evidence he could find on Geller's allegedly paranormal powers. Of the nineteen contributors to this erroneous volume, well over half are physical scientists, who are completely unqualified and lacking expertise in the relevant disciplines of psychology and magic. Significantly, only one psychologist and two magicians are represented in the book and frankly, they should have

known better. Only one of the studies (Targ and Puthoff's) has ever seen
the light of day in a reputable science journal. The rest belong to oblivion.
We shall not try the reader's patience* with critiques of all the
contributions to Panati's volume. This would require a short book of its
own. We shall consider, however, three of the least transparent
contributions (other than Targ and Puthoff's, which is already discussed in
chapter nine).

The first of these is by Eldon Byrd, who describes "Uri Geller's Influence
on the Metal Alloy Nitinol." Byrd (born 1939) has a B.S. in Electrical
Engineering and a M.S. in Medical Engineering. He is a member of Mensa
and a Mormon. Three sets of tests occurred between October 1973 and
October 1974 involving several different wires made from the alloy nitinol.
Byrd concluded his investigation: "Geller altered the lattice structure of a
metal alloy in such a way that cannot be duplicated. There is no present
scientific explanation as to how he did this." In Panati's opinion, Byrd's
paper was the most impressive in the book and according to Panati,
"appears here with the official approval of the Naval Surface Weapons
Center...The paper represents the first time parapsychological research
conducted at a government facility has been released for publication by the
Department of Defense." Sounds impressive doesn't it? But let's take a
closer look at what actually happened.

In the first test, which took place in Silver Spring on 29 October 1973,
Byrd presented Uri with a small block of nitinol and two wires, one 1.5 mm
in diameter, the other 0.5 mm in diameter. Nitinol is an alloy of nickel and
titanium which has a "memory" for a particular shape. A straight nitinol
wire can be bent while cold, but after heating it, it normally should become
straight again. Uri handled the block and the thicker wire but nothing
happened. Then Geller rubbed the thinner wire for twenty seconds and
produced a small bump in it. When Byrd immersed this wire into boiling
water, instead of becoming straight, it went into a right-angle shape. Byrd
claims that several metallurgists of the Naval Surface Weapons Center
where he worked could not remove the kink after putting it under tension
in a vacuum chamber and heating it until it glowed. In an official four-page
"Memorandum for the Record" (dated 19 July 1976), the Public Affairs
Officer of the Center, Mr. J.P. Smaldone, flatly denied that such tests had
been carried out by the laboratory's metallurgists. Moreover, Byrd didn't
conduct the tests in the Naval Surface Weapons Center as stated by Panati;

*Or our own!

he conducted them at the "Isis Center for Research and Study of the Esoteric Arts and Sciences" (now defunct), which had no connection with the Naval Laboratory.

Martin Gardner* reports how he discovered that, with the help of pliers, he could bend the wire at a sharp angle and then straighten the wire. By holding the wire between the thumb and first two fingers and pressing with his thumbnail, Gardner reports he could easily create a bump at the wire's center. Placing the wire in boiling water, *Gardner found the wire assumed a right-angle shape, just like the Gellerized wire.* (The delayed control group procedure wins again.) The shape remained unaltered by heating in a match flame. Gardner found the same results (a "permanent" kink) using pennies and by biting with his teeth! In the confusion that reigns in all of Geller's demonstrations, Geller could easily have substituted his own wire or prepared Byrd's by switching wires and excusing himself for a couple of minutes.

After the Navy Lab's denial that reannealing tests had been run, Byrd sent the wire to Ronald Hawke at the Lawrence Livermore Laboratory in Livermore, California and asked him to arrange for a reannealing of the wire. The wire was heated under tension to 900° C and normally should have become straight when cooled. Byrd was hoping the wire wouldn't go straight so that his original claim in the Panati volume would still be valid. Unfortunately for Byrd, Hawke reported that the wire lost its kink during reannealing so nothing paranormal had happened after all.

The second and third tests are equally flawed. For the second "test" Byrd told Martin Gardner that *Geller actually took the wires home and had a whole month in which to work on them.* Small wonder that they came back bent permanently out of shape. As there were no controls whatsoever in this second test, and Byrd wasn't even present during the bending to see how it was done, this "test" can be discounted completely out of hand.

The third test took place in the Connecticut home of writer John G. Fuller in October, 1974. Three more wires, each four inches long and 0.5 mm in diameter, were used. In the Panati article, Byrd says he left one piece of wire behind as a "control," but there's now some doubt over when Byrd cut the wires and how many control wires there were. In trying to establish the facts of this case Philip J. Klass, a technical journalist and author of *UFO'S Explained* (Random House), was told two different accounts by Byrd of the control conditions used. In one conversation (11

* *Humanist,* May/June, 1977.

October 1976), Byrd said the wire was cut into four pieces at Fuller's house. In a second conversation (29 November 1976), Byrd reverted to the story of cutting off a control wire in his laboratory before going to Connecticut and then cutting off a second control wire in New York, where he spent a night on the way to Connecticut. These forgettings of important points of procedure make the credibility of Byrd's report rather low. Byrd claims Geller "kinked" all three wires by rubbing or stroking them. As the audio tapes of this session are inaudible (Philip J. Klass, personal communication) and as several of Geller's aides and assistants had access to the wires prior to the tests (reported by Klass), the third "test" must also be discounted as poor science.

To be fair to Byrd, he is now certainly aware of the fact that his experiments were not flawless. Byrd admitted to Klass that he likes Uri, but that he's not sure if people are hoodwinking him. "I tend to take people at face value," he said.

A third unfortunate Gellerite is the late Wilbur M. Franklin, recently Chairman of the Department of Physics at Kent State University. Dr. Franklin was present at SRI in November 1972 when Geller purportedly cracked a platinum ring and then broke a small segment out of the shank. Franklin photographed the ring at high magnification using a scanning electron microscope (SEM). Examination of these photographs led Franklin to conclude that one region of the ring was almost melted while a neighboring region showed a low-temperature cleavage. On the basis of this remarkable discovery of simultaneous melting and freezing and of other Geller effects, Franklin received a grant from the Ford Foundation and initiated a new course at Kent State on "teleneural" physics. All on the basis of one uncontrolled experiment. Franklin didn't bother to take photographs of *other* broken rings at magnifications of up to twelve thousand times before rushing into print with the conclusion that Geller had performed a miracle in producing "unusual fracture surfaces." What is deemed "unusual" must surely depend upon what is usual, and it seems that Franklin didn't bother to find this out before publishing this conclusion in the Panati volume.

In a letter to the *Humanist* (September/October, 1977) Franklin admitted that, when scientists expert at analyzing SEM photographs studied the fracture surface, they attributed the "unusual" surface to *"an incomplete braze at the point where the jeweler attached the shank of the ring to the portion holding the gemstone."* To make things even worse, *evidence of fatigue through mechanical bending was present* around the brazed region. Hopefully "teleneural" physics is to be based on more solid foundations than bent and broken objects such as this ill-fated platinum ring.

A fourth Gellerite from within the ranks of science is Professor John Taylor of King's College, London. Taylor, another physicist, is well known in Britain as a television personality and has written books with titles as varied as *Black Holes: The End of the Universe?, The Shape of Minds to Come,* and in 1975, *Superminds,* which deals exclusively with the paranormal. Taylor's early endorsement of Geller on a national television program was a major factor in Geller's wide acceptance and credibility in the United Kingdom.

There seems to be no doubt that Taylor became acutely afflicted with a bad dose of Gelleritis following his participation in a BBC television program on 23 November 1973, in which Geller demonstrated his powers. Taylor recounts his interpretation of Geller's performance in the first chapter of *Superminds,* confidently stating that Geller couldn't have tricked him. Just like Byrd and Franklin, Taylor could hardly have been expected to know if he had been tricked. Academic qualifications in physics or math have no relevance to conjuring. Yet, Taylor launched into a major research project on the paranormal without first properly checking for trickery by consulting the appropriate experts, magicians, and psychologists. In fact, one distinguished magician, The Amazing Randi, was rebuffed several times by Taylor when he attempted to educate Taylor on this matter.

In one episode described by Randi in his book *The Magic of Uri Geller* (Ballantine, 1975), Taylor showed Randi some "cheat-proof" apparatus consisting of a test tube containing a metal strip sealed with wax. Randi, in Taylor's presence and without detection, was able to open the tube, take out the metal strip, bend the metal out of shape, photograph it, and reseal the tube. Even though his manifest and proven inability to notice trickery was pointed out to Taylor by Randi and others, he continued his involvement into the physics of metal bending for several years. Like converts to a new cult religion, Gellerites seem blinded by the faith that something miraculous is about to be discovered. We are still waiting for that miracle.

Following Geller's national television appearances, hundreds of spoon-benders emerged all over Britain, astonishing their more naïve friends and relatives with amazing feats of "psychic" skill. The "Geller effect" seemed to be contagious. When Uri bent cutlery, cutlery all over the nation seemed to bend, and other benders discovered their "powers."

Taylor reports his laboratory research with thirty-eight of these "superminds," thirty-four of whom were under the age of seventeen. Taylor's näivete is astonishing. It reaches epic proportions in Taylor's description of the bending process: "One curious feature of the bending process is that it appears to go in brief steps; a spoon or fork can bend through many degrees in a fraction of a second. *This often happens when the observer's attention has shifted from the object he is trying to bend.* Indeed this feature of bending not happening when the object is being watched —'the shyness effect'—is very common *(sic)" (Superminds,* p.69). Despite the "shyness" of metals to bend when directly observed, incredibly, Taylor concluded his treatise with the view that "the whole question of deception either intentional or unconscious, can be dismissed as a factor, at any rate in the majority of instances" *(Superminds,* p.83). Taylor had so much faith in his young benders' honesty, he allowed some subjects to take home metal strips sealed inside tubes (just as Byrd had given nitinol to Uri to bend at home) and accepted the bent metal returned after one week as evidence of the paranormal. Taylor's theory that metal benders' don't cheat received a serious blow when Harry Collins, a sociologist at the University of Bath, observed young metal benders through a one-way mirror. In association with psychologist Dr. Brian Pamplin, Collins reported in *Nature* (Vol. 257, p.8) that he observed six young benders, five of whom successfully bent metal rods or spoons. This bending occurred, however, *only while the observers in the room with the subject deliberately looked away.* (Shyness effect?) In every case the subjects were observed cheating by the experimenters on the other side of the mirror. (See Fig. 20 for one typical case.) Pamplin and Collins asserted that "in no case did we observe a rod or spoon bent other than by palpably normal means." This was a bitter pill even for Collins to swallow, as he'd fully expected to observe genuine psychic spoon bending.

Undeterred, Taylor continued his study of spoon bending and other allegedly paranormal effects. Together with E. Balanovski, Taylor* tested the curious hypothesis that the only force that could conceivably be involved in metal bending and other psychic phenomena (psychokinesis, psychic healing, and dowsing) is electromagnetic radiation (EM). Taylor and Balanovski reasoned that the other forms of energy—radioactivity, nuclear and gravitational—could not be used by humans. So they set

* *Nature,* 276 (1978), 64-67.

about looking for unusual signals of EM while subjects performed various psychic effects. This three-year project involved an elaborate range of sophisticated equipment measuring a wide range of EM frequencies (d.c. to ultra-violet). In all of the tests conducted the subjects claimed that they were in a good psychic state. In some cases subjects achieved successful results, but only when the conditions were relaxed à la Pamplin and Collins. In none of the tests conducted was there any evidence of abnormal EM activity, even in cases where successful performance occurred.

On the basis of the absence of unusual electromagnetic radiation while their subjects performed, Balanovski and Taylor finally reached the conclusion that *none of the metal bending, psychokinesis, healing, or dowsing they observed was paranormal.* This conclusion is based on the deduction that paranormal effects must result from unusual electromagnetic radiation.

This is surely an amazing chain of reasoning. First, Taylor confidently ignores the possibility of cheating, in spite of evidence of hoax accumulating around Geller and the child spoon-benders, and even a demonstration of conjuring by Randi in Taylor's own laboratory. Next Taylor confidently assumes that psychic phenomena *must* work by EM force, thus ignoring the possibility that paranormal communication might use *any* known or unknown energies in ways not yet understood. The absence of EM signals is no more a disproof of psychokinesis than the absence of magnetic fields around a hypnotized person is a disproof of hypnosis, except for Taylor. To say that Taylor has now "seen the light" is a risky conclusion, for we cannot predict the next step in his peculiar logic.

4. The Media, Science Journals, and Books

Everybody loves a sensational, unusual story. Especially the media. No field has greater potential for increasing sales than the world of the psychic. The media can be held responsible for propagating Gelleritis, and other irrational beliefs in UFO's, the Bermuda Triangle, Big Foot, and the like, throughout an already superstitious society. Not that we are suggesting deliberate deception or hoaxing is normally involved in media coverage of psychic phenomena. Like many scientists attracted to the study of psychic effects, the average journalist is simply poorly equipped to deal with what he observes.

To see how perfectly sincere reports can manufacture a psychic event, consider a newspaper story that appeared in a small city just before a Uri Geller performance. Along with a glowing front page story about the miracle man, the paper (which can remain nameless since it could have happened in most newspapers) presented the three photographs that the reader can see in Figure 20A-C. These were presented one above the other with the comment: "The cook (left) seems somewhat skeptical as Uri sets to work on the hapless utensil—a heavy ladle. A spot of concentration and finger-stroking produces a marked curve in the spoon handle. More concentration, and disbelief turns to astonishment as the handle turns a 30-degree angle." Looking at these pictures, it obviously seems that Geller just stood there in front of the reporter, photographer, and hotel cook, holding a huge kitchen ladle which melted before everybody's bulging eyes.

However, one of us (RK) took a quick trip to the same hotel three days later and interviewed the cook shown behind Geller's shoulder, one Mr. Stewart Shaw. According to Shaw, this bending episode took fifteen minutes, and between photographs Geller raced around the kitchen asking for metal (practically everything in sight was metal!) before switching to a cry for water and then a refrigerator. Consequently, everybody had to run along behind Geller's back, and when they caught up, the big spoon was bent further. After each dash the photographer urged Uri to return to the starting place and pose the next picture in the sequence. Notice how the ceiling lights and shelves in the background change from shot to shot.

The photographer himself subsequently confirmed Shaw's story, although he and the reporter still believed that Geller had done the effect by mind-power. An examination of the negatives revealed the three photographs published were numbers 2, 4, and 10, in a series of at least ten shots, and that the roll of film was changed between shots 6 and 7.

Shaw also believed Geller at the time, but he was not dazzled. He said he had no idea how or why he made such a face in the last picture shown. But he asked Dick Kammann how anybody could bend such a thick solid piece of metal, if it wasn't psychic? Dick asked, "How did you straighten it out?" His expression froze for a moment and then he laughed, "With my hands."

The problem with news stories like this is that one reporter's private illusion becomes one more piece of psychic evidence in the individual minds of hundreds of thousands of readers or TV viewers. Photographs can be highly misleading as the above case shows but most people accept them as documentary proof of whatever the storywriter's description suggests.

Another problem with this whole area is that a skeptical viewpoint is not very popular with most people. As chapter one indicates, the majority of the population believes in ESP, and so anybody who wants to publish a skeptical viewpoint starts off at a disadvantage. Over thirty different publishers were approached before Prometheus Books agreed to publish this book. The most commonly cited reason for rejecting our manuscript was that a "pro-ESP" book was already on their lists or in the pipe line, and they didn't think this and the "pro" book would make very friendly neighbors. We don't have any hard statistics on sales, but we strongly suspect that skeptical books, which debunk the paranormal and the occult are not big sellers. Phillip J. Klass, author of *UFO's Explained* (Random House), had this to say: "Good luck in your efforts. The 'debunker's' lot is a lonely one—and a pro-Geller book will outsell yours 10-1, as is the case for UFO's, but I know that neither of us would change to the other side of the street."

Scientific journals should, of course, remain free of bias and not be swayed by the normal pressures of the market place. There is, however, a tendency not to publish negative results. It is much easier to publish a paper concluding that something is the case, than one trying to prove a negative. Negatives are in fact impossible to prove conclusively because observations must always be limited by constraints of time, economics, and human endurance. But that white crow might be just around the next corner.

Our own experience with two science journals in connection with our Geller research indicates that editors may be unsure about what to do with this kind of material. Following publication by *Nature* of the SRI research with Geller, we decided to submit our delayed-control group experiments on Geller's ability to reproduce sealed drawings and start watches. The editor's decision was that our data were "insufficiently conclusive." We believe that, in the total context presented in this book, our data are more than sufficient. In the brief report submitted as a letter to *Nature* we could, of course, give only a fraction of our evidence and we would not quibble with the decision. The reason for rejection, however, is one that plagues researchers who would want to question an established finding.

Having failed to gain acceptance of our Geller research in *Nature**, we decided to submit the research report to *Science*. We received two reviews

---

* *Nature* later accepted our critique of the SRI remote viewing experiments with Pat Price (see *Nature,* 17 August 1978, 680-1).

by independent scientists, one reservedly positive, and the other laudatory, saying he'd wished he'd done the experiments himself. Editor Philip Abelson overruled his reviewers, however, and rejected the paper with the following terse comment: "We are not interested in this topic." This was indeed strange. Anthropologist Margaret Mead was that year President of the American Association for the Advancement of Science (the publishers of *Science)* and herself an active proponent of psychic research. In fact, Mead had herself written a highly positive introduction to Targ and Puthoff's book, *Mind-Reach.* Moreover, some years earlier, Mead had helped lobby the AAAS for acceptance of parapsychology as a legitimate branch of science. Clearly the editor of *Science* was not in tune with his publisher. Or perhaps he didn't want to cause unnecessary controversy or embarrassment. After all, SRI physicists had "validated" Geller, and surely two psychologists from remote New Zealand couldn't know better, now could they?

The news that Geller's powers had been scientifically "proven" traveled fast. The SRI research and tests by other scientists with Uri provided a good story line for journals, magazines, and books, and Geller himself made the most of the opportunity in promoting his career in showbiz. Sociologist Marcello Truzzi and psychologist Ray Hyman collected a basic bibliography* on Uri Geller and his scientists listing almost two hundred items published between 1972 and 1978, including eleven books. Geller commanded more attention from science than any other psychic in history. Gelleritis was contagious and spread everywhere, finding representatives in most universities around the world.

5. Other Gellers

As Gelleritis reached almost epidemic proportions, it went beyond the worlds of science and literature. Other people came forward claiming similar powers to Geller's, powers that remarkably had lain dormant until Geller appeared on the scene. Professor Taylor studied a number of these cases and reported his findings in *Superminds,* as described above.

A young psychic, not included in Taylor's survey, was an Englishman, Matthew Manning (born 1955). In his book *The Link* (New York: Holt,

* Published in the *Zetetic Scholar,* Volume 1, 1978.

Rinehart and Winston, 1975), Manning presents his own story about poltergeists and other strange happenings that took place at home and at school from the age of eleven. Like Geller's *My Story, The Link* is an autobiographical account and, therefore, is of minimal scientific value.

Manning describes how, after watching Geller perform on television, he discovered that he too could bend cutlery and other metal objects. Physicists, like Nobel laureate, Professor Brian Josephson F.R.S., and mathematicians like Dr. A.R.G. Owen, flocked to study Manning's miracles. Josephson is reported by the *Daily Mail* of London to have concluded: "We are on the verge of discoveries which may be extremely important for physics. We are dealing here with a new kind of energy." The introduction to *The Link* promises a series of "learned papers" following research on Manning's powers by "twenty-one giants of science" in Toronto during June and July, 1974. Five years later we are still awaiting these publications with great interest. Unfortunately, paraphysicists seems to be perpetually "on the verge of discoveries" and no closer to actually making one.

If Manning is the English "Geller" then the French "Geller" is Jean-Pierre Girard. According to Marcel Blanc, writing in the *New Scientist* (16 February 1978), Girard decided to copy Geller and take in scientists to prove how easily misled they are. While Girard may have got off to a reasonable start, fooling a few scientists like Charles Crussard of Pechiney and Z. Wolkowsky of the Sorbonne, he has consistently failed tests conducted under controlled and supervised conditions. Leading French physicists Bernard Dreyfus and Yves Farge have used protocols designed with the assistance of professional magicians Randi and Klingsor, and in none of these tests has Girard performed successfully. Of course, Geller couldn't either, when tested under properly controlled conditions.

6. "Gelleritis" as Pathological Science

What conclusions can be drawn from "Gelleritis" in relation to modern science? A number of characteristics emerge that have much in common with Irving Langmuir's concept of "pathological science, the science of things that aren't so."* Of Langmuir's list of symptoms of "pathological science," we shall briefly mention four:

*Langmuir's discussion of "pathological science" was developed in an unpublished address delivered to the Research Laboratory of the General Electric Company in Schenectady, New York, on December 18, 1953.

(i) "The maximum effect that is observed is produced by a causative agent of barely detectable intensity, and the magnitude of the effect is substantially independent of the intensity of the cause." Geller's effects are produced by a causative agent that cannot be detected by physical science. The effects are seemingly independent of distance from the cause and normal physical barriers.

(ii) "Fantastic theories contrary to experience." Puharich's theories about Geller are as fantastic as anyone could find in contemporary science. The influence of Puharich in arranging Geller's "validation" by science should not be underestimated. Other Gellerites' theories are all contrary to experience.

(iii) "Criticisms are met by ad hoc excuses thought up on the spur of the moment." Geller and Gellerites always find reasons, which we term "special pleading," for why the effects tend to disappear and reappear from moment to moment (e.g., "not in the mood," "too tired," "takes a long time," "must be near metal," "must be near water," "people too negative" or "too skeptical," "too crowded," "not enough people," etc.). In Langmuir's words, "They always had an answer—always."

(iv) "Ratio of supporters to critics rises up to somewhere near 50 percent and then falls gradually to oblivion." The exact incidence of Gelleritis in the scientific community when it reached its peak is unknown, but the shape of the curve is correct. Oblivion is just around the corner. Again we quote from Langmuir: "The critics can't reproduce the effects. Only the supporters can do that. In the end, nothing was salvaged. Why should there be? There isn't anything there. There never was. That's characteristic of the effect."

Pathological science has no cure and there is no universal immunity. It is a function of fallibilities in human cognition associated with strongly held beliefs. Commitment to beliefs of any kind occurs only at a cost—and a high one. In a word, that cost is rationality. Paradoxically, as science grows, so does the risk of irrationality. We shall explore this further in the next three chapters.

11

THE ROOTS OF COINCIDENCE

One thing, however, remains to be explained—the Geller effect. By this I mean the ability of one able though perhaps not outstanding magician (though only his peers can judge that) to make such an extraordinary impact on the world, and to convince thousands of otherwise level-headed people that he is genuine, or at any rate, worthy of serious consideration.

Arthur C. Clarke

The short answer to Arthur Clarke's question is that Geller succeeded because the public wanted him to. As we have seen (chapter 1), most people are believers, and Geller (or Kreskin or remote viewing) is only "proof" they are right.

The real puzzle is why so many people believe in supernatural effects for which there is so little evidence. Is this our answer to the hard seats and dull arithmetic of schooldays past? No area of science could survive such a long history of high hopes and poor results, so many false alarms, so many hoaxes, and so little visible progress (Hansel, 1966). We have examined the three most spectacular psychic claims of the 1970s, only to find three more duds. While most scientific fields change so fast that only experts can hope to cope, psychism has a Brigadoon indifference to time while it awaits its first reliable result.

It would be foolish to deny the *possibility* of ESP, or for that matter, the fountain of youth. We must acknowledge that most wonders of modern science were once crazy conjectures: atoms, meteorites, germs, artificial fertilizers, genes, antibiotics, and all the rest. Who among us wants to be the historic fools of our era, like those who doubted the round earth of Columbus, the centrality of Copernicus' sun, Fuller's steam engine, or NASA's moon landing?

On the other hand, our history books forget to mention all the false theories that have been believed, sometimes by quite large followings, a deficiency that has been much corrected by Martin Gardner's skeptical classic, *Fads and Fallacies in the Name of Science* (Dover, 1957). Contrary to the where-there's-smoke theory, the number of people believing an idea is not much evidence for its truth value.

Just for the sake of argument, let us imagine that *there really is no such thing as ESP*. In that case, how could we explain the widespread conviction that there *is?* This turns our attention from psychics to the psychology of psychic belief.

One likely explanation is motivational. We seem to have a profound yearning for a magic formula that will free us from our ponderous and fragile human bodies, from realities that will not obey our wishes, from loneliness or unhappiness, and from death itself. This idea is especially compatible with the broader occult spectrum including astrology (which relieves us from responsibility for our actions and moods), spiritualism, reincarnation, and faith healing. In this sense, the occult serves as a sort of underground religion. It is less clear, however, what wish is fulfilled by ESP or UFOs, which seem rather to be superstitious conjectures of modern thought. We think the motivational hypothesis deserves much more study, but at the moment it is only an enticing speculation.

We move onto firmer ground with the cognitive hypothesis that psychic belief follows from natural fallacies of human thought. Our starting point is the common experience of stumbling onto a mysterious event that defies explanation and seems supernatural. These are the stories that people say "could not be a mere coincidence." But what is a coincidence, and what are the roots of coincidence?

The Case of the Drowning Daughter

We begin with a true story that happened to one of the authors (RK).

I usually forget my dreams, but seven years ago I had a

particularly vivid and disturbing nightmare that turned out to be prophetic. In this dream, I kept running into the bathroom where my seven-year-old daughter was playing in the bathtub. The water level was not very high, but as dreams go, she had somehow shrunk to doll-size and was constantly slipping under the water, so I had to keep sitting her back up to keep her from drowning. I mentioned this bad dream to my wife the next day.

After I had forgotten the dream, we were invited to a garden party at the home of friends who had a swimming pool. The party took place about two weeks later. After most of us had taken a dip in the pool, the adults gathered on the lawn for party talk and drinks. Suddenly out of the corner of my eye I saw my daughter thrashing under water in the deep end of the pool—she did not know how to swim. I broke through the crowd, jumped in beside her, and heaved her up into the arms of a friend at the poolside. After a few gasps and splutters, she got her breath back and was perfectly okay. She had been bobbing up and down alone in the shallow end of the pool and had drifted well beyond the ramp into the deep end.

After I was calm again I remembered the dream of saving her in the bathtub. Coincidence seemed impossible. Why should I, who rarely remembers dreams, who never had a dream like that one, and who rarely went swimming with my daughter, find myself dreaming about her nearly drowning just two weeks before she nearly did? The idea of the pool party could not have caused the dream, because I remembered that the invitation came after it. The idea that the dream caused the pool incident seems absurd—if anything the dream should have made me more careful to prevent any accident. Nor could my memory of the dream have been revised to fit the facts, since I had already told it to my wife. After much discussion, I could only guess that it was precognition, but whatever it was, I never forgot it.

In such stories as this, it is common to say that there was a "striking coincidence," and to turn around and deny that it was a "mere coincidence." This semantic paradox results from different meanings of "coincidence," so we must take a small detour through a definition of our terms.

The dream is event A. The pool incident is event B. They are connected by *similarity* (a drowning daughter in a rectangular tub of water being saved by her father). Thus, events A and B form a *match*.

While life is full of matches, as when the front door key fits the front door lock, this type of match has a distinct quality of *oddity*, because we cannot explain it by any common knowledge. An oddity captures our attention and causes us to search further for an explanation. The more striking the oddity, the longer we think about it and remember it.

Because a psychic anecdote first requires a match, and, second, an oddity between the match and our beliefs, we call these stories *oddmatches*. This is equivalent to the common expression, an "unexplained coincidence." However, we are not just being difficult to insist that *oddmatch* is a better name. You might think of your favorite psychic story to see if it fits our definition of an oddmatch.

All explanations of an event in terms of normal or nonpsychic processes are examples of what we call *N Theory*. All explanations based on psychic or paranormal ideas belong to *P Theory*. But the two types or theories are not equal. If we can explain an event in terms of N Theory, then we do not involve P Theory. An event cannot be "paranormal" unless we can first show that it is not "normal." As a person's knowledge of N Theory expands, the number of oddities decreases and the less often P Theory is needed.

The reason N Theory always dominates P Theory is that N Theory can predict events (i.e., can name the conditions that favor their occurrence), whereas P Theory predicts nothing until after it happens.

Parapsychology is a class of P Theory that studies oddmatches involving thoughts. In *telepathy*, there is an unexplained match between one person's thought A and another person's thought B. In *clairvoyance*, the oddmatch occurs between thought A and object B, as when we can state which card is now on top of a well-shuffled deck. In *psychokinesis*, A is a thought or wish that some object would change (event B)—we might wish that the car engine would fix itself, and it does. Finally, in *precognition*, thought A predicts some future event B, as when a fortune teller says you will meet the love of your life in the next six months, and you do. It is actually difficult to classify many oddmatches. Suppose you imagine that you are about to get a long distance telephone call from your mother, and you do. Is this telepathy from her mind to yours, or clairvoyance that she is dialing, or precognition of the phone call?

One final point. The way we explain an event, whether by N Theory or by P Theory, influences which details are remembered and which are forgotten.

Four Meanings of Coincidence

We have taken the trouble to define oddmatches, P Theory, and N Theory, so that we can make sense of *coincidence,* which has four different meanings.

1. Coincidence as a Match. Coincidence as the coinciding of similar events is a trivial definition because it covers all matches. Thus, a box of chocolates would be a bundle of coincidences.

2. Coincidence as an Uncaused Match. It has been traditional to define a coincidence as the coming together of two (similar or related) events without any apparent cause. This definition is not really complete, because we don't know the cause of a lot of matches. Just because two ships pass each other on the seas, or two friends meet in a store, we do not experience a sense of oddity.

Our knowledge of causes is actually very limited. Why do objects fall to the ground? Because of gravity. What causes gravity? (??) As the parent of a three-year-old child can tell you, we find the limits of our causal understanding very quickly by asking "why" after each explanation.

Furthermore, science has had to go beyond the idea of chains of causes. These have been replaced by other ideas, of which probability and statistics are the most important here. This brings us to the "chance coincidence."

3. Coincidence as a Probability Match. When a person is dealt four aces in a poker hand, we have a very striking match, but it is not a scientific oddity because we say it occurred by chance or the laws of probability. But if it happened five times in a row, we would suspect that something else was going on.

Probability can never predict that a particular event will occur at a given moment, such as which cards will appear in the next poker hand, but it predicts how often events will occur, under certain conditions. For example, if you roll a pair of dice 360 times, then you would expect the sums of the dice to come up this often:

sum of two dice	number of times
2	10
3	20
4	30
5	40

sum of two dice	number of times
6	50
7	60
8	50
9	40
10	30
11	20
12	10

Statistical rules tell us we will usually not get exactly these sums, but they will be reasonably close. The more times we roll the dice, the better the results will agree with the theory.

It is puzzling, of course, how probability rules cannot predict any particular event, and yet can predict the frequency of events. But as long as events fit the expected pattern, we say the particular event is normal within chance. Thus, the "mere coincidence" is a case of N Theory.

A very common use of statistics in research is this. We propose that a certain condition exists (such as, these are fair dice) and work out the expected distribution. If the results differ too much, then we conclude the hypothesis was wrong (the dice are loaded).

4. Coincidence as an Oddmatch. We finally get to the "striking coincidence," which is taken as evidence of a psychic or paranormal happening. Recall that an oddmatch has no explanation, not by cause, not by probability, not by any form of N Theory. Therefore, it supports P Theory.

The failure to distinguish among these meanings of coincidence can lead to tremendous confusion as, for example, in the writings of Arthur Koestler, which we take up shortly. What *we* mean by the roots of coincidence is the explanation of the oddmatch.

In psychic thinking, anecdotes like the dream of the drowning daughter are significant because they baffle N Theory and open the way for P Theory. But this is an illusion. There are biases in human perception and reasoning that hide the role of probability from our view. What seems like an oddmatch must often be a probability match, and our challenge to psychic theory is the challenge of chance.

The Challenge of Chance

We shall use probability theory to explain the results of a major ESP experiment and then a group of personal anecdotes, both of which are given in *The Challenge of Chance* by Alister Hardy, Robert Harvie, and Arthur Koestler (Hutchinson, 1973). Their title has a very different meaning from ours.

Alister Hardy is an eminent British marine biologist who founded the Religious Experiences Research Unit in Oxford, England. As a young man he had experienced a striking odd match that convinced him that telepathy was real. He was also President of the British Society for Psychical Research from 1965 to 1969, and it was during this period that he organized one of the most comprehensive ESP tests on record, an experiment ingeniously designed to snare mental telepathy for once and for all.

In this study, members of the Society for Psychical Research and interested friends were recruited for an experiment in which 120-or-so of them would concentrate in unison on a single target picture while another 20 of them in the same room tried to receive the group message. The receivers were seated in screened cubicles in the center of the lecture hall in Westminster, London, while the senders sat on both sides and in front of the cubicles so they could see the target picture. After each one-minute trial, the receivers came out to look at the target. After ten trials, the 20 receivers traded places with 20 (of the 120) senders, so everybody got a turn as receiver. The experiment took seven Monday evenings to complete.

Hardy enlisted the help of Robert Harvie, a graduate psychology student at the time, for the statistical analysis of the results. Their own judging revealed 35 cases of a match between the response and the target; all of these matches are published in the book for public inspection, and most of them seem very good. But looking at these best cases is somewhat beside the point. *They represent only 1.7 percent of the 2112 responses judged.* That Hardy and Harvie did not point this out is not vital, but is our first sign of the human bias to concentrate on successes and ignore failures. This is the very basis of the psychic illusion.

It was not, however, the 35 target matches that interested the researchers, but the unexpected finding of 260 matches occurring *between receivers.* None of these cross-talk matches had anything to do with the target, but, for some reason, the 1-power thought of another receiver came through more often than the 120-power thought of the senders.

Or so it seems. But to show that cross-talking is stronger than target matching, we should not compare 260 to 35. Rather, we must show that the cross-talks had a greater success rate, and this means we must know how often they failed, as well as how often they succeeded. We have gone back through the Hardy experiment, and found that there were 18,952 cross-talk failures. The success rate is the number of successes out of all possible cases (successes and failures), and *this turns out to be 1.4 percent, which is actually lower than the rate of target matches (1.7 percent).*

The failure of Hardy and Harvie to calculate this reflects again the human bias to look carefully at the successes (they published all 260 cross-talk matches) and to throw the failures into an uncounted scrap heap.

As it turned out, however, Harvie conducted the necessary test for the number of matches that would be expected by chance, using the method of the delayed control group on Hardy's data. He first moved every response from its correct trial to some other trial, on a random basis. Second, he required that no two drawings from the same real trial could get shifted to the same false trial.

The results of this massive shuffle were startling. They now discovered 34 new target matches on false trials, compared with 35 on real trials, and 217 new cross-talk matches compared with 260 original ones.

Naturally, these results were frustrating to the psychic researchers. While the difference between 260 and 217 cross-talk matches was probably not significant, it was at least in the right direction, so they left that result alone. However, 34 accidental target matches was much too close to 35, so they ran some more tests. This is the classic psychic "fishing fallacy," which is searching through the data to find a publishable result, without considering that the more times you analyze the data, the more chances you have of finding a "result" that is merely an unusually large but random fluctuation in the numbers. Some social scientists do it too.

First, they looked for so-called *precognitive* target matches, that is, a match between any drawing on one trial and the target of the *next trial.* That only produced 16 cases, so they tried out precognitive matches going back two trials, and then three, four, and five trials, but the number of precognitions in each test varied randomly around an average of 13, or only 0.6 percent. As they stated, they would also have tested for postcognitive matches (getting the target from a *preceding trial* by ESP), but they had allowed the subjects to see the target after each trial, so this test would have been meaningless.

So the next thing to do was to repeat Harvie's control test with a new shuffling of the data, but they still got 30 control matches, compared with the original 35 target matches. So, they shuffled the data three more times, which finally produced the result they were looking for—they got only 16, 16, and 22 control matches. So they could now *average* the number of matches on different control runs, giving an average of 24, and that, of course, is "only about two-thirds" as large as 35.

Throughout this entire experiment, it never occurred to the two researchers that there could be anything wrong with the procedure of letting themselves be the judges of the matches. It is a well-established psychological fact that our intuitive standards of judgment change to fit our hopes and our expectations. But we are asked to believe that Hardy and Harvie were not influenced by their knowledge that every match found in these later control runs was a blow against ESP.

To summarize, Hardy and Harvie did not do any follow-up tests on the cross-talk matches, but, counting the precognitions, they ran nine more tests on the target matches—using themselves as the judges—until they got a result that allowed them to conclude, "Perhaps just a small fraction was really due to telepathy?"

But if we stick to the first run of control tests, as we should, it is clear that Hardy and Harvie produced a definitive demonstration of non-ESP. The result is all the more impressive by the fact that the usual psychic rationalizations do not apply. One can hardly say that the researcher was too skeptical, or did not use a good selection of psychic subjects, or that the signal was too weak (with 120 senders), or that the receivers' sensitivity was blunted by boredom, since they had only ten trials and were allowed to see the target (got feedback) immediately after each trial.

But pseudoscience theories are outstanding in their ability to disregard negative findings. In this instance, Hardy and Harvie suspected that something mysterious was producing all those *control* matches (ignoring the simple explanation that they occurred by chance), whereupon Harvie ran some checks on random number tables and found that they were *not quite* random after all. As we are not concerned here with the possible defects of random number tables, we move on to Koestler's anecdotes.

Koestler's Fallacy

Arthur Koestler has long been interested in ESP and other scientific mysteries and has authored several books on the theme that modern science is mechanistic, strait-jacketed, narrow-minded, and is on the brink of a paranormal revolution, or should be.

Koestler is such a fascinating writer that it is hard to tell the difference between his scientific essays and his novels. Unfortunately, his critique of scientific logic stumbles on his failure to understand it. Instead, he uses the same literary formula that generates pseudoscience bestsellers: first, choose an exciting hypothesis and then assemble all facts or quotes that agree with it, and ignore any that don't.

For example, in *The Roots of Coincidence* (Hutchinson, 1972; Pan Books, 1974), he takes us through an uncritical acceptance of ESP experiments, some paradoxes of modern physics, the paranormal speculations of a lot of scientists, but most especially of physicist Wolfgang Pauli, biologist Paul Kammerer, and psychoanalyst Carl Jung, through his own concept of "holons," and, finally, the lurking suspicion that Darwin's theory of evolution must be wrong. The conclusion is that there are more things under the stars than are dreamt in our philosophies, a platitude with which we can readily agree.

This intellectual casserole is seasoned with a sprinkling of personal anecdotes of the oddmatch variety. The first two come from Kammerer's personal logbook.

While seated in the doctor's waiting room, Kammerer's wife comes across the name of a painter named Schwalbach in a magazine, whereupon the receptionist appears and asks if a patient named Frau Schwalbach is present, as she is wanted on the telephone.

Again, Kammerer's wife reads the name, Mrs. Rohan, in a magazine, later that day she sees a man who looks like her friend, Prince Rohan, and that evening, Prince Rohan himself actually drops in for a visit. In the same day the name of the village Weissenbach on Lake Attersee also occurs twice. As Koestler then says, "Most of [Kammerer's] other examples are even more trivial."

Two more of Koestler's favorite examples come from Carl Jung, the pro-mystic psychoanalyst. While talking with Freud about ESP, Jung felt a red-hot sensation in his stomach, and there was abruptly a loud report from Freud's bookcase. Jung predicted it would happen again, and immediately it did. Apparently Freud was unimpressed, and it appears that neither of them bothered to see if any books had fallen over or if a mouse was encountering some mousetraps. Regrettably, we do not have Freud's account of the incident.

On another day, one of Jung's patients was recounting a dream involving a golden scarab (a black dung beetle that was a religious symbol in ancient Egypt), and a few moments later, Jung discovered a scarab beetle trying to get into his window.

When Koestler picks up the challenge of saving the Hardy-Harvie results from psychic oblivion, he now has a much wider field of anecdotes from his fan mail and from Hardy's files in the Religious Experiences Research Unit. Over forty of these personal oddmatches are recounted in detail.

But all this requires that oddmatches cannot be explained by chance, which is to say they could not arise from time to time in the normal progression of natural events.

If we think about the movement of the moon around the earth, and of the earth around the sun, it seems very unlikely that the three balls will ever be found lying in a straight line. Indeed it *is* unlikely, because it happens so rarely, but it is also perfectly predictable that it will happen—which produces an eclipse of the sun or the moon.

By "Koestler's fallacy" we mean the mistaken assumption that oddmatches cannot arise by chance. It is a simple deduction from probability theory that an event that is very improbable in a *short run* of observations becomes, nevertheless, highly probable somewhere in a *long run* of observations. For example, if we flipped five coins at once, the probability of getting five heads is $1/32$ or about .03. But if we repeated the flipping of five coins ten times, the probability of getting five heads *somewhere* in the ten tests is about .27. If we ran 100 tests, the probability of five heads rises to .96, which is highly probable indeed. But if we stopped anywhere in these 100 tests and asked, what is the probability of getting five heads on the very next trial, we are back to the starting probability of .03 because we have switched from a long run question to a short run question.

This example also shows the basic error made by Hardy and Harvie in conducting ten different searches for ESP in their data. It is standard practice to reason as follows. If I assume that only chance is operating here, I can calculate how likely I am to get a difference between the experimental and the control group results of any particular size. (If the difference is small, the probability of it occurring is large, but if the difference is large, the probability is small.) So I shall say that if any large difference occurs that has a chance probability of .05 or less, then I can reasonably conclude that it is most likely not chance but is a real ESP effect. But this reasoning is correct only for the first test. The probability that the researcher will get a difference *that large* somewhere in ten different tests is actually .40. It is incorrect to interpret the results of a long run as if they came from a short run.

The principle of the long run is easy to understand in simple coin/dice/card situations where all the choices are well defined, but it is less visible in the chaotic world of human experiences. Something is happening all the time to every living person, but we do not see these events as a long run because so many *different kinds* of things are happening. Thus, when we come across an oddmatch, we suffer from a *short run illusion,* because there is nothing before or after that looks at all related. We can now show how this comes about.

Let us do a simple mental experiment on Koestler's 40-or-so anecdotes. Assume that at the end of an ordinary day, a person can recall 100 distinct events if prompted by questions. Since an oddmatch requires, first of all, a match between an event A and an event B, we need to know the total different number of PAIRS of events available from the 100 single events. The first event can be paired with each of 99 others. The second event can be paired with each of 98 others (because it has already been paired with the first event). Proceeding in this way we see that the total pairs is given by: 99+98+97+96+...+3+2+1. The total is 4950 pairs of events for a single person in a single day.

We have already noted that oddmatches will be remembered for years to come (witness the dream of the drowning daughter), so we may estimate that a person can remember all the important oddmatches over the past 10 years (about 3650 days). Let us assume further that Koestler has access to 1000 people through his personal life, his books, his fan mail, and Hardy's files. We are now ready to multiply: 4950 x 3650 x 1000, giving us 18,067,500,000 pairs. That Koestler should find 40 (or even 400) amusing oddmatches out of 18 billion pairs of events is not sufficient cause for a paranormal revolution.

It may be argued that 100 simple events a day is too many, but is it? Most people do things like read newspapers, magazines, and books, receive letters, answer the telephone, talk to family, friends, and work associates, listen to the radio, watch TV, and travel around town for work, leisure, and shopping, and thus receive countless thousands of bits of information of which 100 might well be memorable at the end of the day. By memorable, we mean that if event B occurs that is surprisingly like event A, then A will be recalled too. Furthermore, oddmatches are not always confined to a single day (e.g., the dream of the drowning daughter). But even if we allowed only 10 events a day, and only 5 years, and only 100 people, we still get a long run of over 8 million pairs of events to give rise to Koestler's 40 interesting stories.

Of course, these nonevents seem irrelevant because, for example, there were not thousands of patients talking to Jung about scarab beetles, nor did Jung notice thousands of such beetles over the years. Perhaps only one patient mentioned a golden scarab, and perhaps Jung had only seen ten in his whole life.

But one oddmatch is just as good as another. It doesn't matter whether the match is between beetles, claps in bookshelves, names in a magazine, or dreams about daughters—they are equally good as psychic mysteries. We call this the *principle of equivalent oddmatches.* It is not the probability of a *particular* oddmatch that matters, but the probability of *any* oddmatch. Statistician-magician Persi Diaconis (1978) has called this the problem of "multiple end points," which frequently crops up in psychic research.

Clusters and Gremlins

The perceptual basis of Koestler's fallacy is this. It is easy to see something happen, but it is hard to see something NOT happen. We notice that two events are a *pair* if they are alike, but not if they are different. This bias has several applications.

Koestler is much intrigued by Kammerer's "law of series" that says, essentially, that things come in clusters or runs, or as we all know, it never rains but it pours.

A doctor or dentist gets a run of the same rare problem after he has not seen it for months. A typewriter repairman notices that he gets a run of the same brand of typewriter, or else a run on the same defect across different brands. Nurses notice that a full moon produces a surge of births in the maternity ward. We call this the *clustering illusion.*

Why does the phone always ring when I'm in the bathtub? Why does the vacuum cleaner (oven, refrigerator, blender) always break down just before a dinner party? Why does it always rain on my vacation? Why do I get a flat tire on the very day I left my jack at home? We call this the *gremlin illusion.*

There is a special case of the clustering illusion, which is the *new word effect.* One day you learn a new word, and to your surprise, it crops up a few days later, and then again a few days after that. But maybe it was cropping up just as often *before* you learned it as it does afterwards.

To illustrate, one of the authors (RK) moved from America to New Zealand, and after he was there about six months, he learned the new word *ta,* which is the New Zealand equivalent of "thanks." From that day on he ran into *ta* practically every day, but during the first six months he had not "heard" it once. We notice things that have meaning, and not the ones that do not.

Birthdays and Committees

No matter how good human intuition may be for some purposes, it can be disastrous in estimating combinations of events and, hence, certain kinds of probabilities.

How many people do you need to have together in one room before you have a fifty-fifty chance of finding two people born on the same day of the year (ignoring the year)? Surprisingly, the answer is only twenty-two people.

Koestler says this birthdays problem is a silly puzzle that has nothing to do with his judgment of probabilities. Let us try a much more basic estimation problem.

You are a member of a secret club of ten people who want to organize some big happenings. You are going to need a lot of committees, and each person will have to be on several committees, but you don't want any two committees to have exactly the same people. That is, comparing any two committees, there must be at least one person on the first committee who is not on the second.

For certain jobs, you need teams of only two people. How many different teams of two can you make out of ten people?

For other jobs you want committees of three people. How many different committees of three people can you make out of the ten?

How many different committees of four people? Five people? Six people? Seven people? Eight people?

Psychologists Amos Tversky and Daniel Kahneman gave this problem to college students, and it is interesting to compare their average guesses with the correct answers:

Committee Size	Correct Number	Average Number Guessed
2	45	70
3	120	50
4	210	40
5	252	26
6	210	26
7	120	29
8	45	20

(Tversky and Kahneman, 1973.)

We usually underestimate the possible number of combinations rather badly. The only exception is for pairs, and even that overestimation may only apply when the starting number is small, such as ten in this case.

Tversky and Kahneman suggest that we base our guesses on how easily we can think up the first few examples. It is easy to visualize a lot of different pairs in a set of ten people, but difficult to imagine different committees of eight. Only when we stop and think—for each unique committee of eight there is a unique pair left off the committee—do we begin to see why pairs and eights must both have the same total number (forty-five). But the students guessed that there are seventy pairs and only twenty octuples.

The lesson is clear enough. Before we say that an event could not happen by chance, we should try to work out the number of chances it had—on paper. Our impressions are not good enough.

The First Root of Coincidence

We can summarize as follows. The first root of coincidence

(oddmatches) is simple probability.

Koestler's fallacy refers to our general inability to see that unusual events are probable in the long run. We call it "Koestler's fallacy" because Arthur Koestler is the author who best illustrates it and has tried to make it into a scientific revolution. Of course, the fallacy is not unique to Koestler but is widespread in the population, because there are several biases in human perception and judgment that contribute to this fallacy.

First, we notice and remember matches, especially oddmatches, whenever they occur. Second, we do *not* notice nonmatches. Third, our failure to notice nonevents creates the *short-run illusion* that makes the oddmatch seem improbable. Fourth, we are poor at estimating combinations of events. Fifth, we overlook the *principle of equivalent oddmatches,* that one coincidence is as good as another as far as psychic theory is concerned.

Our human ability to see positive cases and inability to see negative ones tends to put us all in the position of the fool who believed that everybody spoke the same language he did, because he had never met anybody who didn't. Nor is it so surprising that many people believe that islands float on water, rather than recognizing that they are the upper tips of submerged mountains or land masses.

For the same reason, it is *ingenuous* (although very human) to believe that the plants and animals we see are the only ones that have ever been, whereas it is *ingenious* to visualize the vastly greater number of vanished species that were the stepping stones to the current living assortment. It is no wonder that evolutionary theory was a late development in human thought, that Darwin's theory was later still, and that many people still reject the whole idea out of hand.

The Second Root of Coincidence

Up to this point, we have simply assumed that every event is independent of every other event, just as we might imagine rolling two dice in separate shakers and counting up how often we get a matched pair. But life is not a random collection of unrelated events, but a highly organized process.

Usually we can see clearly what leads to what, but there are exceptional cases where invisible chains of cause and effect bias the probabilities, so that matches are made more probable than simple chance would predict.

The second root of coincidence is the *unseen cause*. With Koestler's pardon, we shall illustrate these with anecdotes and practical cases.

A simple example of the unseen cause, especially in scientific research, is an *equipment malfunction*. For example, in *Learning How to Use Extrasensory Perception* (1976), parapsychologist Charles Tart, a good friend of Targ and Puthoff, reported a successful ESP experiment in which his subjects scored above chance in guessing which of ten digits (from 0 to 9) was being displayed on special apparatus in another room. But later, three of Tart's colleagues at the University of California at Davis discovered that the machine, which was supposed to choose the digits purely randomly, was badly biased because it tended to avoid using the same digit twice in a row from one trial to the next. It just so happens that people have exactly the same bias. Since the ESP subject was always given feedback (was told the correct target digit) after his guess on each trial, his natural tendency to choose a *different* digit for the next trial agreed perfectly with the bias in the random number generator. When Tart repeated these experiments with proper controls, the ESP result disappeared but his original incorrect finding will be quoted for years to come.

Deliberate *deception* is another unseen cause, as Kreskin and Uri Geller have amply demonstrated. The stories of the pool hustler who misses his shots until the stakes are high enough, or the poker shark who uses marked cards are legendary. Even in the cultured atmosphere of international tournament bridge, a few teams have recently resorted to hand and posture signals to convey their hands to their partners.

We should as well beware of whimsical *pranks*. After Geller made his big splash in England, there was a boom of psychic spoon-bending children. During a radio show on Uri Geller in New Zealand, a child psychic was rushed into the studio for our attention with a huge bent fork (scratched by plier marks). It is difficult to estimate how many poltergeists might turn out to be ten year olds living three or four doors down the block.

Not long after we had completed our Geller studies, a local professor of chemistry called us for our opinion about an old friend of his who had recently been discovered to be a psychic spoon-bender. The man was then holding a job of high responsibility and seemed sane in every respect, but one evening he turned ashen white while several spoons melted in his hand in front of his wife and a visitor. Our advice to the professor was to interview the man for more details, whereupon the budding psychic sheepishly admitted that his face had only gone pale from the amazing discovery that he could so easily fool his wife and friend with pre-bent spoons.

One of the greatest psychokinetic events of all time took place at a suburban party in 1959 on a hilltop looking out over Cincinnati, Ohio. A crowd gathered on the veranda as one Max Brill waved his finger about in slow circles, then suddenly stabbed his finger at the sky, producing an instant distant clap of thunder. Not once, not twice, but again and again. Some observers were awed, some scoffed, and some remained silent, but there was no denying that Brill was poking distant booms out of the sky.

Max Brill's view of the situation was entirely different. He had spied a fireworks display going on in the baseball park down in the valley and used the flashes of light to cue his arm thrusts. At that distance, the lag between sound and light was enough for Brill to jab a fraction before the sound arrived.

One of the authors was in Ann Arbor, Michigan, in the early 1960s when the newspapers reported a rash of UFO sightings. The next day he learned that an enterprising team of students were trying to figure out how to attach candles or flashlights to light a cluster of helium balloons they planned to release that night.

Even more subtle as an unseen cause is the *self-fulfilling prophecy,* which occurs when a person has a belief or makes a statement about the future and then acts unconsciously to make it come true. For example, consider a man who believes that people in general are selfish and incompetent; he then approaches a workmate, a sales clerk, or a waitress with his demanding and distrusting attitude. Naturally this breeds resentment, which escalates into open hostility, and then the grouch goes home more convinced than ever that people are rotten.

The self-fulfilling prophecy can be far more powerful than this. In a voodoo or black magic culture in which a sinner "knows" he cannot escape the edict of magical revenge, grown men have been reported to collapse in fear and die within a few days.

Most self-fulfilling prophecies are less dramatic, but let us consider. Arthur Koestler writes a book on the mysteries of strange coincidences, and, sure enough, his fan mail includes a rash of new cases. If you happen to be a person lacking in odd matches you are somewhat less likely to read Koestler, and you are certainly less likely to write him a letter telling him that you have nothing to report.

One unseen cause we cannot fully explain is the *population stereotype* that we encountered in Kreskin's circle-triangle and number-37 tricks. To be fair, Uri Geller uses it too. On one radio talkback show, Geller announced he had made a drawing, whereupon one of us bet it was a sailboat against the other who bet it was a flower. It was a flower. Then we really had a laugh when Geller next said he was thinking of two geometric shapes that (lo and behold) turned out to be a "circle and a pyramid."

Simple curiosity goaded us to do a further experiment on population stereotypes, which we pitted against an ESP effect, but population stereotypes won hands down. The details of this experiment are given in Appendix I.

Our analysis of *unseen causes* has covered several types: equipment malfunction, deliberate deception, whimsical pranks, self-fulfilling prophecies, and population stereotypes. To this ragbag of illusions we must add one or two more that have no simple labels.

It is commonly said that ESP is more likely to occur between two partners in love than two acquaintances, and this is attributed to their psychic rapport. Alternatively, it might be attributed to:

a. having more experiences in common;
b. being more familiar with each other's habits of thought;
c. thinking about each other more often;
d. all of the above.

Similarly, the prophetic dream about the drowning daughter becomes a little less mysterious when we fill in some missing details. The father had been late in learning how to swim in his own childhood and had resolved that his daughter should learn as early as possible. But over the preceding summer, he had not made time for it and felt concerned to do so as the new summer came in. His daughter was now seven years old. The problem was thus half-consciously on his mind, and it is often the case that unresolved worries express themselves most clearly in a dream. Furthermore, it is not certain, after all, that the party invitation had not at least been mentioned shortly before the dream occurred, in which case the thought of his daughter at the swimming pool would have intensified his guilty feelings.

While this does not explain the incident at the pool, it does suggest that the dream was part of a recurring thought pattern that anticipated certain risks coming up that summer. That the father was the first person to see the daughter in trouble, although many adults were closer to the pool, suggests that the worrying was not without its uses.

But what details are perceived and remembered depend importantly on how the odd match is interpreted at the time. To a surprising extent, you see what you believe. We take up this theme in the next chapter.

12

SELF-PERPETUATING BELIEFS

By the eagerness of the human mind things which are obscure are more easily believed.

Tacitus

The oddmatch illusion gives us an alternative model for ESP in everyday life. But it is not a complete model of paranormal belief. It does not give an adequate account of astrology, UFOs, biorhythms, fortune telling, graphology, palmistry, poltergeists, and so on.

Now there are three possibilities. The first is that some of these psychic and occult beliefs have a basis in fact, but as far as we know there is no scientific evidence for any of them. The second is that each one is based on a different kind of illusion. The third possibility is that there are some common psychological processes, or cognitive fallacies, that contribute to all of them.

In this chapter we explore some case studies and a few psychological experiments to see if it is possible to develop a more comprehensive model of paranormal belief. In doing so we shall end up with a grand sweep of skepticism that will seem very prejudiced, as if we think that science now knows all there is to be known. Actually, science knows very little—especially about the meaning and management of our own lives—but we shall indicate why we believe that stars, biorhythms, and UFOs are unlikely places to get any real answers to our uncertainties.

Our goal here is to understand the difference between *rationality* and *rationalization*. By rationality we mean a self-correcting system of discovery, while rationalization refers to all processes that make beliefs self-perpetuating regardless of the evidence.

The biases in human perception and reasoning not only cut into

174

paranormal thought but also into everyday human affairs, into the professions, into psychology itself. It would be premature to venture very far into these orthodox fields, but we shall signpost some of the possibilities in this chapter and the next.

The term "magical thinking" has been used to describe our tendency to take correlations or similarities and treat them as cause-and-effect relationships. For example, a mother may say that her daughter's fear of heights comes from her father, and that it runs in his side of the family. She does not mean that the daughter "caught" her fear from her father (although that is a more reasonable theory in its own way), but that it was transmitted by heredity. Seeing the father-daughter similarity as cause-and-effect is magical thinking, and spelling that out in terms of heredity is providing a subjective explanation.

The explanation is only subjective because it has no predictive power. It is a string of words. However, this string of words can have far-reaching implications. If everybody in the family agrees with it, then the daughter is stuck with her fear of heights because it's "in her genes." If she makes any effort to get rid of the fear, the skepticism of the whole family will persuade her to give up quickly and submit to her fate. Since she never gets rid of the fear, the string of words is "proved" to be right. This is the perfect example of the self-perpetuating belief, because it permits no test of its validity. It is a self-fulfilling prophecy.

An explanation has no meaning unless it can predict something (without forcing it). It says when something will or won't happen, or will happen more and less often. It does not need to predict the future—as in archeology, it can predict what you will find when you look into the "past." It can always be translated into an *if-then* format, as IF I put this dough in this oven, THEN I will get a loaf of bread. It makes predictions that are sufficiently clear-cut that it is possible for them to turn out to be wrong.

It could be argued that the hereditary explanation of the daughter's fear was very predictive since she didn't get rid of it. This is true. But the explanation is very bad at predicting who else will get what kinds of fears and what will happen when they try to get rid of them, and so on. It's ability to predict depends on everybody believing it and never putting it to any further test.

Our concern is not so much with the goodness of a particular explanation as with the attitude that allows it to be put to the test. Scientists talk about hypotheses, models, and theories. These words imply that they have only a working explanation, a best guess at the moment, that is always subject to testing and revision. The life expectancy for most scientific models is very short.

We are concerned here with various devices of the mind that make beliefs self-perpetuating rather than self-correcting. In the last chapter we said that odd matches foster a belief in ESP. In this chapter, we discover the reverse—that the belief in ESP encourages the finding of odd matches. Or more generally, that beliefs influence the evidence that is found. We are pleased to acknowledge the contribution of our colleague, Peter Bradshaw, for helping select some of the material we include.

Subjective Validation

One person walks out of a Kreskin show saying, "I used to *think* ESP was real, now I *know* it is." Another person says, "Just what I thought, a bunch of stage tricks." But, says the believer to the skeptic, how can you explain those things—how did he get "551026" ? I don't know, says the skeptic, I'll bet he has an accomplice. If he has ESP why doesn't he go to Las Vegas and get rich? If he wanted to he would, says the believer.

What happened and what we think happened are often not the same thing. What we see is partly determined by what is going on in our heads at the time of observation and afterwards. Our perceptions are shaped by our expectations, our beliefs, our motives, our past experiences. The two people above, with opposite prior beliefs, saw the "same" happening but each ends up more convinced about his own theory.

Our beliefs are not automatically updated by the best evidence available. They often have an active life of their own and fight tenaciously for their own survival. They tell us what to read, what to listen to, who to trust, and how to explain away contrary information.

Selective exposure is a well-documented psychological principle that says we choose our newspaper reports, our magazine stories, our TV channels, our lectures, our books, and our authorities in such a way as to confirm our views. People with an occult bent of mind read *The Bermuda Triangle*. People with a rational bent of mind read *The Bermuda Triangle Mystery—Solved*. (Only the first is a bestseller.) Give a lecture on ecology and you have an audience of ecologists. Put on a TV series to praise different ethnic minority groups, and each week the audience consists primarily of the group being featured. We are always preaching to the converted.

People cannot always predict, however, what they will read or hear, and they often end up facing information that does not agree with their views. In this case, they fall back on a second line of defense—they actually misperceive or misunderstand the data. Whenever a person misreads unfavorable or neutral evidence as giving positive support to his beliefs, we say that he has found or made a *subjective validation*.

In a classic experiment, psychologists Hastorf and Cantril (1954) took advantage of a rivalry football game between Dartmouth and Princeton in 1951. The game had been a tough one, with escalating rough play, rule violations, and penalties. Among the several injuries, the star Princeton quarterback was put out of action. Surveys of students after the game showed each side was convinced the other side was guilty of foul play.

Since the entire game had been filmed, Hastorf and Cantril had fifty students from each college watch the movie soon after to detect as many violations by *both* sides as they could. Even though the students were now in a laboratory experiment requiring accurate perception, they saw that more infractions were committed by the other team than by their own. After all, if you want to count violations you should look at the team that is making them!

In other cases we cannot assume that people turned their eyeballs in the wrong direction. We have already seen an outstanding example in the judging of the SRI remote viewing transcripts. The judge, perhaps a friend of the experimenters, is handed a set of ESP records to match them up with target locations provided in their correct order. While reading over the transcripts the judge comes across phrases that suggest their order. Thus, he gets some ideas about which goes with which, but he assumes he is still capable of judging them objectively. He will take each location on its own merits.

As the judge gets to each location, he finds rather amazing evidence that his casual guesses were absolutely correct. Just how striking these similarities can be is illustrated by the photographs (taken after the fact) published by Targ and Puthoff along with excerpts and drawings from the transcripts. We can report from our own experience, once you know which ESP record goes with which park or building, it seems impossible that anybody could mismatch them. On the other hand, if you are judging them blind, you get a completely different set of matches, and the reasons, the similarities, are just as convincing.

It seems preposterous that one or two casual bits of information (the cues) could organize a whole fifteen-minute monologue (the ESP record).

But remember the ESP record is vague, rambling, and impressionistic like the passage that follows:

> With hocked gems financing him
> Our hero bravely defied all scornful laughter
> That tried to prevent his scheme
> Your eyes deceive he said
> An egg not a table correctly typifies
> This unexplored domain.
> Now three sturdy sisters sought proof
> Forging along sometimes through calm vastness
> Yet more often over turbulent peaks and valleys
> Days became weeks
> As many doubters spread fearful rumors
> About the edge
> At last from nowhere winged creatures appeared
> Signifying momentous success.

If you did not find a satisfactory meaning for this pseudopoem, read it again but ignore the phrase "the voyage of Christopher Columbus" while you do so. It won't help at all. (Passage from James Dooling and Roy Lachman, 1971.)

Illusory Correlation

In the Draw-A-Person test, a subject or mental patient is asked to draw a picture of a person. The rules for interpreting a drawing are not all that difficult. We illustrate by listing six features of drawings and six mental symptoms. We present both in a random order, to allow the reader to match them up.

Drawing Sign	Patient's Mental Symptom
large head	worried about his manliness
unusual eyes	suspicious of other people

Drawing Sign	Patient's Mental Symptom
unusual ears	concerned with being fed and taken care of
muscular with broad shoulders	worried about his intelligence
emphasis on mouth	problem with sexual impotence
emphasis on sexual area	worried that people are saying bad things about him

Most people line these up as follows: (head) intelligence, (eyes) suspiciousness, (ears) people saying bad things, (muscular) manliness, (mouth) being cared for, (sexual) impotence. The only problem is that *there is no such pattern in the drawings of real patients.* The only things the drawings reveal are drawing habits.

When the negative results came out on the Draw-A-Person test, some clinical psychologists could not believe them. They said, I have seen too many cases in which the drawing was a perfect reflection of personality—and my patients agreed that my diagnosis was correct. Psychologists Loren and Jean Chapman, at the University of Wisconsin in 1966, made the radical guess that clinical experience was producing an *illusory correlation.* Clinical experience was fooling itself.

To test this idea, they presented a number of drawings and mental symptoms to a group of students. The students' task was to decide, for every drawing, which of two listed symptoms was the more likely one. The Chapmans made sure that there was no correlation in their examples between the mental symptoms and the drawings. For example, the symptom "is worried about his intelligence" was shown just as often with small heads and medium heads as with large heads. After the students had gone through a number of these examples, they were asked what they observed in the data. Right. They observed that worrying about intelligence produces big heads! And so on for the other drawing signs.

In the next experiment, the Chapmans made the drawings go against the expected symptoms. For example, "is worried about his intelligence" was only offered as a symptom with small heads. But the students still found, although not as strongly as before, that worries about intelligence produce *big* heads.

Still other experiments showed that the illusory correlation could not be easily dispelled. They tried giving the students more practice, offering them a prize for the best answer, and letting them compare all the examples against each other, but they could not get rid of the false effect. The students maintained that worries about intelligence produce big-headed drawings. They always found the match they expected to find.

Illusory correlation is thus a type of subjective validation in which expected matches are imagined to occur more often than they really do.

Getting the Best of Nostradamus

Our understanding of subjective validation is much enriched by watching an intelligent man, and a superb writer, explain his belief in the prophecy of the seers—when he does explain it. The author is Charles N. Gattey, and the book is *They Saw Tomorrow: Seers and Sorcerers from Delphi Till Today* (Harrap, 1977). Gattey digs out the background stories on the Oracle at Delphi, Nostradamus, Cagliostro, Cheiro the English palm-reader, who ended up in America, Krafft ("Hitler's Astrologer"), and even that unsinkable rubber duck, Jeane Dixon, on whom he reports a few successes with no mention of any of her blunders.

Gattey comes to his writing task a committed believer. The jacket says he "knows from his own experience that telepathy exists and it was the fulfillment of certain predictions made to him personally that led to occult research—and this book." Although Gattey clearly believes his prophets most of the time, his examples of their successes are so sketchy that it is usually impossible for the reader to judge for himself. It is with Nostradamus that Gattey gives us the best chance to assess his logic, so let us take a brief look.

Nostradamus was no fool. In the introduction to his great work of prophecies called *Centuries* (1555) he explains, "...but so as not to upset my present readers I would do this [set of predictions] in a cloudy manner with abstruse and twisted sentences, rather than the plainly prophetical." Gattey buys this explanation, adding, "The language is enigmatic, at times almost unintelligible, as if written in code. The verses are not in chronological order and jump about in time and subject." And again, "Everywhere we find mystifying puns and anagrams."

Gattey does not recognize that unlimited metaphorical interpretation, versatile punctuation, and letter shuffling give him endless opportunities to force matches. Let us consider Quatrain 51 of Century II, which is bound to be quoted by unsuspicious readers as predicting the great fire of London in 1666 as Gattey claims.

Le sang du juste à Londres fera faulte,
Bruslés par fouldres de vingt trois les six,
La dame antique cherra de place haute,
De mesme secte plusieurs seront occis.

The blood of the just shall be demanded of London,
Burnt by fire in thrice twenty and six,
The old cathedral shall fall from her high place,
And many [edifices] of the same sect shall be destroyed.

We get our first hint of opportunistic translation from Gattey's offhand claim that Nostradamus often used "dame" to mean a cathedral, in this case, St. Paul's. Acting on this cue, we gave the same quotation, without comment, to a local French scholar, who gave the following as a straightforward translation.

The blood of the just man will be missing in London.
Burnt by thunderbolts of twenty-three and six,
The ancient lady will fall from her high place,
Of the same sect, several will be killed.

Showing him Gattey's version, our consultant said it is not reasonable to translate *fera faulte* as "will be demanded" of London. The number is twenty-three and six and almost certainly refers to the length of the thunderbolts with the unit of length understood. In fact, if there was an acute over the *e* in *les,* it is an old measure in the rough vicinity of two or three feet, so the phrase would sound very much like twenty-three feet six (inches). Gattey's translation as "thrice twenty and six" is not impossible, but it is very farfetched. Since the final word means "killed" and not "destroyed," the attempt to transform the old lady and her sect into stone buildings is a semantic insult.

Such effort after matches can even be detected when the original French is not given. Consider Century X, Quatrain 39.

The eldest son unhappily married leaves a widow
Without children, two islands in discord,

Before eighteen, an incompetent age.
The younger earlier shall be the betrothal.

Gattey says this verse describes the marriage in 1558 of Mary, Queen of
Scots, to the Dauphin, later Francis II of France, when the boy was
fourteen years old. He died at sixteen without leaving any children. The
last line is supposedly about the next king of France, Charles IX, who was
betrothed at age eleven.

Why is the French version not given? Why is the last line awkwardly
translated? Perhaps we should look more closely. The second line ends
with a comma, and the third line with a period, but it reads even better
when these are reversed, in which case "Before eighteen" would not refer to
"Francis" but to "Charles."

The death of Francis leaves two islands in discord, but Scotland and
France are not islands and they were not in discord. Gattey tells us, this
really means the subsequent feud between Mary, Queen of Scots, and
Elizabeth, Queen of England, because it involved two kingdoms on the
same island. Was Francis II unhappily married? Gattey doesn't comment
but our history books tell us he was "madly in love" with Mary.

We are next told that we can find out more about Charles IX in Quatrain
47 of Century IV, which is six centuries earlier! It turns out that *any* verse
in all of *Centuries* can be matched on a time-free basis with *any* historical
event. This is another example of Koestler's fallacy. We leave it for the
curious reader to figure out how many possible pairs there are between ten
prophecies and ten historical events, and then again between a thousand of
each. Against this second result, consider that Gattey reports about thirty
examples of successful prophecies.

But probability matches aside, Gattey's examples reveal what might be
called progressive match making. First one finds an apparent similarity
between one or two notable facts in a quatrain and a historical event. Given
this organizing theme, like a cue in a remote viewing transcript, one can
then shape up both verse and history to maximize an apparent agreement.

If this is correct, then Gattey has helped us discover the micro-
machinery of subjective validation. The rule is simply—keep searching for
similarities until an overall match has been made *(cherchez la
correspondance)*. Once the match is presented it will be hard to see how it
could be any other way.

It is easy enough to test the validity of Nostradamus's prophecies by
using several control groups. For example, one could take five groups of

history students with specialties in different areas, and provide them with the predictions of Nostradamus (without naming the source) to see how many prophecies are fulfilled for different historical periods in different regions of the world. If just as many prophecies are fulfilled in the pre-Christian middle east, or in ancient Greece, or in the middle ages of Scandinavia, as in post-sixteenth century Europe, then we would have to say that Nostradamus doth predict too much.

For our next example of subjective validation we go back into the psychological laboratory, this time of Baruch Fischoff at the Hebrew University in Jerusalem. Fischoff (1975) was interested in finding out if people could judge the strength of evidence for a conclusion without being biased by knowing the conclusion.

To test this idea he gave his students some passages to read, each about four to five paragraphs long. These stories described such things as a military battle, or a riot situation, or the case history of a person. These were all real cases, but they were unfamiliar to the students. For each passage, Fischoff listed four possible outcomes. For example, after the military battle, the choices were: a British victory, a Gurka victory, a stalemate with a peace settlement, a stalemate without a settlement.

The students' task was not to guess which was the correct outcome, but to judge how probable each outcome was on the basis of the evidence given in the story. If they are objective about this, then their probability judgments should be the same whether or not they happen to know what was the actual outcome. However, if subjective validation is taking place, then if they know the outcome, they should "see" the evidence as favoring that conclusion over all the others.

For a random half of the students, Fischoff included the correct outcome as the last sentence in the story, while for the other half this was left out. When the outcome was omitted the students gave it the same probability as the other outcomes. That is, for four possible outcomes A/B/C/D in which A happens to be correct, the average probabilities were .25/.25/.25/.25. But for the students who knew the outcome, the average probabilities were .40/.20/.20/.20. Furthermore, when the students rated the usefulness of each sentence in the passage, the ones who knew the outcome gave higher ratings to sentences that agreed with the stated result. Once they knew the answer they saw plenty of evidence to support the outcome. This is like the strong impression of inevitability that occurs in remote viewing transcripts or in Nostradamus's prophecies, once they have been matched.

Another case history takes us into the physics laboratory of Professor M. Rene Blondlot at Nancy University in 1903. It was not long after X rays had made their scientific debut, and many scientists were vying for the honor of discovering the next ray, which would bring the discoverer international acclaim. Blondlot discovered N rays.

According to the professor, N rays are given off most strongly by metal objects and have the important property of enhancing human vision. He had measured this effect (by his own eye) with calibrated precision in his spectroscope. Soon, there was a burst of N ray reports from other French laboratories, and Blondlot was quickly offered a high scientific award. However, English and American physicists were having trouble getting the effect. (The power of suggestion seems to follow an inverse distance law.)

The next year, 1904, an American physicist by the name of Robert W. Wood visited Blondlot in his laboratory where he observed, among other things, that Blondlot continued to call out different brightness readings after Wood had deftly lifted a necessary prism from the apparatus, so that no brightness differences were possible. By these and other tests Wood discovered that Blondlot was seeing only what he expected to see.

After Wood published all his findings in *Nature* that same year (without mentioning Blondlot by name), the N ray effect vanished itself. In ESP theory this would be attributed to Wood's negative vibes, but in physics it was accepted as a disproof of N rays. A fuller account of the incident is given by Phillip J. Klass in the Fall/Winter 1977 issue of *The Zetetic,* since renamed *The Skeptical Inquirer.*

Superstitious Thinking

Superstitious thinking is a special case of magical thinking in which a person believes that his actions determine the course of events, when in fact they don't. A familiar example is the tribal dance or sacrifice of a goat or a virgin girl to persuade the gods to deliver rain. The fact that nothing happens is not a disproof of the ritual, but a demand that it be done better. Sooner or later of course it rains, and this is taken as evidence that the gods are now pleased. The ritual is subjectively validated.

Behaviorist B.F. Skinner was able to demonstrate a striking analogy with this effect in pigeons. It is a well-established Skinnerian principle that behavior that occurs just prior to the click of the food dispenser in the animal's cage acts as a reward, which is to say that that behavior will tend to occur more often.

In his demonstration of superstitious behavior, Skinner put the food machine on a clock schedule which completely ignored the pigeon's behavior, just as weather patterns ignore the sacrifices of a particular tribe. But the pigeon was always doing something when the dispenser clicked, and was then more likely to repeat that last action, making it more likely to occur again at the time of the next click, which made the pigeon repeat it still more often. In a short time it was found that one pigeon was constantly turning circles, another was pecking obsessively in one corner, and another was repeatedly flapping its wings.

It might be going too far to say that the pigeons were subjectively validating a belief. It is apparent, however, that a random behavior that had been accidentally rewarded was now being repeated over and over. The fact that forty-nine repetitions produced no effect was no match for the fiftieth repetition that did. Thus, animals demonstrate even more clearly than people, attending to positive cases and ignoring negative ones.

Patterns

Students watching a football game on film see more violations by the other team.

Remote viewing judges with cues find strong matches between ESP records and target places. Judges without the cues find different matches more convincing.

Students expecting to find a correlation between mental symptoms and drawing features find it in data where the correlation is zero or even negative.

Students who know the outcome of a military battle find the outcome is well predicted by the story. Students who don't know the outcome find other results just as likely.

The ambiguous verses of Nostradamus are shown to have striking similarities with historical events. But a fresh look shows that each prophecy can be interpreted in many different ways, but only the matchmaking interpretation has been reported.

A physicist discovers N rays that change the visibility of objects. His brightness readings reflect his expectation of how strong the rays should be at the moment.

Native tribes go through rain dances to get rain; pigeons go through food dances to get food. Both dances get positive results.

In every case, a belief or expectancy of a cause-effect relationship is confirmed by a misperception of the data. More specifically, there is an exaggeration of the correlation, a making of matches, and a failure to grasp the anticorrelational evidence, the nonmatches. Whether it is the more basic error to see similarities at the expense of dissimilarities or to see positive evidence for the belief at the expense of negative evidence may depend on the strength of the belief, among other things. We can see, however, that subjective validation is a pervasive human fallacy.

Mistories

Subjective validation is particularly hard to escape when it comes to us ready-made by a creative author. If we need any more case studies in the art of rationalization, there are plenty of natural specimens to be found in Martin Gardner's compendium of pseudoscience, *Fads and Fallacies in the Name of Science* (Dover, 1957).

As we said in the last chapter, the formula for writing a pseudoscience bestseller is this. Choose an exciting hypothesis and then assemble all the facts or quotes that agree with it, and ignore any that don't. Latch on to the affirmative, eliminate the negative, and don't mess around with Mr. In-Between.

We list here three examples of popular *mistory* and the *mistorians* who have gotten rich by pawning them off as science.

The most outstanding example must be Erich von Däniken's *Chariots of the Gods?* (Corgi, 1971), not to mention his popular sequels, that weaves together a potpourri of history and archeology to suggest that man has been under UFO observation for many centuries. The curious reader will find a sufficient antidote in Ronald D. Story's *The Space-Gods Revealed* (Harper and Row, 1976; Barnes and Noble, 1978).

Carlos Castaneda's books on the teachings of don Juan, his never-seen Yaqui Indian sorcerer in Mexico, are so convincing that the third book was awarded a Ph.D. thesis in anthropology by the University of California at Los Angeles. If one takes Castaneda's works as an imaginative challenge to human consciousness, they are uplifting, like any good novel. But as anthropological research they belong in a separate reality in which fact and fiction are the same thing. One cure for Castaneda's psychedelic trip is given by Richard de Mille in *Castaneda's Journey: The Power and the Allegory* (Capra, 1976).

In some ways, the most transparent abuse of rational thought is provided by the Bermuda Triangle mistorians, such as Charles Berlitz. The theory is that ships and planes have been disappearing for a couple of centuries out of a particular area of the Caribbean Sea with the suggestion that they are being whisked away by outer-spacelings. In these stories there is a blatant disregard for elementary historical facts that point toward simple shipwrecks and airplane crashes, usually in stormy weather. Some of the demystifying details have been assembled by Larry Kusche in *The Bermuda Triangle Mystery—Solved* (Harper and Row, 1975)

A Personality Reading Just for You

We are now going to describe *your* personality. Ridiculous? We ask you to try to put your prejudices aside and read on with an open mind.

You have a need for other people to like and admire you, and yet you tend to be critical of yourself. While you have some personality weaknesses you are generally able to compensate for them. You have considerable unused capacity that you have not turned to your advantage. Disciplined and self-controlled on the outside, you tend to be worrisome and insecure on the inside. At times, you have serious doubts as to whether you have made the right decision or done the right thing. You prefer a certain amount of change and variety and become dissatisfied when hemmed in by restrictions and limitations. You also pride yourself as an independent thinker and do not accept others' statements without satisfactory proof. But you have found it unwise to be too frank in revealing yourself to others. At times you are extroverted, affable, and sociable, while at other times you are introverted, wary, and reserved. Some of your aspirations tend to be rather unrealistic.

Well, that's it. The next question is, how well does it fit you? Would you say:

EXCELLENT
GOOD
FAIR
POOR
WRONG

Now try to imagine how you would feel if you had answered a personality test for us three days ago, and this was our official report. Unless you are being very skeptical (skeptics will be the end of us), chances are you would at least say "FAIR" and more likely you would say "GOOD" or "EXCELLENT." At least, that is what college students do. Here is an example of what sixty-six students felt (data collected by RK in 1974).

Rating of Personality Report	Number of Students	%
EXCELLENT	20	44
GOOD	30	45
FAIR	6	9
POOR	1	2
WRONG	0	0
	66	

Oh, those New Zealand students, you say, a very gullible lot. Good thinking. You get A for prejudice. This result has been found repeatedly by psychologists all over America for the past thirty years. Or you might imagine that the result is produced by females (A for male chauvinism). There is no difference between men and women on this. Here are some examples of U.S. student reactions to the false personality report in their own words:

....a fine job with the material you had to work with... agree with all your statements.

....on the nose. Very good... all true without a doubt.

....brought out points which had worried me because I was not sure if I had imagined these to be personality traits of mine.

....I believe this interpretation applies to me individually, as there are too many facets which fit me too well to be a generalization.

....surprisingly accurate and specific in description.

(Ulrich, et. al., 1963)

After giving each student the *same* personality report, we reveal the hoax immediately by asking if any student will volunteer to read his or her "personality" to the class. As the reader gets into the sketch there is a restless titter, then some groans, then laughter, reading in chorus, and finally applause. When the exercise is well handled, students strongly approve of the ten-minute deception as an excellent lesson in fallacious thinking.

This all began in Los Angeles in 1948 when psychologist Bertram Forer accused a nightclub graphologist of peddling statements that were true of everybody—the handwriting expert replied that his art must be valid because his clients said his readings were correct. This made Forer wonder, do people really buy such general statements as being uniquely true for them? To find out, he bought an astrology book from a newsstand and wrote out the personality sketch we presented above and, sure enough, the students were completely taken in (Forer, 1949).

From our point of view, Forer's result is a special case of subjective validation in which we find ways to match ourselves up with the description given. Our personalities are not as fixed and constant as we usually imagine. Everybody is shy in one situation, bold in another, clever at one task, bumbling at another, generous one day, selfish the next, independent in one group of people but conforming in another group. Thus, we can usually find aspects of ourselves that will match up with a vague statement, although the specific examples of self will be different from one person to the next.

If you are told, "You have a great need for other people to like and admire you," you can recall your own particular thoughts of wanting to make friends or be more popular. If you are told nearly the opposite, for example, "You don't need other people to be your true self," you can recall personal times when you spoke your mind without regard for popular opinion, or alternatively, times when you just enjoyed being alone.

When we examine Forer's sketch more closely, it actually has several near opposites in it.

    a. You have personality weaknesses.
    b. You compensate for them (i.e., you have strengths).

    a. You are disciplined and self-controlled.
    b. You prefer change and variety, not restrictions and limitations.

    a. You need other people to like you.
    b. You do not accept others' statements without satisfactory proof.

    a. You are extroverted, affable, sociable.
    b. You are introverted, wary, reserved.

If somebody ever says, "Will the real (you) please stand up?" you would be perfectly right to reply, "What, *all* of us!" But most of us think in terms of a constant self, a predictable personality. We also imagine that certain people have the special power to see through our social pretenses and mind-read our private thoughts and feelings. The problem is, it is we who are doing all the matching up.

Forer's effect (he called it "the fallacy of personal validation") casts a whole new light on occult effects that tell people who they are, such as *astrology* and *horoscopes, biorhythms, palmistry, graphology, Tarot cards,* and *fortune telling.*

In each of these cases, a person is told (ambiguously) what kind of a day to expect, what kind of a person he is, or what the future will bring. But life itself is a fluctuating stream of diverse moments, and there is a good chance we can remember, or shall come upon, events that agree with the diagnosis. And, like students who get the Forer effect, we end up saying, but it was so specific, it was right on the nose! Meanwhile, the evidence against the validity of these occult prophecies keeps accumulating. (See issues of the *Skeptical Inquirer* for some of the negative evidence.)

Every time the victim gets personal validation he not only fools himself, but he gives the personality reader a dangerously false confidence in his powers of diagnosis. This is not only an occult problem, but applies to the personality descriptions that are thrust on people by psychologists, psychoanalysts, psychiatrists, doctors, lawyers, social workers, bureaucrats, teachers, and families. (Let's see, is there anybody we missed?) It spares no one who offers diagnoses about other people and their problems and who takes acquiescence by the victims as evidence that the diagnostician knows what he is talking about. There is even some suggestive evidence that these prophecies can become self-fulfilling, that people will see themselves in a new light and try to live up to, or down to, the diagnosis (Delaney and Woodyard, 1974).

Forer's result did not immediately make scientific history. Over the next twenty-five years there was a bare trickle of one-shot studies, and it languished as a curiosity item. Starting in the early 1970s, psychologist C.R. Snyder at Kansas State University picked up the banner and began to explore Forer's effect more systematically. To sketch out what is known about the effect, we borrow from an excellent review of the field by Snyder, Shenkel, and Lowery (1977), supplementing with some results of our own.

It doesn't matter very much what ritual is used to make a diagnosis. One can be just as convincing by asking for *birthdays* (especially to the hour and minute), for a sample of *handwriting,* for a *dream,* or for answers to a *personality test.* The test does not have to be the least bit reasonable—for example, the reader can use the North Dakota Null Hypothesis Brain Inventory in which the victim is asked to say true or false to items like, "I think beavers work too hard," and "I am never startled by a fish." (This pseudotest is another joke by campus humorist Art Buchwald.)

It is usually better to give the victim a favorable sketch than an unfavorable one because it is more likely to match the person's view of himself. In this case, it is not at all necessary for the reader to have high status or professional standing. However, if the report is a very negative one, status is useful. Psychiatrists are the best diagnosers for convincing people they are insane, after which they may well be.

To these findings we can now add a few of our own. (Research by RK.) We tried out drastically different wordings of the Forer sketch. For example, we gave one group of students a completely reversed sketch, in which every sentence was opposite to what Forer had written. This only reduced the average rating from GOOD+ down to FAIR+.

We then translated each Forer item into a very specific statement.

Instead of saying, "You have a tendency to be critical of yourself," we said, "Last year you were critical of your ability at sports." But even this unlikely sketch produced a FAIR+ rating.

We then tried out a sketch that was designed to be as wrong as possible. In a previous survey, we had asked 360 students to go through a list of sentences and check off any that applied to them. The list was a mixture of Forer sentences and of sentences that were thought to be very unlikely, which turned out to be correct. A typical Forer item was checked off by 60 percent of the students, while a typical bad item was checked by only 12 percent. Two of these items were, "Your boundless energy is a little wearisome to your friends," and "You seem to find it impossible to work out a satisfactory adjustment to your problems."

With a new group of students, we then went through the usual Forer procedure—collecting from each student a dream in his own handwriting (our standard procedure). But we gave back the 12 percent personality sketch a week later. The average rating was FAIR-. Out of fifty-two students, two rated it as EXCELLENT and nine rated it as GOOD.

This aroused our curiosity. If it doesn't matter so much what you say, what *does* matter? We got a strong answer in the next experiment.

Again, we went through the Forer procedure (collecting dreams in the students' own handwriting) and gave back personality sketches. But this time we broke the personality report into a long list of separately numbered sentences. Half these items were the sentences from Forer's sketch (60 percent sentences) and half of them were the bad items (12 percent sentences) from the last experiment. Some students found all the Forer items circled in pen as their report, while the others found all the bad items circled.

After the students made the usual overall goodness ratings, we asked them to go through the whole list carefully and place a check by each item we *should* have circled to be most correct.

The results were striking. Students given the Forer sketch agreed with us that, on average, 91 percent of the Forer sentences did apply to them, and also found that only 5 percent of the bad items should have been added. But the students given the unlikely personality sketch felt that only 16 percent of the Forer items should have been added, but they agreed that 50 percent of the bad items did apply to them as we had indicated. In other words, whatever we said was true, was true.

The conclusion is clear. While some statements are indeed more effective than others, the more important fact is whether or not some person takes the role of personality-teller and declares that certain statements are true. The Forer effect relies heavily on the power of suggestion. And as we have seen before, it doesn't seem to matter much if the reader has high status or not (except for very negative reports) or what pretense he uses for making his "diagnosis."

Personal validation has also cropped up in two studies of *biorhythm* readings. In both studies, college students were given an explanation of biorhythm theory and predictions about their high and low days (Bainbridge, 1978) or their "critical days" (DeMuth, 1979). Although the predictions were phony because they ignored biorhythm theory, students usually felt that they were correct. It may be added that both Bainbridge and DeMuth provide enough additional evidence to allow us to classify biorhythms as one of the sillier pseudosciences going today.

The point is this. The validity of fortune telling, horoscopes, biorythms, palm reading, psychological tests, and other diagnoses is in no way supported by the fact that people feel the readings are true.

Plausibility and Confidence

It is rarely indeed that people can collect the hard evidence needed to back up any of their beliefs. We are forced to take most of our knowledge on other people's word. But some beliefs remain very weak, while other ones seem more plausible, and still others have our absolute confidence. Once the belief reaches a high enough confidence level, subjective validation starts to work.

We now want to argue that the amount of time we put into reading or hearing about one theory or another builds up our associations to that idea, and then we use these associations to decide how plausible it is in a given case. This is an extension of the research and theory of Tversky and Kahneman (1973, 1974), the psychologists we met in the last chapter when we were trying to estimate number combinations (committees). Recall that Tversky and Kahneman said that the more easily we can think up examples of something, the more impressive it seems. Let us see how this might work more generally.

Consider the imaginary case of Albert the alcoholic. Albert's father has a head full of biblical phrases and religious rules. For him, Albert's problem is that he has drifted from God's ways and will not stop drinking until he returns to the fold.

Meanwhile, Albert's doctor, with a head full of physiology and neuroanatomy and biochemistry and pharmaceuticals, sees Albert's problem as a defect of body chemistry, which requires a different diet (and some medicine).

One type of psychiatrist has a head full of defense mechanisms, unresolved conflicts, and disease labels. He suggests that Albert is mentally ill and needs psychotherapy (at least) to get at the root problems.

Albert's social worker is educated to think in terms of social class, family problems, drinking buddies, and alienation from society. He thinks Albert needs a new "social support system" and recommends that "Albert join the A.A."

Obviously Albert's saviors cannot all be right, and they may all be wrong. But each one has bolstered his viewpoint with readings and shoptalk with colleagues and finds his own theory highly convincing.

In like manner, the UFO addict can rattle off a long history of close encounters and comment sagely on the number of stars in the universe that could have life-bearing planets. The astrology expert can amaze us with an elaborate discussion on the complex synchronies of the planets. The devotee of palmistry knows more about wrinkles on the hand than you have ever thought about and may further explain why these wrinkles have evolved as the only true signs of a person's destiny. Most convincing to some people is the graphologist who sees bold personalities in bold strokes of the pen, and careful personalities where the *i* is neatly dotted and the *t* is neatly crossed, and so on and on.

Unfortunately, it is not the *quantity* of evidence that makes an idea correct, but the *quality* of the evidence. Of course, the more that newspapers and TV bombard the public with unchecked occult happenings, the more believable they become, not by quality, but by quantity.

Betting on Yourself

In order to understand how people rate their confidence in their ideas and beliefs, let us take five examples of knowledge questions that differ in difficulty. The reader is invited to choose an answer for each one.

1. Three-fourths of the world's cocoa comes from:
   a. Africa
   b. South America

2. Which causes more deaths in the United States?
   a. appendicitis
   b. pregnancy, abortion, and childbirth

3. Adonis was the Greek god of:
   a. love
   b. vegetation

4. Kahlil Gibran was most inspired by:
   a. Buddhism
   b. Christianity

5. Potatoes are native to:
   a. Ireland
   b. Peru

Probably you feel more confident about your answers for some of these questions than for others. One way to get information on your confidence is to ask how much money you would bet on your different answers. More exactly, we can ask what odds you would give if somebody came along and bet you one dollar that your answer is wrong. If you bet only one dollar, then you are saying you are just as likely to be wrong as right. If you bet five dollars, your confidence is stronger. If you were willing to bet fifty dollars, your confidence is very high. To get the feel of this, go back and place your odds against one dollar for each of your answers. You can bet any sum you like.

Psychologists Fischoff, Slovic, and Lichtenstein (1977) used this betting method to find out if people's confidence in their beliefs is justified by their correctness. These researchers made up a long list of questions similar to the examples we gave above and presented them to students at the University of Oregon.

On each question, the student first chose his answer and then wrote down how many dollars he would bet that he was right against a one dollar bet that he was wrong. Now for each level of odds, there is a percentage of the time that one needs to be right to break even. For example, if you bet three dollars on each of one hundred different questions, you need to be right on seventy-five of them to break even. On the seventy-five right answers you will make seventy-five dollars, but on the twenty-five questions you get wrong you will also lose seventy-five dollars. The psychologists calculated these break-even percentages for all the different odds that the students used. Then they calculated the actual percent of the time that students were correct at each betting level, to see if they at least reached their break-even points.

There was, of course, a tendency for the students to be correct more often when they gave high odds than when they gave low odds. But the important finding was that the higher the odds they gave, the further they fell below the break-even percentage, and the more money they would have lost in real bets. A general summary of several of these experiments is given in Table 9.

TABLE 9
Results Showing Overconfidence in Belief

Bet Against $1	Break Even %	Average % Correct	% Over – Confidence	$ Lost Over 100 Bets
$ 1	50 %	53%	(none)	$ 6 (gain)
2	67	63	4 %	- 9
5	83	72	9	- 68
10	91	76	15	-164
20	95	78	17	- 362
50	98	79	19	- 971
100	99	80	19	- 1920
1000	99.9	81	19	-18919

Taking the third row in the table, we see that for 5 to 1 odds, the students should have been correct 83 percent of the time just to break even, but they were only correct 72 percent of the time. Thus, they were overconfident by 9 percent and would have lost sixty-eight dollars over 100 such bets. As we go up the betting levels, we see that the students' accuracy fell further and further behind, and their gambling debts shot up astronomically. Only 10 percent of the students did not make at least one extreme bet of five dollars or more while choosing a wrong answer.

Of course, when it comes to betting real money, college students can't afford to risk one hundred dollars or one thousand dollars. But when the Oregon psychologists' team set up an easier gambling situation, in which the students could win or lose about five dollars, the students were willing to bet real money on themselves—and lost about three dollars on average.

Oh yes, the answers to the five problems above are: 1-Africa, 2-appendicitis, 3-vegetation, 4-Christianity, 5-Peru. Admittedly, we chose these questions to trap you, but let us be clear about one thing: the Oregon psychologists showed that overconfidence occurred even when they did *not* ask trick questions.

It should not surprise us that people become overconfident about their pet ideas. According to subjective validation, a strong belief persuades people to notice the agreeable evidence but not the other kind. Consequently, we should be able to talk ourselves into believing we are right even when we are wrong.

Psychologist Stuart Oskamp captured subjective validation in action. Oskamp used the 1952 case history of Joseph Kidd, a twenty-nine-year-old veteran of World War II, a college graduate, and a business assistant in a flower decorating business. The details of the case history were revealed to Oskamp's students in four stages of Kidd's life up to age twenty-nine. After reading each stage, the students were asked to predict how Kidd usually behaved in certain other situations, which were not given in the story.

Over the four phases of Kidd's life, the student's accuracy in predicting his behavior remained constant at just above the chance level. At the same time, their confidence in their answers moved steadily upward to a very high level. In our terms, the students kept getting subjective validation of their initial beliefs about Kidd's personality.

The best example of overconfidence takes us back into the world of ESP. Barry Singer and Victor Benassi at California State University, Long Beach, put on a magic show involving a few simple tricks for a group of students. When the psychologists gave no explanation, 75 percent of the students said it was done by psychic powers. In other demonstrations, they explained to the students that the show they were about to see would be done by magic tricks, but about 60 percent of the students still said afterwards it must have been done by ESP. In the next group, they really emphasized that by magic tricks they meant only simple trickery, but 50 percent still rejected their explanation and said it had to be psychic. Since Benassi and Singer were certainly in the best position to know which it was, it seems rather incredible that the students insisted on their own false perception. Self-perpetuated beliefs die hard.

Looking Back

Somebody is sure to argue that we commit one of the very errors we have described—we have assembled all the evidence for self-perpetuating beliefs and not any evidence for true and accurate beliefs.

But let us remember, we set out to develop a working theory that would account for *false* beliefs, not beliefs in general. If we had set out to prove that people are fundamentally irrational, then we would indeed have built a one-sided case, but that was not our goal.

The fallacies we have taken up in this chapter have picked up on some quite new lines of psychological research. We have a number of "demonstration cases" of subjective validation, personal validation, and overconfidence but we can't yet say when and where they will occur.

The obvious thing to do is to remind ourselves of all those areas of human thought in which our beliefs are accurate, rational, and self-correcting. Let us remember that, when it comes to intelligence, no species of animal can hold a candle to the human mind, its language, its inventions, its discoveries, its ability to take control over nature.

But wait a minute, man has produced both good and ill effects with his ingenuity. And how do we know that we aren't just committing more self-perpetuating beliefs with these glib generalities. Which of the following would you be willing to describe as a fully rational human activity:

science?	medicine?
technology?	psychiatry?
commerce?	religion?
law?	education?
government?	family life?
news media?	personal life?

No one can deny that each of these activities and endeavours is based on a lot of human learning and experience, and each one "works" in some socially accepted fashion. But at the same time, each area may be plagued by mythologies and superstitions that have not been examined.

In this chapter, we went fishing to catch a salmon, but we seem to have hooked onto a whale, which is ripping our craft across the seas. Rather than cutting the line, perhaps we should hang on for one more chapter to see where the whale might be going.

13

THE ART OF DOUBT

...man's cognitive capacities are not adequate for the tasks which confront him.

K.R. Hammond

We started out to study ESP and ended up with a big question mark about the rationality of mankind. To do justice to this new topic would require several years more research and another book.

But there are important problems and challenges facing modern man, and we feel some responsibility to sketch out a positive approach to getting rid of self-perpetuating beliefs that stand in the way of a better future. We do this not only as research psychologists but also as human beings, interested in helping shape more rational solutions to the many social and psychological problems of our times.

The first thing we suggest is to reverse the negative connotations that are placed on *skepticism.* We shall argue that skepticism is an adaptive, creative, liberating, and positive mental attitude, and that we need to develop *the art of doubt* to get unstuck from some of our self-defeating practices. Once we learn to question our assumptions, we are free to apply our most creative tool: *the power of alternative thinking.*

The Power of Alternative Thinking

The British psychologist P.C. Wason (1960) has demonstrated how difficult it is for us to think of alternative explanations for a phenomenon once we hit on our first guess. He gave his students the following kind of problem.

I am thinking of a rule about numbers, about a series of three numbers. An example of the rule would be the numbers 2-4-6. Your job is to figure out what the rule is in as few tests as possible. You can test me asking any three numbers you want, and I will say YES if they agree with the rule and NO if they do not.

Most people notice that in 2-4-6 the numbers go up by twos. So they ask, 6-8-10? YES. 11-13-15? YES. "The rule must be numbers that go up by two."

But this is the wrong answer. The student has failed to consider what *alternative* rules could agree with his positive results.

We may offer the general proposition that positive cases, which seem to support our beliefs, make it all the more difficult to think up alternative explanations.

Consider a different student, who is not blinded in this way. He tests the theory of twos by trying not-twos. 10-15-20? YES. He tests the theory of equal intervals by trying unequal ones. 1-2-9? YES. He tests the theory that the numbers must increase. 7-5-3? NO. Thus, he homes in on the correct rule—any set of increasing numbers.

From this demonstration we learn a basic lesson. Any plausible theory can be supported by an endless stream of positive cases, just as there are endless trios of numbers that go up by twos. But it takes a special act of imagination—it takes alternative thinking—to see that a different theory could cover the same cases, and if it's any good, it will also cover negative cases that have previously been ignored.

All great scientific discoveries illustrate this point. Our direct perception tells us that the sun drifts overhead from east to west every day. At night time, the whole sky drifts overhead in the same direction. It took the brilliance of Copernicus to see that one gets the same effect by a rotating world, and one gets the seasons by placing the sun at the center of the "universe," with the earth revolving around it. The Church nearly put Galileo on the rack at age seventy for agreeing with this heresy.

Until Newton, people confidently explained the color effect of prisms by saying that the glass "darkens" white light according to its thickness, until Newton demonstrated that this was nonsense, and that the prism separates out the components of white light. Newton further went on to show that gravitation on earth was no different from the sun's pull on planets, both following the law that attraction is inversely proportional to the square of the distance.

Direct perception tells us that when two parents mate, their characteristics will be "averaged" in their offspring. But Mendel doubted this, and simply by keeping careful tallies over *two* generations of garden peas discovered the principle of dominant and recessive genes. Direct perception tells us that there are just so many species, presumably created by God, until Darwin and Wallace suggested you could get the same effect, and many other observable results, by a theory of natural selection.

Of course, few people are scientists at all, let alone great scientists. The power of alternative thinking can apply in anybody's life. We are overschooled in knowing the facts, having the answers, pretending to be "right." What if we had a system of education that insisted that we suspend judgment and question our assumptions? Psychiatrist R.D. Laing quotes from educator Jules Henry, and finishes the quote his own way:

> *If all through school the young were provoked to question the Ten Commandments, the sanctity of revealed religion, the foundations of patriotism, the profit motive, the two-party system, monogamy, the laws of incest, and so on...*
>
> *...there would be such creativity that society would not know where to turn.*

> R.D. Laing *(Politics of Experience,* 1967, p. 71.)

For the rest of this chapter, let us consider the possibilities of applying the art of doubt and alternative thinking against some conventional views of our own time. This is not to minimize human achievements, but to illustrate the difference between dogma and doubt, between rationalization and rationality, between subjective validation and alternative thinking.

Professional Overconfidence

One of the pioneers of American medicine was Dr. Benjamin Rush, an honest man and a patriot of the War of Revolution, whose clinical judgment told him that some diseases are best cured by draining blood from the patient. When Rush himself got sick, he demanded a personal bloodletting, and, although he nearly died from the treatment, he survived as another positive case in support of his theory. As for the many patients who did die, the negative cases, why, Rush declared the disease was too strong even for his cure. He didn't think of running a control group of unbled patients, and after all, how could he withhold his "cure" from the people who "needed" it? (Eisenberg, "Social Imperatives," 1977.)

Is this medical overconfidence a thing of the past? In a brilliant exercise in the art of doubt, Bakwin (1945) did a study on 1000 eleven-year-old children and found that only 390 still had their tonsils, due to the medical theory of the day. He sent these 390 children for medical check-ups and almost half were recommended for immediate tonsillectomy. He then sent the kids with "good" tonsils to another group of doctors, and again, nearly half needed tonsils out, the doctors said. By the end of the third round of check-ups, only 65 of the 1000 children would have had their tonsils if the doctors had been taken seriously, and with further check-up trials the number might have approached zero.

It is obvious that the doctors were not responding to a visible sign in the tonsils, but to their own expectations of how many tonsils ought to be bad. What, then, is the difference between bad tonsils and N rays?

The spirit of Benjamin Rush may still be with us in modern surgery. In 1978, the doctors in the Los Angeles area went on strike for over a month. Dr. Milton Roemer of the University of California noted that the rate of surgical operations fell by 60 percent during that period, and the overall death rate in Los Angeles fell by 27 percent. The death rate recovered to its normal level when the doctors went back to work. Perhaps, it is time that surgeons published their batting averages (against control groups) so that the public can judge whether they are practicing medicine or mythology.

The *power of the control group* to reveal the fallacy of "positive cases" is shown in a study of over 1000 heart attacks by a team of 13 physicians in England led by Dr. H.G. Mather of Southmead Hospital in Bristol. Until the Mather study, it seemed obvious that the only place to recover from a heart attack was in the engineered safety of the hospital. In the Mather study, about half the patients went home, sometimes because they chose to, and sometimes because they were ordered to. Half stayed in the hospital. A year later, 20 percent of the at-home patients had died, while 26 percent of the hospital patients had died (Cochrane, "World Health Problems," 1975).

Notice that *without* the control group, a doctor could honestly be impressed by the fact that hospital care had saved the lives of three out of four patients. Positive cases! Alternative thinker Ivan Illich (*Limits to Medicine,* 1976) suggests that this is only the tip of the iceberg, that medicine is detrimental to your health and a hazard to your life. Does this sound absurd? Well, we shall leave it to the reader to decide whether this is worth finding out.

In no sense are we saying that medicine is *all* mythology. Rather, we are noting that in our highest and most scientific profession it is not difficult to find self-perpetuating beliefs, and at the same time some impressive examples of alternative thinking. We cannot say whether or not Ivan Illich's all-out skepticism is totally justified, but in terms of our picture of subjective validation, it is certainly possible that a profession that has a total monopoly (or as Illich explains it, a radical monopoly) could be badly lacking in self-criticism and the art of doubt.

The problem of unreliable and meaningless diagnosis is seen even more clearly in psychiatry. Stanford psychologist D.L. Rosenhan (1973) persuaded eight healthy, normal people to go to hospitals with a single (trumped up) symptom of hearing voices that said "empty, hollow, thud," otherwise correctly reporting all the details of their normal lives. Four of these pseudopatients played the game twice so that twelve different hospitals were tested.

This test produced eleven diagnoses of *schizophrenia* and one diagnosis of *manic-depressive*. The length of hospitalization varied from one week to almost two months, although the actors behaved normally and reported no more symptoms from the time they were admitted. When they were discharged, their records were marked "schizophrenia in remission," meaning that they still had the disease, but the symptoms were temporarily absent.

Upon hearing of this experiment, another hospital declared that they could not be fooled in this way, so Rosenhan promised to send one or more pseudopatients their way. Although he did not actually send any, the hospital identified 21 percent of the real patients over the next three months as probable pseudopatients. In short, in the first experiment, all the sane people were diagnosed as psychotic, while in the second experiment, about one-fifth of the people with real problems were considered as possible fakes.

Many other studies pointing to diagnostic unreliability in psychiatry are reviewed by psychiatrist E. Fuller Torrey (*Death of Psychiatry,* 1975, chap. 4). One of these is particularly interesting because it confirms Fischoff's "hindsight" experiment (chapter 12) in which his students found evidence in a story (e.g., a military battle) that agreed with the outcome— *when* they knew the outcome. A more dramatic example of this effect was found by Temerlin and Trousdale (1969) in psychiatric diagnosis.

In this experiment, psychiatrists listened to a taped interview of a perfectly healthy and normal young mathematician. Half of the doctors were told nothing else. In this case most of the professionals said he was a normal person, a few said he was neurotic, and none suggested he was psychotic. The remaining psychiatrists, however, were told before they listened to the tape that the man being interviewed had been found by his own psychiatrist to be quite psychotic. In this situation, 40 percent of the psychiatrists listening to the tape found the man to be neurotic, while 60 percent agreed he was psychotic.

Just as medicine has found its total critic in Ivan Illich, psychiatry has been challenged *across the board* by three of its own professionals: Thomas Szasz (1961), who refers to the myth of mental illness; R.D. Laing (e.g., 1967), who describes psychiatry as inducting the hapless person into the role of mental patient; and E. Fuller Torrey (1975), who pronounces the imminent death of psychiatry as a profession. Again, we leave the task of judging the credibility of these massive reconceptualizations for the interested reader.

What we are seeing is that experience with positive cases can create self-perpetuating beliefs and overconfidence. When somebody comes along and applies the art of doubt, usually by running a control group experiment, the most basic claims to expertise, widely shared by the whole profession, may evaporate. We shall not try to document this for other professions, but one or two imaginary cases will make the point.

A business manager firmly believes that his judgment of human character is infallible. After interviewing thirty people for a job he hires fifteen. A year later, two of them have been dismissed (not to mention three who "left for good reasons"). The manager considers that thirteen out of fifteen is an outstanding performance. But since he never tries out anybody who doesn't please him, he can not discover that thirteen or even fifteen out of the fifteen he *didn't* hire would have been just as successful.

Based on his personal prejudices, a judge sends some people to jail for two years and lets others off with a warning, for the same offense. He is not surprised that two to three years later, the ones he sent to jail are back in court for another offense. Just what I thought, mutters the judge. It does not occur to him (alternative thinking) that jail is creating criminals, or that the police watch ex-convicts like hawks and arrest them on the least suspicion.

Of course, mental patients and criminals have subjective validation too and readily believe what people in authority tell them. So in a sense, we have a system of social roles and institutions that more or less works. Our point is simply that, until one applies alternative thinking, until one runs a control group experiment, the validity of professional dogma remains untested. Where the profession interferes with the lives of people and is backed up by the authority of the state, a system of alternative thinking, a devil's advocate wing, should be mandatory.

The Problem of Drug Abuse

Once we acknowledge that professions and the government have self-perpetuating beliefs, we begin to see things in a new perspective.

Consider four drugs which people take because they like, or once liked, their effects: alcohol, tobacco, marijuana, and tranquilizers. Of these, there can be no doubt that the first two are major public health problems (Miller, *Living in the Environment,* 1975, pp E120-E127). Alcohol not only destroys the liver, the brain, and the heart, it is strongly linked up with social and domestic violence. Tobacco doesn't contribute to violence, but its contribution to lung cancer, emphysema, and heart failure are widespread, and recent data suggest that cadmium is boosting hypertension. These two drugs are not only freely available on the market place for the profit of their industries, but until recently they were two of the most widely advertised products in all the media.

Tranquilizers (and antidepressants) also have initial pleasurable effects that soon become dependency problems. These are not advertised on the free market, but are freely dispensed by your doctor for the usual office fee and pharmaceutical mark-up.

Marijuana follows a similar pattern—novelty and euphoria gradually giving way to dependency and a felt need. In this case, however, distribution is a crime, and possession is at least a misdemeanor. Fifteen years of research on the genetic and social evils of "grass" have not confirmed the special health hazards it was assumed to have—at the same time, no comparable efforts have been made to determine the long-term hazards of tranquilizers. So, whether a mind drug is pushed, professionalized, or persecuted depends on who gets hold of it first—manufacturers, doctors, or youth cultures—not on how dangerous it has proved to be.

Thinking about the Future

ESP and other psychic fantasies seem to act as a kind of escapism from the really big issues of our times. For the first time in the history of two million years of evolution, man has created such a massive technological impact on nature, on his environment, on his life support system, that painful boomerang effects are probable unless we promptly reorganize our behavior and our technology.

The past successes of industry have generated a whole structure of overconfident assumptions of which the two most dangerous are *technological optimism* and *economic growthmania*.

An example of alternative thinkers in this situation are the ecologists. The attitude that distinguishes ecologists is their drive to get hold of The Big Picture. To an ecologist there are no independent sciences, there are no independent nations, there are no independent human activities, there are no independent processes in nature. Everything is intertwined. The power of the ecologists' arguments, the high batting average of their predictions, their sense of the human condition, are steadily winning recognition by alternative thinkers in every walk of life. They are as diverse in their testaments as Ivan Illich's *Tools for Conviviality* (1973), Ehrlich, Ehrlich, and Holdren's *Ecoscience* (1977), and the late E.F. Schumacher's *Small is Beautiful* (1974), to mention only five of the most visible new thinkers.

Early ecological messages were gloomy, and early ecological predictions were crude approximations. But in the brief span of one to two decades, this science and this movement have risen from total obscurity to a position of high credibility and leadership. Optimism and positive programs of action are now emerging at a rapid rate.

For a while technological optimism was like the mythical Gorgon— every time an ecologist cut off one head, two more grew in its place. People believed the most incredible fantasies about how we could export the surplus human population into space, or feed the masses by farming the ocean, or discover new oil fields as fast as we used up the old ones, and on and on. Patiently, the ecologists considered each of these engineering solutions and patiently showed how each one was preposterous or self-defeating, Gradually, the message has begun to seep into public awareness: man does not control nature; nature controls man. Unlimited wasteful technology contradicts itself by destroying its own resources.

To take just one example of technological overconfidence, the nuclear power industry has bombarded the public with its scientific razzmatazz about its fail-safe nuclear electricity plants. What greater glory (and profit) could there be than to supply people with a new source of energy? The bottom line in these predictions was the promise that a serious nuclear accident has the same remote probability as a meteorite landing on a major city. In that case, a big meteorite landed outside Harrisburg, Pennsylvania in April 1979 when the Three Mile Island nuclear plant had a crash that just barely escaped a meltdown and possibly one of the biggest man-made catastrophes in human history. In America alone, there are about sixty other such plants humming away today with the same lethal potential.

Even more amazing is that all of these plants have been built *before anybody has figured out what we are going to do with the radioactive wastes they are producing, which will be lethal for hundred or thousands of years to come.* Oh yes, we are going to shoot them off into space, or drop them in the antarctic icecap, or bury them in salt mines—there are lots of plans on the drawing boards, but as each one is investigated, it turns out to have crucial loopholes and risks. The technological Gorgon is finally running out of heads.

Most of the people who are called "scientists" today are actually technicians, paid to do a job by some industry or government department. In that role, their consciousness and purpose is restricted by the assumptions and profit goals of company managers or government departments. Thus, the vast bulk of "science" today is organized into the service of technological production. Even the company managers cannot afford to inquire about the social value of their products—that is to be decided in the free market place.

> *The social scene today is nowadays characterized by the existence of a large number of self-maximizing entities which, in law, have something like the status of "persons"—trusts, companies, political parties, unions, commercial and financial agencies and the like. In biological fact these entities are precisely not persons and are not even aggregates of whole persons. They are aggregates of parts of persons. When Mr. Smith enters the board room of his company, he is expected to limit his thinking narrowly to the specific purposes of the company or to those of the part of the company he "represents."*

Gregory Bateson *(Steps to an Ecology of Mind, 1973, p. 421.)*

Even where scientific research is not so tightly controlled by the man who pays the salary, there remains the danger of overspecialization and short-sightedness. When new high-yield varieties of rice and wheat were developed, it was boldly announced that the Green Revolution would solve the world's food problems. This has turned out to be a false prophecy because the Green Revolution requires high inputs of fertilizers, pesticides, irrigation water, and generally works best with westernized farming technology. Even where these problems have been solved, the new farming methods have sometimes created social and economic disruption. While the Green Revolution is indeed an important step forward, it has not changed the fact that greatest famine in human history is happening today.

Economist E.F. Schumacher points out the problem of short-sighted thinking in his own field.

> *About the* fragmentary *nature of the judgments of economics there can be no doubt whatever. Even within the narrow compass of the economic calculus, these judgments are necessarily and methodically narrow. For one thing they give vastly more weight to the short than to the long term, because in the long term, as Keynes put it with cheerful brutality we are all dead.*

> E.F. Schumacher *(Small Is Beautiful,* 1974, p. 35.)

With science so heavily implicated in the fallacies of technological optimism and its ecological follies, the very concept of science as a rational activity has come into question. We could almost ask if science is rational? But ecology is also a science, an alternative thinking science. We must not confuse science with technology.

> *It is said that science will dehumanize people and turn them into numbers. This is false, tragically false. Look for yourself. This is the concentration camp and crematorium at Auschwitz. This is where people were turned into numbers. Into this pond were flushed the ashes of some four million people. And that was not done by gas. It was done by arrogance. It was done by dogma. It was done by ignorance. When people believe that they have absolute knowledge,*

with no test in reality, this is how they behave.

J. Bronowski *(Ascent of Man,* 1973, p. 374.)

Deception and Society

Some people have argued that it doesn't matter if Uri Geller is only a magician, because in that case he has played an excellent and entertaining joke on society. Perhaps. But it seems wrong to us to wink at deception used in support of a false scientific theory.

Whatever dangers there may be in subjective validation, they are multiplied many times over when combined with deception and information control, so that they cannot be checked by alternative thinking.

We expect a magician to deceive us, but we do not expect him to carry out the game when he goes offstage, thus misrepresenting himself as a person and the meaning of what he is doing. It is not clever magic to say that one's magic is not magic, it's just cheating.

How far should we excuse deliberate deception? For three years of Watergate investigations, Richard M. Nixon tried out a whole series of maneuvers that were sufficient to cause any reasonably skeptical person to see that he wasn't going for an open disclosure. First the bugging was passed off as some local amateur job. That didn't hold, so Nixon hired his own special prosecutor with limited powers, and then he fired that one and got another one. Eventually some tapes were released and they contained erasures, and other tapes were held back for "national security" or by presidential privilege. Meanwhile Spiro Agnew, the Vice President, had to resign for previous swindling, and eventually, on top of the Watergate debacle, Nixon was caught in apparent tax evasions.

All the while large segments of the public refused to believe that Nixon was directly involved. Or they said he was only doing what the other side wanted to do. And then they said that impeachment would hurt the prestige of the American presidency. And finally the process of public disclosure was brought to a halt by President Gerald Ford's act of pardon. Shortly after, deception and cover-ups were found in the CIA, the FBI, the Lockheed scandals, and so on. It appears that we are gradually accepting the philosophy that cheating is normal and is okay if it supports our personal interests, our team, our loyalties, our beliefs, or the status quo. In the long run, a society that does not place truth above all current beliefs may discover too late it has been living on illusions.

Rationality and Personal Happiness

Nothing we have said suggests that people should spend a lot of time trying to make their personal lives into a scientific enterprise. On the contrary, it is man in the service of technology and commerce who endangers his sensibilities, his emotional richness, his love, his humanity.

One of the self-perpetuating beliefs of the modern industrial society is that happiness is gained through money and possessions. In fact psychologist Angus Campbell (1976) has found that there is very little connection between family income and happiness. At every level of income in American society, we find the same distribution of life feelings, from misery to joy. Nor does it matter whether one is a man or a woman, young or old, well educated or poorly educated.

We do find, however, that happiness depends on how each person views his or her life situation. Those who are constantly striving to have more than they can get are consistently unhappy. Even more than this, happy people have different assumptions about life.

To illustrate, consider ten statements that are *examples* taken from a happiness questionnaire by one of the authors (Kammann, 1979).

Everything is going right for me.
I feel loved and trusted.
My work gives me a lot of pleasure.
I feel I'm a complete person.
My future looks good.
I'm making the most out of life.
I think clearly and creatively.
I smile and laugh a lot.
I feel life is meaningful.
The results I have obtained make my efforts worthwhile.

These items weren't just made up arbitrarily. They were discovered to be the kinds of feelings about life that happy people have. By happiness we don't mean here a momentary state of joy or elation, but rather a general sense of well-being and harmony with life. It is a state of being from which joy may often spring up.

Now based on Campbell's data, it isn't our life situation that matters, but how we view it. Or as Shakespeare put it, "There's nothing either good or bad but thinking makes it so." But what kind of thinking helps people be happy? We are just beginning to get an idea on this.

Psychologist Wayne Dyer (1977) wrote a popular book, *Your Erroneous Zones,* that distills a lot of current psychological thinking into everyday language for the purpose of helping people improve their happiness and mental health. But first of all, how do we know that Dyer is right, and second, how much do people get out of reading a book if they don't stop and think about it? So just about simultaneously, both authors and one of our students thought of running a discussion group course mainly using Dyer's points, to see if anybody's happiness actually improved. Here is a *sample* of Dyer's pro-happiness beliefs we used as discussion topics:

I value my own happiness and mental health.
I can choose my emotions and feelings.
I can change my personality.
I accept myself with my imperfections.
I don't need the approval of others.
I can be free from guilt and worry.
I can live in the present.
I can accept the world as it is without complaining.
I can act independently on my own feelings and beliefs.
I am ready to try out new experiences.

Now if Dyer's approach is correct, then we should expect that people who agree with beliefs like these are happy people. And that was the first result we got in a group of twenty-four people—the more they said they "definitely agree" with the kinds of beliefs shown above, the higher they scored on the happiness questionnaire. In fact there was almost a one-to-one correspondence between having the pro-happy beliefs and actually being happy. This was before the "happiness course" started.

The next result was that when twenty people went through the discussion group, not only did they increase their agreement with the pro-happy beliefs, but their happiness also increased. Finally, *how much* their happiness increased corresponded very closely to *how much* they increased their acceptance of the pro-happy beliefs (Lichter and Kammann, 1979).

One swallow doesn't make a summer, and one experiment doesn't make a psychological theory. But these first results suggest that people may develop self-perpetuating beliefs that sometimes get them into a rut of misery and depression. These include demands that one's self or the world should be different than it is, and that one cannot change one's self, one's situation, one's activities, or one's view of the world. These are self-defeating beliefs.

Meanwhile, David Marks, together with Paul Sulzberger and Ian Hodgson, has been finding out what makes it possible for people to give up smoking (Sulzberger, Marks, and Hodgson, 1979). Again, we find that there are beliefs that get in the way of change, the belief, for example, that it takes a high degree of will power, because quitting is always very difficult. Then, when the person tries to quit he finds many rationalizations, such as, "One more won't hurt," or "I can reward myself with a cigarette now that I have kept off them for a half of day," or "I'm under such pressure that I need a cigarette to calm my nerves," and so on.

The starting premise in the Isis Smoking Cessation Program is that anybody can quit smoking and do so effortlessly and without will power, using a variety of methods of cognitive control. In the course of five sessions over one week, the volunteers begin to replace their old habits of thought by memorizing a few simple instructions that they rehearse during the day. Each cigarette from that time on is smoked very consciously and deliberately, with full awareness of what one is doing. Techniques of meditation and relaxation are introduced to make the transition smooth and painless. By the end of the week, 83 percent of the group have quit smoking (a result observed in well over one thousand people) and of these people 54 percent are still totally abstinent one year later.

These two experiments, one on happiness and one on quitting smoking, illustrate powers of the mind that, unlike ESP, are real, observable, and personally useful.

A Skeptical Model of ESP

We have taken a long detour through a kind of dialectic seesaw between two kinds of mental attitudes. The first is the self-perpetuating belief, subjective validation, rationalization. The second is the self-correcting belief, alternative thinking, rationality. We did this because, having raised the question of the first case, we had to consider its possible significance. It is time to get back to the problem of ESP.

Subjective validation is no evidence one way or the other about the truth of ESP. That can only be decided by the evidence for or against ESP itself. We have found the evidence to be unconvincing. Rather, it follows the same pattern of deception and error that Hansel (1966) demonstrated for the best ESP experiments in earlier days. Consequently, we have the problem of explaining the prevalence of its belief, and this led us to our concept of subjective validation.

We end up with an alternative model of psychic belief. In our view, the initial stimulus is the oddmatch illusion, which is a common experience in everyday life. It is an illusion because we cannot see the processes that allow it to occur as a probability match. Interestingly, many or most parapsychologists and psychic buffs report some amazing personal experience that set off their search for ESP.

Once the theory of ESP (or any other psychic and occult belief) becomes established, it is susceptible to subjective validation, which allows it to build up to a high level of overconfidence. Positive cases are noted, while negative ones are overlooked or explained away.

Some of the people who have these compelling oddmatch experiences will be scientists, and some of these will go into the laboratory to study the phenomenon they and so many other people have experienced.

In the systematic observation of the laboratory, however, the ESP effect turns out to be extremely elusive. Since the scientist "knows" it is there, endless runs of negative results are merely interpreted as failures to capture the "right conditions."

At this point, the normal fallacies of human observation begin to creep back into the picture in a new and subtle way. Multiple tests are run on the data for psi-missing as well as psi-hitting, or for precognition or postcognition. Experimental controls are not kept tight because the researcher is not exercising the art of doubt, he is not trying to convince himself, but to find the evidence that will verify everybody's experience. Occasionally, a statistically significant effect crops up, as it is sure to do given enough opportunities, and the more so when the data are double-checked on negative findings but not so on positive ones. These now-and-then results get published often enough to keep the field alive.

The overconfidence that ESP is "there" drives some researchers to minor fudging of the data and a few to outright fraud. J.B. Rhine, the founder and undisputed leader of scientific parapsychology, has forthrightly described the difficulties of keeping dishonesty out of his ESP laboratory at Duke University. In one paper Rhine ("Security versus Deception," 1974a) describes twelve cases of would-be parapsychologists whose conduct ranged from highly suspicious to those who were directly caught cheating (four cases). In a subsequent paper Rhine ("Case of Experimenter Unreliability," 1974b) describes a new case, Walter J. Levy, whom Rhine had considered an able colleague and a trusted friend, but who had been caught red-handed fudging his data.

By no means are these pitfalls of research, including fraud, unique to parapsychology. Psychologist Theodore X. Barber, already well recognized for his research in hypnosis, has conducted a superb exercise in the art of doubt, detailing the fallacies and pitfalls that can plague research in mainstream psychology (Barber, *Pitfalls in Human Research,* 1976). Like Barber, we know that psychological research can be fallible, and that we ourselves are fallible. At the same time, psychological research has many well-replicated findings. We are suggesting the possibility that parapsychology's difficulty in obtaining a repeatable effect under tightly controlled conditions is that there is no real phenomenon to be found.

This is a heretical position to take when so many scientists have moved toward a position of "open-mindedness." We also are open-minded but, so far, we keep finding deception and experimental errors. Nothing would please us more than to see a reliable demonstration of a new channel of human perception and communication, for at that moment, we could all study it to explore its properties. In the meantime, it appears to us that the study of ESP is a study of human illusion, sometimes fostered by human deception.

Subjective validation is not unique to psychic belief, but is a regular part of human life and thought. While the belief in ESP may itself be a harmless illusion, we have tried to indicate how the same cognitive fallacies may have real importance in our social institutions and in the way we shape our future.

APPENDIX I

POPULATION STEREOTYPES AND ESP

In chapter 5 ("Kreskin's Riddle Solved"), we reported a preliminary experiment on population stereotypes. We then decided to conduct a follow-up study to be sure that the result was reliable, even if we could not explain it.

At the same time, we had an opportunity to see if we could get any evidence for ESP by instructing the senders to concentrate on certain target messages.

We chose five problems of the type which Kreskin and Geller have used. They were:

1. *I am thinking of a number between 1 and 10, for example, a number like 3, but it's not 3. Write down the first number which comes to your mind.* (The sender concentrated on 4.)

2. *I am thinking of two simple drawings. I will concentrate on both of them for about two minutes. I'm concentrating now.* (One sender concentrated on an axe and an umbrella; another concentrated on a lamp and a kettle.)

3. *I am now thinking of any two-digit number, I am concentrating on it. Write it down.* (One sender concentrated on 43, another on 61.)

4. *This time I am thinking of two simple geometric forms, and one is inside the other. You can write down which shape is inside the other one—you don't need to draw them.* (One sender concentrated on an oval inside a cube, another on a rectangle inside a star, and another on a trapezoid in a hexagon.)

5. *I am thinking of a number, this time between 1 and 50. However, in this number, both digits are odd, but they are not the same odd digits. For example, the number could be 15 because it has two different odd digits, but it wouldn't be 11 because both odd digits are the same. Okay? I am concentrating on the number now.* (The three different senders concentrated on 15, 17, and 19 respectively.)

The senders in these experiments were five psychology or education instructors at other universities whom we did not know personally. We got their cooperation through their department heads. Not all senders were given all five problems. We were worried that the results of one number problem might be influenced by another number problem, so we deleted some problems at some universities. These experiments were run in large lecture classes in introductory psychology or education and the results were sent back to us for analysis. As a result of our experimental plan, and of the two universities that did not answer, the number of students answering a problem varied from nearly two hundred (problem 1) up to about seven hundred (problem 2).

According to most varieties of ESP theory, not everybody has or uses ESP ability. So, we asked how often each student experienced ESP. Students who said *never* or *very few times* were classed as Insensitives, whereas if they said *many times* or *very frequently,* they were Sensitives.

In addition, whenever a student felt that a particular response might have been received by ESP during the experiment, he made a checkmark by his answer. We called these "tingle" responses.

The Population Stereotypes

The strength of the stereotypes was impressive. On the number between 1 and 10 (but not 3), there was a cluster of responses at the numbers 6-8 with a peak at 7. This cluster accounted for 62 percent of all answers, instead of the 30 percent expected by chance.

For the two simple drawings, the most popular responses were: house, circle, square, stick figure of a person, triangle, boat, tree, and cat. These eight choices covered 69 percent of the drawings.

For the two-digit number from 10 to 99, there was a strong cluster at 21-23 with a peak at 22, and a second cluster at 11-13 with a peak at 12. These six numbers accounted for 43 percent of all replies, instead of the 7 percent expected by chance. These choices were "stolen" from the multiples of 10—not one student in 350 chose 30, 40, 50, 60, 70, or 90 (one chose 80).

For the two geometric forms, the circle-triangle combination accounted for 34 percent by itself, with the triangle *inside* circle on 25 percent of all choices.

For the number between 1 and 50 with the two different odd digits, the most popular choice was 37, accounting for 33 percent, with numbers 35 and 39 being the next in line.

These patterns of stereotypes were very consistent from one class of students to another and from one university to another. The basic results are shown in the tables at the end of this Appendix.

The ESP Results

For our ESP targets, we made an effort to avoid choosing stereotypes, and succeeded all too well. On the problems with many possible choices (two drawings, geometric figures, any number from 10 to 99), there were only 4 target matches out of 1642 responses. Even these 4 cannot be reasonably interpreted as ESP since there were also 6 probability matches (in the same 1642 responses) in which a student's response matched up with a target that was not being sent in his room, but that was designated as the target for another group.

When the number of choices was very restricted, as for the number from 1 to 10, or the two-odd-digits-between-1-and-50, there were of course more target hits, but they were still well below chance levels if all choices had been equally probable.

The two-odd-digits problem gives us a special opportunity to test for ESP, because there were three different targets sent at three different universities: 15, 17, or 19. Together, these three numbers were chosen by 83 students, which is sufficiently large for further analysis. If ESP is working, we must expect that these numbers will be chosen more often when they are used as targets than when they are not. The number of students (out of 682) choosing these numbers when they were targets was 27, for a success rate of 4.0 percent. However, the number choosing them when they were not targets was 56, or almost exactly double, which results from the fact that there were always two numbers acting as nontargets in each group. The success rate for these accidental matches is 4.1 percent. Once again we find no evidence of ESP.

The percentage of students who were Sensitives was 19.5 percent, leaving 80.5 percent as Insensitives. Of the total of thirty-eight target matches on all problems, we should therefore expect, on a random basis, that about seven should come from Sensitives and about thirty-one should come from Insensitives. The actual results were five and thirty-three, respectively; there was no tendency for Sensitives to be on target more often. When we looked at all responses, we found that the Sensitives conformed almost perfectly to the same stereotype patterns produced by Insensitives.

The percentage of all responses which were marked as psychic tingles was 21.3 percent, leaving 78.7 percent non-tingles. There was only a small tendency for tingles to occur more often among Sensitives (31.7 percent) than among Insensitives (18.8 percent), so it seemed worthwhile to analyze tingles as a completely separate test of ESP. Based on the overall tingle rate, chance leads us to expect that about eight target matches should have been tingles, leaving thirty to come from non-tingles. The actual results were seven tingles and thirty-one non-tingles, showing again no evidence for ESP. Instead tingle responses merely conformed to the basic pattern of population stereotypes.

In all the 2521 responses which we collected in this experiment, we did not find a single statistical trend that pointed toward psychic communication. Although we were open-minded, we minimized the possible charge of skeptical influence by having the experiment conducted remotely by people we did not choose or know. We also gave separate attention to the answers of psychic Sensitives, and to those answers checked as psychically significant, with no better results. Our negative results agree with Hardy and Harvie (chapter 11).

It might be argued that the population stereotypes reflect bursts of cross-talk ESP among the students. (In ESP theory, anything is possible.) This would not explain, however, why exactly the same stereotypes occurred in different classes and different universities.

We must ask why students who felt they frequently had ESP experiences (the Sensitives) showed no sign of it in this experiment. One obvious answer is that we (and Hardy and Harvie) did not capture the right conditions. We have no objection to this reply as long as psychic researchers will start tallying failures and not just the apparent successes. But what if there is no ESP? Then we would have to guess that our

Sensitives are people whose beliefs persuade them to interpret their oddmatch experiences as examples of ESP.

We are more in the dark on the cause of "tingles," the illusion that a particular answer was possibly psychic, but we can hazard the following guess. It is well known that reaction times are faster on some trials than others, in a somewhat random fashion. It is possible that when students got particularly fast (or subjectively clear) associations, they took that as evidence of ESP.

In contrast to the imaginary ESP signals, the population stereotypes came through loud and clear. Unfortunately, there has been very little theoretical research on these associative clusterings, so we cannot yet name the factors that govern them. They do, nevertheless, illustrate the second root of coincidence, the unseen cause which produces unexpected results.

POPULATION STEREOTYPES
Two Simple Drawings

house, building	94
circle	93
square	77
stick figure	61
triangle	57
boat	40
tree	38
cat	26
Star of David	17
face	16
fish	16
flower	15
cube	13
sun	12
dog, horse	10
car	10
apple, pear	7
all other	100
	702

POPULATION STEREOTYPES

Number from 1-10 (not 3)		Two Geometric Forms		Odd Digits Number (1-50)	
Response	No.	Response	No.	Response	No.
1	4	circle-triangle	203	13	28
2	6	circle-square	146	15	9
3	10	triangle-square	66	17	51
4	7	two of the same		19	23
5	25	figures	28	31	51
6	37	all other	147	35	159
7	63			37	226
8	23			39	100
9	21			Other	35
10	1				
	197		590		682

Any Two-Digit Number
(N = 350)

Response	No.	Response	No.	Response	No.
10	5	40	0	70	0
11	17	41	0	71	1
12	24	42	2	72	2
13	12	43	5	73	2
14	7	44	2	74	0
15	4	45	2	75	0
16	4	46	3	76	0
17	5	47	7	77	1
18	5	48	0	78	2
19	3	49	0	79	2
20	4	50	0	80	1
21	18	51	4	81	2
22	45	52	3	82	0
23	34	53	2	83	0
24	9	54	3	84	2
25	4	55	5	85	0
26	4	56	5	86	3
27	16	57	3	87	2
28	2	58	1	88	1
29	3	59	0	89	0
30	0	60	0	90	0
31	1	61	3	91	0
32	3	62	1	92	0
33	5	63	3	93	0
34	2	64	3	94	0
35	3	65	1	95	1
36	5	66	2	96	0
37	7	67	3	97	0
38	0	68	1	98	3
39	3	69	2	99	5

APPENDIX II

RULES FOR RATIONALS

Having confronted so many varieties of rationalization we wondered, almost whimsically, if we could construct a set of rules for rationals. While very few people can be scientists, and very few really want to be, anybody can be rational if he wants to.

The art of doubt can be fun, like having the only pin at a balloon party. But it is important to make a distinction between confronting an idea and confronting a person. It is one thing to show that an idea is wrong and quite another to show that a person is wrong. The object is never to win, only to learn. When you win, you lose.

For some unknown reason a lot of people have got it into their heads that they have to "be right" in order to be lovable, respectable, and happy. And yet who is more lovable and worthy of our respect than the person who says, "Say, you're absolutely right. Fancy that, all my life I have believed just the opposite, and I was completely wrong." This is a person with real self-confidence, with humility, with flexibility. For him it is more important to learn the truth of things than to appear to be right.

For a rational person, no idea is sacrosanct or above challenge, including his own ideas. For him, "being right" is a posturing game, and a serious source of human frustration and confusion. The rational person finds it equally amusing to discover that his opinions and views are right *or* wrong.

When two rational people sit down to talk, they have a wonderful freedom to play with ideas. One can offer a proposition, while the other can be the devil's advocate who tries to destroy it. In the middle, they can switch roles. Or they can jointly brainstorm an idea to see how far they can push it.

When a rational person meets a rationalizing person, he finds discussion to be a waste of time, because it is not a learning opportunity, except to learn how this person carries out his rationalizations. Having no interest in "being right" or in causing useless upset and distress, the rational person drops the discussion.

1. If-what-then-what. Many beliefs are stated in such vague terms that even the author doesn't know what they mean. They are judged on their esthetic merits, like a painting. To bring a belief down to earth you can ask what it predicts, what it means in terms of if-what-then-what. For example, a person offers the opinion that we have hardly begun to grasp the possibilities of cosmic consciousness. You ask what he means, and get another string of words you don't understand. So then you might say, if I have cosmic consciousness, how will my life be different?

2. Disprovability. This is another way of stating rule 1. Instead of repeating if-what-then-what, you may need to shift gears and ask, what piece of evidence would make your theory incorrect? For example, the believer says, lots of people have mental telepathy. You can startle his logic by asking, what kind of evidence would make him change his mind. Since he has only thought in terms of positive cases, this will add a new dimension to the discussion.

3. The Burden of Proof. The burden of proof is on the believer. A person asks, why are you so skeptical about UFOs. It is easy to fall into the trap of trying to give reasons why UFOs are improbable. The best answer is, why do you *believe* in UFOs?

4. Alternative Thinking. When evidence is presented, you may ask (or just wonder) if there is any explanation that could produce the same results. For example, the advocate says, modern medicine has increased our life expectancy from thirty-five years to seventy years. You could ask if anything else could have done it, even if you don't have a hypothesis, like diet, sanitation, housing, immunity, etc. *Alternative thinking is your most creative tool.*

5. *Missing Negative Cases.* This rule has three applications.

a. Probability Matches. We demonstrated in chapter 11 that one needs to count all possible events including negative cases to see how often a result might occur by chance in the long run.

b. Sometimes negative cases are ruled out by an escape clause. For example, the reason that UFOs are never photographed clearly is that they always run away from cameras. People may see them clearly, but bring out a camera and away they go. This is like the "negative vibes" clause in ESP theory.

c. Sometimes the negative cases have been literally eliminated. An educator reports a survey showing that senior students all love high school, overlooking the fact that all the drop-outs were not interviewed. The story is told of a British officer who proposed to add armor plates to certain sections of Royal Air Force planes during World War II. He presented a diagram showing the regions with a high density of gunnery scars after combat missions. But Winston Churchill said maybe he should put the armor everywhere else because he had only studied the planes which came back.

6. *Personal Observation.* What a person has observed in his personal or clinical experience is no evidence for his belief. Unless he has at least kept a written tally of positive and negative cases, you can reasonably assume he is giving his subjective validations.

7. *Testimonials.* The worst kind of evidence for a belief about human nature comes from people's experience of themselves. We recently met a man who claimed that the key to giving up smoking was simple will power, which he had demonstrated himself. As the story went on, it turned out that he had developed a chronic chest complaint that got worse, and his doctor told him that if he didn't quit smoking he would soon die. Above all, remember the Forer effect—fortune tellers (even in plain clothes or white coats) always seem to be right.

8. *Sources.* It is always helpful to find out where a person got his ideas. This may turn out to be a completely frivolous source like a newspaper or a TV program. If the source sounds more credible than that, you may decide it's worth looking up. But you can always apply the short-cut rule—if the believer can't make a plausible case himself, forget his sources.

9. Emotional Commitment. If the person advocating an idea is committed to it emotionally, if he cannot consider being wrong in a matter-of-fact style, then you are wasting your time for two reasons. First, your questions are threatening his personal beliefs for no good purpose (unless he is doing public harm). Second, you can reasonably assume that his theory is false. Of course, this is not inevitably so. But it is unlikely that an emotionally committed person has weighed his evidence pro and con. He is advocating a belief that feels good to him.

10. The Ad Hominem Technique. This Latin phrase means "to the man." It has many variations. First, a believer may hold certain authorities to be infallible, and quote their opinions as evidence. Second, he may try to place contrary believers into a category of bad people and thus reject their arguments out of hand. Third, he may turn against you, accusing you of bad motives or stupidity. All of these arguments are fallacious, and it is not only important to recognize them, but also not to use them. The object is to learn, not to win.

REFERENCES

Bainbridge, W.S. Biorhythms: evaluating a pseudoscience. *The Skeptical Inquirer*, 2 (1978), pp. 40-55.

Bakwin, H. Pseudodoxia pediatrica. *New England Journal of Medicine*, 232 (1945), 691-697.

Barber, T.X. *Pitfalls in Human Research: Ten Pivotal Points.* New York: Pergamon, 1976.

Bateson, G. *Steps to an Ecology of Mind.* Frogmore, St. Albans, England: Paladin, 1973.

Bronowski, J. *The Ascent of Man.* London: British Broadcasting Corporation, 1973.

Campbell, A. Subjective measures of well-being. *American Psychologist*, 1976, 117-124.

Chapman, L.J. and Chapman, J.P. Genesis of popular but erroneous psychodiagnostic observations. *Journal of Abnormal Psychology*, 72 (1967), 193-204.

Cochrane, A.L. World health problems. *Canadian Journal of Public Health*, 66 (1975), 281-287.

Delaney, J.G. and Woodyard, H.D. Effects of reading an astrological description on responding to a personality inventory. *Psychological Reports*, 37 (1974), 1214.

de Mille, R. *Castaneda's Journey: The Power and the Allegory*. Santa Barbara, California: Capra, 1976.

DeMuth, P. Wobbly biorhythms. *Human Behavior,* April 1979, pp. 53-55.

Diaconis, P. Statistical problems in ESP research. *Science,* 201 (1978), 131-136.

Dooling, J.D. and Lachman, R. Effects of comprehension on retention of prose. *Journal of Experimental Psychology,* 88 (1971), 216-222.

Dyer, W.W. *Your Erroneous Zones*. London: Sphere Books, 1977.

Ehrlich, P.R., Ehrlich, A.H., and Holdren, J.P. *Ecoscience: Population, Resources, Environment*. San Francisco: W.H. Freeman, 1977.

Einhorn, H.J. and Hogarth, R.M. Confidence in judgment: persistence of the illusion of validity. *Psychological Review,* 85 (1978), 395-416.

Eisenberg, L. The social imperatives of medical research. *Science,* 198 (1977), 1105-1110.

Evans, C., Parapsychology—what the questionnaire revealed. *New Scientist,* 25 January 1973.

Fischoff, B. Hindsight   foresight: The effect of outcome knowledge on judgment under uncertainty. *Journal of Experimental Psychology, Human Perception and Performance,* 1 (1975), 288-199.

Fischoff, B., Slovic, P., and Lichtenstein, S. Knowing with uncertainty: the appropriateness of extreme confidence. *Journal of Experimental Psychology, Human Perception and Performance,* 3 (1977), 552-564.

Forer, B.R. The fallacy of personal validation: a classroom demonstration of gullibility. *Journal of Abnormal and Social Psychology,* 44 (1949), 118-123.

Fuller, U. *Confessions of a Psychic*. Box 433, Teaneck, New Jersey 07666: Karl Fulves, 1975.

———. *Further Confessions of a Psychic*. Box 433, Teaneck, New Jersey 07666: Karl Fulves, 1979.

Gallup, G.H. *The Gallup Poll: Public Opinion 1972-1975*. Vol. 1. Wilmington, Delaware: Scholorly Resources, 1978.

Gardner, M. *Fads and Fallacies in the Name of Science*. New York: Dover, 1957.

Garwood, Superstition and half-belief. *New Society*, 31 January 1963.

Gattey, C.N. *They Saw Tomorrow: Seers and Sorcerers from Delphi till Today*. London: Harrap, 1977.

Hastorf, A. and Cantril, H. They saw a game: a case study. *Journal of Abnormal and Social Psychology*, 49 (1954), 129-134.

Hammond, K.R. Human judgment and social policy. *Program of Research in Human Judgment and Social Interaction, Report 170*. Boulder: Institute of Behavioral Sciences, University of Colorado, 1974.

Hanlon, J. Uri Geller and science. *New Scientist*, 64 (1974), 170-185.

Hansel, C. E. M. *ESP: A Scientific Evaluation*. New York: Charles Scribner's Sons, 1966.

Hardy, A., Harvie, R, and Koestler, A. *The Challenge of Chance*. London: Hutchinson, 1973.

Illich, I. *Limits to Medicine*. London: Marion Boyars, 1976.

———. *Tools for Conviviality*. New York: Fontana, 1973.

Jahoda, Gustav. *The Psychology of Superstition*. Gretna, La.: Pelican, 1970.

230 *References*

Kammann, R. *Sourcebook for Affectometer 1.* Dunedin, N.Z.: Why Not? Foundation (P.O. Box 8010), 1979.

Klass, P.J. N-rays and UFOs: are they related? *The Zetetic* (since renamed *The Skeptical Inquirer),* 2 (1977), 57-61.

Koestler, A. *The Roots of Coincidence,* London: Hutchinson, 1972; London: Pan, 1974.

Kreskin. *The Amazing World of Kreskin.* New York: Random House, 1973.

Kusche, L. *The Bermuda Triangle Mystery—Solved.* New York: Harper and Row, 1975.

Laing, R.D. *The Politics of Experience.* New York: Ballantine, 1967.

Leland L.S., Jr., Patterson, J.R., and Clark, J.R. "Incidence of (Self-report) Supernatural Powers among University of Otago Undergraduates." Paper presented at the New Zealand Psychological Society, August 1974. Professor John Clark, who initiated this work, is now at Highlands University, New Mexico.

Lichter, S. and Kammann, R. A demonstration course for improving happiness and psychological health. Unpublished manuscript, Department of Psychology, University of Otago, Dunedin, New Zealand.

Miller, G.T. *Living in the Environment: Concepts, Problems and Alternatives.* Belmont, California: Wadsworth, 1975.

Mitchell, Edgar D. and White, J., eds. *Psychic Exploration: A Challenge for Science.* New York: Putnam's Sons, 1974.

Oskamp, S. Overconfidence in case-study judgments. *Journal of Consulting Psychology,* 29 (1965), 261-265.

Pfungst, O. *Clever Hans (the Horse of Mr. von Osten).* Holt, 1911; New York: Holt, Rinehart, and Winston, 1965.

Puthoff, H. and Targ, R. The record: eight days with Uri Geller. In *The Geller Papers*, edited by Charles Panati, Boston: Houghton Mifflin, 1976.

Randi, J. *The Magic of Uri Geller*. New York: Ballantine Books, 1975.

Rhine, J.B. Security versus deception in parapsychology. *Journal of Parapsychology*, 38 (1974), 99-121 (a).

————. A new case of experimenter unreliability. *Journal of Parapsychology*, 38 (1974), 215-255 (b).

Rosenhan, D.L. On being sane in insane places. *Science,* 179 (1974), 250-258.

Schumacher, E.F. *Small is Beautiful: A Study of Economics As If People Mattered*. London: Sphere Books, 1974.

Snyder, C.R., Shenkel, R.J., and Lowery, C.R. Acceptance of personality interpretations: the "Barnum effect" and beyond. *Journal of Consulting and Clinical Psychology,* 45 (1977), 104-114.

Story, R.D. *The Space-Gods Revealed*. New York: Harper and Row, 1976.

Sulzberger, P., Marks, D.F., & Hodgson, I. *The Isis Smoking Cessation Program*. Dunedin, New Zealand: Isis Research Centre, 1979.

Szasz, T.S. *The Myth of Mental Illness: Foundations of a Theory of Personal Conduct*. New York: Harper and Row, 1961.

Targ, R. and Puthoff, H. Information transfer under conditions of sensory shielding. *Nature*, 251 (1974), 602-607.

————. *Mind-Reach*. New York: Delacorte, 1977.

Tart, C. *Learning to Use Extrasensory Perception.* Chicago: University of Chicago Press, 1976.

Temerlin, M.K. and Trousdale, W.W. The social psychology of clinical diagnosis. *Psychotherapy: Theory, Research and Practice,* 6 (1969), 24-29.

Torrey, E.F. *The Death of Psychiatry.* New York: Penguin, 1975.

Tversky, A. and Kahneman, D. Availability: a heuristic for judging frequency and probability. *Cognitive Psychology,* 5 (1973), 207-232.

– – –. Judgment under uncertainty: heuristics and biases. *Science,* 185 (1974), 1124-1131.

Ulrich, R.E., Stachnik, T.J., and Stainton, N.R. Student acceptance of generalized personality interpretations. *Psychological Reports,* 13 (1973), 831-834.

von Däniken, E. *Chariots of the Gods?* London: Corgi, 1971.

Wason, P.C. On the failure to eliminate hypotheses in a conceptual task. *Quarterly Journal of Experimental Psychology,* 12 (1960), 129-140.

Wilhelm, J.L. *The Search for Superman.* New York: Pocket Books, 1976.

PAPERBACKS AVAILABLE FROM PROMETHEUS BOOKS

CRITIQUES OF THE PARANORMAL

____ESP & PARAPSYCHOLOGY: A CRITICAL RE-EVALUATION C.E.M. Hansel	$7.95
____EXTRA-TERRESTRIAL INTELLIGENCE James L. Christian, editor	$6.95
____OBJECTIONS TO ASTROLOGY L. Jerome & B. Bok	3.95
____THE PSYCHOLOGY OF THE PSYCHIC David Marks & Richard Kammann	7.95
____PHILOSOPHY & PARAPSYCHOLOGY J. Ludwig, editor	8.95

HUMANISM

____ETHICS WITHOUT GOD K. Nielsen	4.95
____HUMANIST ALTERNATIVE Paul Kurtz, editor	4.95
____HUMANIST ETHICS Morris Storer, editor	8.95
____HUMANIST FUNERAL SERVICE Corliss Lamont	2.95
____HUMANIST MANIFESTOS I & II	1.95
____HUMANIST WEDDING SERVICE Corliss Lamont	1.95
____HUMANISTIC PSYCHOLOGY I. David Welch, George Tate, Fred Richards, editors	8.95
____MORAL PROBLEMS IN CONTEMPORARY SOCIETY Paul Kurtz, editor	5.95
____VOICE IN THE WILDERNESS Corliss Lamont	4.95
____RABBI AND MINISTER: THE FRIENDSHIP OF STEPHEN S. WISE AND JOHN HAYNES HOLMES Carl Hermann Voss	6.95

PHILOSOPHY & ETHICS

____ART OF DECEPTION Nicholas Capaldi	5.95
____BENEFICENT EUTHANASIA M. Kohl, editor	7.95
____ESTHETICS CONTEMPORARY Richard Kostelanetz, editor	9.95
____EXUBERANCE: A PHILOSOPHY OF HAPPINESS Paul Kurtz	3.00
____FULLNESS OF LIFE Paul Kurtz	5.95
____FREEDOM OF CHOICE AFFIRMED Corliss Lamont	4.95
____HUMANHOOD: ESSAYS IN BIOMEDICAL ETHICS Joseph Fletcher	6.95
____JOURNEYS THROUGH PHILOSOPHY N. Capaldi & L. Navia, editors	10.95
____MORAL EDUCATION IN THEORY & PRACTICE Robert Hall & John Davis	7.95
____TEACH YOURSELF PHILOSOPHY Antony Flew	5.95
____THINKING STRAIGHT Antony Flew	4.95
____WORLDS OF PLATO & ARISTOTLE J.B. Wilbur & H.J. Allen, editors	5.95
____WORLDS OF THE EARLY GREEK PHILOSOPHERS J.B. Wilbur & H.J. Allen, editors	5.95
____PHILOSOPHY: AN INTRODUCTION Antony Flew	6.95
____INTRODUCTORY READINGS IN THE PHILOSOPHY OF SCIENCE E.D. Klemke, Robert Hollinger, A. David Kline, editors	10.95

SEXOLOGY

___THE FRONTIERS OF SEX RESEARCH *Vern Bullough, editor*   6.95

___NEW BILL OF SEXUAL RIGHTS & RESPONSIBILITIES *Lester Kirkendall*   1.95

___NEW SEXUAL REVOLUTION *Lester Kirkendall, editor*   4.95

___PHILOSOPHY & SEX *Robert Baker & Fred Elliston, editors*   6.95

___SEX WITHOUT LOVE: A PHILOSOPHICAL EXPLORATION *Russell Vannoy*   8.95

SKEPTICS BOOKSHELF

___ATHEISM: THE CASE AGAINST GOD *George H. Smith*   6.95

___CLASSICS OF FREE THOUGHT *Paul Blanshard, editor*   5.95

___CRITIQUES OF GOD *Peter Angeles, editor*   6.95

___WHAT ABOUT GODS? (for children) *Chris Brockman*   3.95

SOCIAL ISSUES

___AGE OF AGING: A READER IN SOCIAL GERONTOLOGY

  Abraham Monk, editor   8.95

___REVERSE DISCRIMINATION *Barry Gross, editor*   7.95

The books listed above can be obtained from your book dealer
or directly from Prometheus Books.
Please check off the appropriate books.
Remittance must accompany all orders from individuals.
Please include $1.00 postage and handling for each book.
(N.Y. State Residents add 7% sales tax)

Send to _____
(Please type or print clearly)

Address _____

City _____ State_____Zip_____

Amount Enclosed_____

℞ Prometheus Books
Box 55 Kensington Station
Buffalo, New York 14215